D1491510

Julian Hayes is senior partner at Berris Law in London specialising in criminal and child-care law. He has undertaken many of the most high-profile and serious cases seen in criminal courts in the last twenty years, most notably the 'Ricin Case' terrorist trial in 2005, the Graff jewellery robbery and the Vietnamese lorry deaths case. As an author, he is uniquely placed as the son of John Stonehouse's nephew, Michael Hayes, and has in-depth knowledge of the criminal courts and in particular the Old Bailey, where the Stonehouse trial took place. He has used his knowledge and experience to forensically examine the evidence to establish whether Stonehouse worked with Czech State Security, and to provide insight into Stonehouse's disappearance and trial.

Stonehouse

Cabinet Minister, Fraudster, Spy

Julian Hayes

ROBINSON

ROBINSON

First published in Great Britain in 2021 by Robinson

1 3 5 7 9 10 8 6 4 2

A CIP catalogue record for this book
is available from the British Library.

ISBN: 978-1-47214-654-0

Typeset in Electra LT Std by SX Composing DTP, Rayleigh, Essex, SS6 7EF
Printed and bound in Great Britain by Clays Ltd, Elcograf S.p.A.

Papers used by Robinson are from well-managed forests
and other responsible sources.

Robinson
An imprint of
Little, Brown Book Group
Carmelite House
50 Victoria Embankment
London EC4Y 0DZ

An Hachette UK Company
www.hachette.co.uk

www.littlebrown.co.uk

To my children Christian, Patrick and Rachel –
my inspiration and joy

CONTENTS

CONTENTS

PROLOGUE

Pentridge Prison, Australia, 10 June 1975

Pulling the collar of his overcoat tight around his neck, warding off the cold early-morning air, the man faces the forbiddingly austere gates of the Victorian prison. Winter has finally arrived. Shaking off the momentary physical discomfort, he steps towards the jail.

Undeterred by his surroundings, the man strides confidently up to the reception office where he reaches into his overcoat and withdraws a neatly folded document. He passes it across the desk to the uniformed officer, who shakes it out and scans it carefully before giving a nod to a colleague. The heavy jail door swings open ominously, ready to swallow him into the prison's cavernous halls. He is brought to his senses as the gate clangs shut behind him.

His footsteps echo off the institutionally drab and shabby corridor walls as he follows a tall, dour guard towards the hospital wing. As they venture deeper into the prison, the man in the overcoat seems to withdraw further into its folds each time the guard pauses to unlock and relock another door. Turning right, they are confronted by yet another door, but this time the officer knocks and waits. Through the heavy iron, vague sounds can be discerned and, after a short wait, there comes the familiar sound of turning metal tumblers.

A middle-aged man in a nurse's uniform is revealed within and the gentleman again offers the papers he showed at the entrance.

The nurse takes his time reading through the document, checking his visitor's face as if he might find some discrepancy there, then hands it back and waves him inside. The guard's footsteps can faintly be heard retreating as the door is locked firmly behind the visitor.

As taciturn as his colleague, the nurse ushers the man through the hospital wing to a grey, metal door, which opens into a dimly lit room, furnished only with an iron bedstead and a mattress with crisply starched but slightly greying sheets. As they enter, a man springs from the bed, looking rather dishevelled in a pair of rumpled pyjamas and a threadbare dressing gown.

The two men weigh each other up for a moment before the visitor recovers his demeanour and extends a hand in greeting. 'Doctor Allen Bartholomew.'

Warily, the other man responds with a curt handshake, simultaneously sinking down onto the bed, eliciting indignant squeaks from the springs.

'How are you feeling today? Is there anything you need?'

Frowning, the patient puts a finger to his lips and from a small bedside cabinet snatches up a pad and a stubby pencil. Scribbling an answer, he holds it out to his visitor. And so the scene was set for the next two days, the doctor probing, the patient responding in urgently scrawled notes.

* * *

The doctor was the eminent Australian forensic psychiatrist, A. A. Bartholomew. The patient was the English MP, privy councillor and former cabinet minister, John Stonehouse.

How had Stonehouse come to find himself in such a state, in such a place?

1

NEW BEGINNINGS?

Miami, 20 November 1974

The Plymouth saloon swept up the driveway of the Fontainebleau Hotel, gliding to a halt outside its imposing facade. The driver, a tall, handsome man in a grey suit, an unfashionably skinny silk tie and a crisp, white shirt, leapt out, tossing the car keys to the concierge. His passenger stepped stiffly from the vehicle. Together, the men strode through the hotel's luxurious lobby towards the reception desk, casually discussing plans for the evening. Giving a smile and a nod to the desk clerk, each man collected his key and, with a friendly pat on the back, they went their separate ways.

An observer of the scene would have noticed the tall man's relaxed facade immediately falling away, to be replaced by a look of steely determination as he strode off urgently.

Darting upstairs to his room, he walked over to the window, where he remained, lost in a long, lingering look at the view, the dazzling light glinting on the ocean enticing but somehow sinister. Though the day was glorious, the beach was almost deserted out of tourist season. Eventually, he sighed and fresh resolve broke his reverie. Rapidly and methodically, he moved about the room gathering documents, among them a passport bearing the name Stonehouse and traveller's cheques. He placed these carefully into a briefcase, the snap of the latch and click of the combination breaking the silence. On the bedside table he placed an airline ticket from Miami to London, patting it almost superstitiously. Crossing to the wardrobe, he put the briefcase on a shelf before kicking off his shoes and slipping out of his suit and tie, taking care to hang them neatly. He picked out another hanger holding casual clothes, then paused to run his hand over the jacket he had just taken off. Composing himself, he put on swimming shorts under casual trousers and a patterned shirt.

He looked back over the room, readying himself for the next step.

He walked back down to the hotel lobby where, rather than simply leaving his key on the counter, he rang the bell for the clerk and handed it to him in person.

He walked towards the hotel's private beach, strolling past the empty, still swimming pool. At the entrance to the beach, he signed in with the bored member of staff sitting in the shade of a beach umbrella. Undressing quickly, he deposited his clothes with the beach attendant and, pausing briefly to greet a passer-by, ran across the warm sand towards the sea. Wading into the water he surrendered his body to its soothing embrace.

When later interviewed on television, the lifeguard on duty claimed not to have noticed the man enter or leave the sea. If he had been paying attention, he might have seen the man swimming parallel to the shoreline before walking back out of the water, up the beach and into the grounds of the neighbouring Eden Roc Hotel, which was closed and deserted.

With familiar assurance, he skirted the sunbathing area around the abandoned swimming pool and made his way to a phone kiosk in which he had placed a towel, freshly washed clothes and sandals. He towelled himself dry and got dressed. Patting his damp hair into place, he made his way to Collins Avenue and hailed a taxi, directing the driver to drop him at the arrivals door of the airport.

He followed the signs to the left-luggage area, where he retrieved a large suitcase and a leather briefcase. He unlocked the briefcase to reveal a British passport in the name of Markham, a plane ticket and some cash.

Pocketing the ticket, briefcase gripped tightly, the man disappeared into the relative anonymity of the commuter and tourist traffic.

So began one of the most peculiar chapters in British political and legal history, the opening pages of which had been written many years earlier.

2

KOLON

1925–59

What had led up to that fateful November day? What had forced a man who, on the surface, had everything, to take such drastic steps? What storm was brewing in his mind?

The seeds had been sown many years before, in the fertile ground of childhood.

Born in Southampton on 28 July 1928, John Thomson Stonehouse was the third child of two staunchly socialist parents. Both were from families of skilled dockyard workers: John's father, William Mitchel Stonehouse, was the son of a shipwright, as was his grandfather before him. After his apprenticeship in Her Majesty's Dockyard Sheerness, William moved to the Royal Navy dockyard in Portsmouth. John's mother, Rosina, maiden name Taylor, was the daughter of an East End boilermaker and Irish mother from Tipperary. Rosina, having been born and initially raised in London, met William after her father took a job at Portsmouth dockyard.

Stonehouse grew up in a household that valued books and learning, yet only the two sons, John and his eldest brother George, went to the fee-paying Taunton's Grammar School due to limited funds. Keeping with prevailing social expectations, the boys were chosen over their two sisters. My grandmother Elizabeth, Stonehouse's eldest sister, had to make the best of the basic education provided by the state. As children, he and his siblings were involved with the Woodcraft Folk, a socialist alternative to scouting. They were brought up as practising Catholics and, in her later years, Rosina received the honour of a papal medal for her good works through the church.

At the outbreak of the Second World War, Stonehouse found himself stranded in France, where he had been holidaying with a French family. Even at the age of fourteen, John had the wit and resources to find his own way home.

Family members have observed that John appeared to be his mother's favourite. They were close and he sought her approval in all his ventures. John also enjoyed a close relationship with his eldest sister, my grandmother, who was said to dote on him. When she met and married my grandfather, Tom Hayes, he was welcomed into their close circle and, on my father Michael's birth, the excited teenager rushed to visit him in hospital when he was only two days old. This initial enthusiasm developed into a strong bond between uncle and nephew that would prove to be significant years later.

His mother, Rosina, was a formidable woman. Stubborn and taciturn, she disliked displays of emotion, whether in affection or anger. In 1959 she became the first female Labour mayor of Southampton, having been, alongside her husband, a prominent member of the Co-operative movement. In 1927 the Co-operative Party had made an electoral pact with Labour not to stand against each other, with candidates described as being members of the Labour and Co-operative Party.

Throughout his formative years Stonehouse was immersed in the political ideology of the centre left and it is unsurprising that this was to influence his career. Although called up to the RAF during the war and undertaking flying training in the United States, he saw no active service. Taking up an armed services sponsorship, Stonehouse entered the London School of Economics (LSE), gaining a degree in economics and politics. He found this new world intoxicating and threw himself into student life. Having been temporarily constrained by the war, his interest in politics re-emerged and he became chairman of the LSE Labour Society. Britain had entered a new era with the establishment of the NHS, free secondary education and legal aid providing access for all to basic needs for the first time. As chairman Stonehouse came into contact with a great number of young people similarly excited by the idealistic vigour of post-war socialism. One of these was Donald Chesworth, who was to become his lifelong friend.

Chesworth was a secretary of the International Union of Socialist Youth from 1947 to 1951, and chairman of the National Association of Labour Student Organisations in 1947. He was to be a lifelong Labour Party activist, developing a career in London politics as alderman of Kensington and Chelsea and playing a very active part in the Greater London Council (GLC), forerunner of the London Assembly. Chesworth held various roles, and most significantly became chairman of the anti-poverty charity War on Want. He and Stonehouse bonded over their shared political beliefs and a keen interest in colonial affairs. Below Chesworth's surface, however, lurked something darker: a less innocent motive in nurturing his relationship with Stonehouse.

It was also at this time that Stonehouse met Barbara Smith, intelligent, beautiful and loyal. She was the perfect foil to the brash and at times impulsive young man. They married in 1948. Her calmness and strength, coupled with the quiet ambition that she held for her husband, provided the foundations that enabled him to pursue his political aims.

Stonehouse twice stood for parliament at by-elections, first in Twickenham in 1950 and again in Burton the following year. Following a brief stint in the probation service in Southampton, he secured a managerial position within the Co-operative Society in Uganda in the early 1950s, rising to be president of the London Co-operative Society in 1956, a post he held until 1964. During his time with the Society he successfully headed off an attempted coup by communist members, lending him some kudos among the more centre-left members.

Through perseverance and patience, Stonehouse eventually suc-
ceeded in his political ambitions when, in 1957, he was returned as
Labour Co-operative Member of Parliament for the constituency of
Wednesbury in the West Midlands, making him, at thirty-two, the
youngest MP at the time. For the next few years Stonehouse would
juggle his responsibilities as an opposition backbench MP and president of the London Co-operative Society. Throughout his political
career there is no doubt that Stonehouse worked hard and conscien-
tiously for his constituency and many of his former constituents
remembered him fondly. He continued, even to the very end of his
time in parliament, to contribute regularly to parliamentary debates,
particularly on issues concerning the former British colonies. He
maintained a strong anti-colonial stance and celebrated the fact that
so many colonies were gaining independence. He was especially
interested in Africa, and living in Uganda had provided him with a
comprehensive insight into African affairs and the leadership of political groups such as the African National Congress. Before becoming
synonymous with South Africa, the ANC had been a continent-wide
organisation and many of its prominent members had gone on to lead
newly independent countries. He would regularly take the British government to task when he considered that it was continuing to interfere
in the politics of these new nations. He was particularly concerned at
how the new constitutions were manipulated to allow white minorities to maintain their privilege and control.

Immediately after his election, Stonehouse set about trying to raise
the profile of his constituency. Part of that process involved finding
various towns and cities that could be 'twinned' with Wednesbury.

When Stonehouse was invited to a house party thrown by his good
friend, Donald Chesworth, there is no doubt that this was largely
contrived to fulfil a very specific purpose. Chesworth had been
recruited by Czech State Security (*Státní bezpečnost*, StB), for whom
he had become an agent codenamed Knight. The aim of Chesworth's

house party was to introduce Stonehouse to a Czech StB agent codenamed Majer, masquerading as a diplomat. Clearly Stonehouse impressed Majer, who reported favourably on his new contact to fellow operatives at the London embassy.

Stonehouse's activities had been observed and, it would transpire, assisted by other quarters. The Cold War was at its height in the 1950s and early 1960s. The capitalist/communist stand-off had erupted into a number of regional conflicts, including the imposition of the Soviet-dominated buffer zone in Europe, the Berlin Blockade, the Korean War between 1950 and 1953, the construction of the Berlin Wall in 1961, the Cuban missile crisis in October 1962, and the conflict in Vietnam was simmering. The world teetered on the brink of a nuclear catastrophe.

Behind the conflicts there was a more insidious type of warfare, principally concerning the USA, its allies and the Soviet Union. The rival nations were fixated on espionage and counter-espionage, developing zones of influence and enlisting sympathetic governments in strategically useful parts of Africa, the Middle East and South-east Asia.

Formidable security services operated within all the communist-controlled countries of Europe, their purpose as much to monitor and keep in check their own populations as to spy on the West. A further significant part of their remit was to target individuals in influential positions with the aim of recruiting them as agents. Information is power and, in the ruthless pursuit of intelligence, prominent politicians and trade unionists were of particular interest. Stonehouse was regarded as a rising star in the Labour Party; it was no surprise that he had attracted the attention of the Czechs.

Buried deep in the StB archives in Prague are many secrets: confidential files concerning the hidden work behind the scenes from 1945 to the end of the Cold War in 1988. Some of those secrets are buried in file 43075, relating to the activities of agent Kolon.

In the same year that Chesworth had thrown his house party, Stonehouse visited Czechoslovakia with a delegation from the Co-operative Society. It is alleged that, in the course of this trip, he was the victim of a honey trap, his hosts completing his embarrassment by filming the whole episode. File 43075 offers no detail but it is suggested that Stonehouse included a fictionalised account of this incident in his 1982 novel, *Ralph*. In it he describes how the hero is lured into a compromising act by the femme fatale, realising too late that he had been filmed and become the victim of an elaborate sting. Whether this took place in reality and whether the perpetrators confronted him is unclear, as Stonehouse took the truth with him to the grave.

His holiday to Czechoslovakia had given Stonehouse the idea to twin his constituency with a Czech town. Kladno, situated approximately twenty miles from Prague, was similar to the Black Country town he represented, reliant on the heavy industries of coalmining and steelworking. On his return to London, Stonehouse was targeted by Vlad Koudelka, who introduced himself in November 1957. Using the codename Kugler, Koudelka was a captain in the StB who operated from the Foreign Affairs Department in the Czechoslovak embassy in London. A shrewd operator, he was a busy man, having ingratiated himself into political circles. Stonehouse was not the only politician on Koudelka's radar; he had managed to turn Harold Wilson's private secretary, Ernest Fernyhough, and the backbench MP Will Owen, known as agent Lee, who was to play a role in the Stonehouse saga. Koudelka was also keen to engage civil servants and trade unionists.

The men's relationship started innocently enough with Stonehouse's ambitions to promote his constituency and, no doubt, his own political cause by suggesting the twinning of Wednesbury with Kladno. He invited the Czech to listen to a speech he was giving in parliament, expressing interest in what views Kugler may have about his performance. That invitation was followed up with lunch on 19 November

1957, where the twinning and Stonehouse's speech were discussed. From this initial contact Kugler sensed that, with a little work, the MP might be susceptible to 'cooperating'. Kugler saw that, in the absence of a political mentor, he might be able to fill that role.

Stonehouse initially regarded Kugler with justified suspicion. Kugler's first objective was to ascertain whether the young politician might be susceptible to manipulation and over a period of the next couple of years the two met at various restaurants throughout west and central London, with Kugler assessing Stonehouse's potential and his areas of vulnerability.

If Kugler and the StB did in fact possess anything compromising on Stonehouse they chose not to blackmail him into working for them, preferring to adopt a stealthy approach. Stonehouse only ever knew Kugler by the name of Vlad Koudelka, and that was how he referred to him both in his 1975 autobiography, *Death of an Idealist*, and in correspondence that he sent to the Czech agent, which can be found in file 43075.

There were further encounters. At Christmas, Kugler gave Stonehouse two bottles of liqueur and chocolates for his wife. On 30 December the Czech ruefully reported, 'He hasn't even thanked me yet.' Nonetheless, his disappointment was tempered by the potential prospects of these early exchanges: 'He is an interesting deputy, politically immature, on whom there are objective assumptions to do something. Meanwhile, I count on him as a prospective contact on which I am going to work.'

True to his word, he invited the Stonehouses to a private party at his apartment on 14 January. A clear rapport was developing between the two men, although driven by differing desires. Stonehouse naively believed he could use the Czech 'diplomat' to help him not only with his constituency but also his personal and political profile. For the moment, Kugler was happy to oblige. Anything to promote his own objectives and to nurture his network of informants and agents.

12

On 15 March 1958, Kugler further reported 'STONEHOUSE – lunch 11.30, Discussion of his speech in parliament. I criticised him for some of his comments on communism and so on. Familiarity with him is starting to deepen . . . I can already call him a contact.'

With very rare exception, the majority of those who enter politics, and in particular national politics, possess an ego to match their ambition. In those early days, Stonehouse was fuelled by an idealistic zeal that made him prepared to take risks and to support causes that were considered unpopular. Throughout the rest of 1958 into 1959 Stonehouse spent a great deal of time travelling to Africa, especially to Rhodesia (now Zimbabwe) on what started as a fact-finding mission into the minority white government.

The young politician created an international stir when he was expelled from Rhodesia for having addressed an African National Congress meeting, announcing to the assembly that they had the support of the Labour Party in Britain and encouraging the black majority to take a stand against the government. His experiences formed the basis of his book *Prohibited Immigrant*, published in 1960. Whether simple idealism or political opportunism, the episode undoubtedly worked to heighten his profile within his party.

Despite Kugler's complaint that, having established the contact, 'he has been weakening recently partly because he is constantly abroad (Africa) and he is politically naive', the operative was not to be deterred. The Czechs were in fact attracted by Stonehouse's expertise in African affairs, having ambitions to set up trade and cultural links with the former colonies. As the countries were still firmly under British influence any tentative steps they tried to make in those territories were immediately thwarted, creating the need for a sympathetic figure within the British political establishment to promote their cause. Young, idealistic, naive John Stonehouse appeared to be the perfect candidate.

In an effort to accelerate matters, Kugler invited Stonehouse to a house party in the summer of 1958, reporting that the MP had 'promised to attend the party I am preparing for 26.8'. Stonehouse himself referred to the invitation in *Death of an Idealist*, in which he recounts how he and his wife had intended to go but had been obliged to prioritise an earlier social event in Twickenham. Exhausted by their schedule the couple decided to go home, unable to face travelling into London to join Kugler. It transpired that the party was a somewhat different affair from that which Stonehouse had anticipated, and Kugler had clearly expected his target to attend alone, having also invited a number of single young ladies, possibly hoping to lure him into another trap.

Stonehouse never set out to be an agent for the StB. Had he been confronted with the prospect in such plain terms as 'Do you want to spy for us?', he would have replied with a resounding no. Knowing this, Kugler employed great skill in manipulating events and weaknesses, and his work would eventually pay dividends.

Throughout 1958 and 1959 Stonehouse continued to meet with Kugler at various upmarket West End restaurants and tearooms, including well-known establishments such as the Café Royal, Bentley's, the White Tower and the Vine. Initially Kugler's reports referred to Stonehouse by his name but, as the relationship developed, he ceased to be considered a simple contact and instead came to be regarded as an informant. A codename was selected for him to prevent the sensitive information passing between them being easily traced to its source. Given Stonehouse's knowledge and expertise in colonial matters, the codename Kolon was selected.

It was at one of their lunch meetings at the White Tower on 14 August 1959 that Stonehouse confided in Kugler his search for an income to supplement his basic MP's salary. Kugler immediately seized the opportunity to casually drop into the conversation that Stonehouse may be interested in undertaking some work on behalf of the Czech embassy. Rather than instantly recoiling from the idea, Stonehouse was not averse and, encouraged by the positive response,

Kugler left the topic open with the assurance that he would look into how this could be put into action.

The promising development was promptly reported to Kugler's superiors in Prague, who responded with cautious optimism:

> STONEHOUSE – Approve the procedure. If Kugler fails to induce a situation to ask S. for a loan, then he must not offer anything to him. He does not realise that he has done anything for us and that an inappropriate offer could complicate further collaboration. Kugler was ordered to review the case and a serious case analysis to send the next post . . . with a plan . . . for which we would offer S. reward and engage in conscious cooperation.

This message showed clearly how Stonehouse was perhaps unwittingly about to be ensnared. He became pressured into undertaking two specific courses of action on behalf of his new associates. The first related to a parliamentary debate regarding the conditions that the Western allies had insisted on before relations could be developed with Czechoslovakia, one of which was the insistence that Soviet troops should leave the country. Stonehouse agreed to challenge this in the parliamentary debate, but the opportunity failed to arise. The second concerned the British government's refusal to allow a Czech trade delegation to travel to Rhodesia, which Stonehouse was able to challenge, pleasing Kugler immensely.

Kugler continued steadily to apply the pressure, noting that the MP had a large personal and political appetite. He had already expressed frustration he could not afford to develop his political career and equally finance the lifestyle that he and his family aspired to on his modest MP's salary. Consequently, he opened himself up to exploitation by the Czechs.

3

CZECH MATE

November 1959–January 1960

Kugler felt he was making significant progress in his engagement with Stonehouse and his confidence soared. Capitalising on his success to date he arranged a lunch date at Bentley's Oyster Bar and Grill for 17 November. 'I consider this meeting to be the most important I have ever had with Kolon,' the excited Czech reported less than an hour after the meeting.

As was his custom, Kugler left the embassy early and took a circuitous route to the planned rendezvous, travelling to another part of London to ascertain if he was being tailed by British intelligence. He arrived at the restaurant early to check whether he had been or could be compromised. When he had satisfied himself that there was no surveillance in place he called Stonehouse from the restaurant payphone to give him the all clear, then took a seat at a table and waited.

The politician arrived a short while later and the two men greeted each other warmly, Stonehouse briefly filling in the StB man with news of his recent tour of Scandinavia, which had appeared to go well. He anticipated that his forthcoming book, *Prohibited Immigrant*, would be translated into Danish and Swedish.

Although he felt that the book would assist his political aspirations, he told Kugler that he did not believe that his championing of colonial affairs was going to progress his career much further. He thought that he should now concentrate on matters closer to home, issues relating to consumer affairs, where he could direct the expertise he had gained from his position with the London Co-operative Society. He was interested in the views of his companion, who seemed highly knowledgeable of British parliamentary affairs. Stonehouse had been impressed when he canvassed Kugler's anonymous opinion with his political colleagues, who had concurred with the Czech's analysis.

Encouraged by Stonehouse's eagerness, Kugler offered to provide advice and assistance in his future endeavours. Pushing aside the platter of empty oysters shells, he suggested that Stonehouse should divide the topics he raised in parliament into three distinct areas. The first should focus on foreign political affairs, where he would take a centre-left stance. The second would be to take a more 'offensive' approach on colonial issues, allowing him scope to give a more passionate performance and show off his oratorial skills. The third and final topic should relate to matters specifically related to his constituency. Stonehouse was impressed, and the other man responded kindly, assuring Stonehouse that he would have come to the same conclusions himself in time. The politician went on to lament that he was swamped with colonial issues and correspondence relating to it, allowing him little time to pursue other matters. Kugler immediately countered this by suggesting that he could perhaps help to give Stonehouse more freedom to pursue other, more advantageous, political avenues.

Stonehouse reacted warily, anxious to avoid the fate of his fellow Labour MP John Baird, who was clearly being fed questions and information by the Chinese and Soviets. Kugler took pains to reassure him that he did not expect the MP to become a spokesman for Czechoslovakia, but merely suggested that he provide him with topics and supporting research material, not only on matters relating to the immediate interests of Czechoslovakia. It was an extremely delicate moment. If Kugler were to set his trap successfully he had to be perceived to treat Stonehouse's fears with sensitivity and seriousness.

After a tense moment, Kugler was rewarded by a placated Stonehouse agreeing to his offer of help on the clear basis that the matters he raised, and when, would be at his discretion. Stonehouse stressed that he would suffer immense personal and political damage within both parliament and his own party if their arrangement were to be revealed. He knew he was playing with fire.

Kugler continued in his report:

> I noted that I myself might be a little too discreet, and that I am worried about the level of discreetness on both sides. He was surprised that I would think he would go and tell someone else about it – he would not undermine his own interests. I told him that something like that could happen, for example if he discussed the details of an issue with me over the telephone or in a letter – I told him I thought that it was not in his best interest. He caught on right away and asked if I thought MI5 could do something in that case. I told him they couldn't afford to resort to an outright representation, but that he might be surprised to have Gaitskell or Phillips [Hugh Gaitskell, Labour leader, and Morgan Phillips, the party's general secretary] show him a recording of the conversation. It could be very unpleasant, and it would not work in the favour of Kolon's interests. He said that if they were interested in our conversation, they could have put a wire in the restaurant we were sitting in. I asked him: 'Who knows that we're sitting here?' Kolon: 'You called me; they could have heard it.' I answered casually: 'I called you from a phone booth,' and I went on talking about food.

Stonehouse expressed his gratitude to Kugler, at the same time laughingly suggesting to the Czech that he was being overly cautious, to which the shrewd spy replied that he did not want his friend's interests compromised by their association. He told the MP that being in a position to help his friends brought him great satisfaction, casually adding, 'I don't mean financial help. That's nothing.'

The intention behind his words was not only to avoid the suggestion that he was buying the MP's services but to sow a seed in the impressionable young man's mind.

They went on to discuss the mechanics by which they could convey the information that Kugler was to feed him. With discretion a priority, it was agreed that the material would be passed to Stonehouse in person or through his parliamentary mailbox without any mark to indicate from whom it was received. The seed was germinating.

Kugler noted: 'Kolon had started to view me with considerable respect, and I felt that our partnership had changed. We had been equal partners up to that point, but he started to feel inferior then. Nothing was said on the matter, it happened naturally.'

Kugler astutely pursued the matter Stonehouse had raised earlier in their conversation concerning the thorny issue of his finances. The MP was feeling overwhelmed, partly because his secretary was provided by the Co-operative Society and did not work exclusively for him. He was having to pay an additional £2 per week, which he complained he could ill afford on his meagre salary, for further assistance with his mounting colonial correspondence. His wife, Barbara, was having to help but she would soon be forced to quit as she was pregnant with their third child, due early the next year. Stonehouse confided in Kugler that they thought they were having twins, in which event an insurance policy would pay out £1,000, substantially easing his financial concerns. As for finding a way of funding the promotion of his political ambitions he was at a loss. Wining and dining prominent figures, sponsoring events and hosting functions were a vital but expensive aspect of his career. His problem was that he 'looked like a Lord', with the use of a chauffeur-driven Daimler, a perk of his position in the Co-operative Society, a profile that didn't elicit the offer of any sympathy from his colleagues in the Labour Party.

Embracing the opportunity, Kugler assured the MP that, should he ever need financial assistance, he could discreetly help him out as a personal friend. Stonehouse thanked him, agreeing to ask for help if it became necessary on the strict provision that it was 'unconditional'. Kugler confirmed that this would be the case and that his offer was entirely altruistic.

The conversation moved on and Stonehouse updated Kugler on the progress of a good friend and colleague, 'Marquis', who was rapidly rising through the Labour Party ranks. It was suggested that Stonehouse should throw a party so that Kugler could be introduced, the Czech generously offering to supply the refreshment for the proposed soirée. Toasting the agreement with the dregs of the Riesling, the two men resolved to meet again on 8 December. The trap had been set.

Just over a week later, an excited Kugler submitted a comprehensive report to his superiors in Prague. It outlined Stonehouse's education, described his political persuasion as 'centre left' and a 'social democrat', and remarked on his having a positive attitude towards Czechoslovakia. It went on to detail his family circumstances, noting he had two daughters, with his wife expecting to give birth in the spring of 1960 (it would turn out to be a boy, not twins), and suggesting that his wife suspected him of having affairs which was consistent with what the Czechs already knew of Stonehouse's weakness for women. Kugler summarised how his relationship with the politician had developed and that 1959 had been a pivotal year, with his political profile developing significantly due to events in Rhodesia. Kugler commented, 'So far, Kolon has been counted as an informant and for implementing active measures. However, the latest development has shown that the possibilities of his involvement are broader.'

Stonehouse was not yet an agent but Kugler was already planning ahead: 'Kolon intends to run for National Executive LP [Labour Party] and assumes, based on the current information he has, that he should be able to succeed in two years. That is what makes him a contact with perspective, strong will and the ability to get to high places.'

In identifying how the next stage of his plan would be achieved, Kugler concluded that the obvious incentive would be financial. He recapped their conversation about finances and explained that there had been some tentative discussions as to how they could help each other politically. With Stonehouse seeking to make inroads into the Labour Party executive within a couple of years, an ambition that would be assisted with his plan to stand for president of the London Co-operative Society, Kugler was feeling no small degree of enthusiasm for the potential to develop their bond further. However, extended delicate work was required. His report concluded:

> I propose to file him for next year as a type for further development. For this purpose, I propose that the first step for typing him is testing his willingness to cooperate based on assigning him such active measures that will not only fulfil our requirements but also increase his prestige in the parliament. After fulfilling 2–3 active measures, he will receive some sort of reward and we will attempt to raise his interest in cooperating with us by political as well as material means.

In a subsequent memo to the bureau in Prague, Kugler updated them on his progress. The Czech agent had researched and formulated questions for Stonehouse to ask in the Commons relating to German trade in the colonies and its increasing influence. The Second World War was painfully fresh in memory, having ended only fourteen years earlier, and huge resentment and mistrust of the newly formed West Germany remained within Europe. East Germany was not even recognised as an independent country by the Western Allies and was deliberately subjugated by the Eastern Bloc, in part as revenge, but also to prevent the emergence of a new and more powerful Germany.

The view among Eastern Bloc nations, perhaps understandably, was that, despite having caused two world wars, Germany was being allowed to prosper at the expense of countries such as Czechoslovakia. Smaller, less forceful states needed policies to be challenged and changed to afford them the same opportunities, and material relating to this was anonymously provided to Stonehouse.

*   *   *

The steps that the MP had taken to pursue these topics were discussed at the next meeting between the two men on 8 December. Kugler had taken his usual precautions to ensure there was no surveillance at the location, the Vine restaurant on this occasion, before Stonehouse arrived and took a seat opposite. As they waited for their starters, Kugler observed that his companion seemed more focused and serious. Having become adept at massaging the young politician's ego he commenced by bringing out a draft of the speech that Stonehouse had made regarding the make-up of the Monckton Commission. This had been formed to consider the constitution of the Federation of Rhodesia and Nyasaland (which would subsequently become Zimbabwe and Malawi). The Hansard reports record Stonehouse asking a question on this topic on 3 December and Kugler praised the MP on how his arguments had shifted the views of Labour's Harold Wilson and Jim Callaghan, who in turn supported Stonehouse's stand in discussion with Gaitskell. The tactics used by the Labour Party to oppose certain aspects of the Commission's review had been very effective and had raised Stonehouse's profile even further within the party.

The young MP thanked Kugler for his help on this and other matters. The Czech had only just got started giving advice to his protégé, listing the sort of matters he should focus on. The MP was to be seen as a moderate, left of centre, and not to align himself with hardliners in order to avoid any suspicion that he was colluding with a communist country. It was clear to the Czechs that, while Hugh Gaitskell was the current leader of the Labour Party, those possessing the greatest potential to succeed him were Wilson and Callaghan, and so Stonehouse was encouraged to nurture friendships with the two men.

Other aspects they addressed covered ways for Stonehouse to maximise his potential through social activities and how to manage this financially. In addition, he needed to develop his standing and influence within the Co-operative movement. They discussed his ambitions to stand for president of the Society in 1960 and how, in the event that he achieved this position, he would have considerable sway over the selection of new Co-operative Members of Parliament. This significant development would also lend weight to his candidacy for the Labour Party executive.

With those goals set, Kugler moved on to the manner in which Stonehouse had received his materials, apologising for the standard of English used. Stonehouse observed that he did not mind this as it ensured he needed to rephrase the material. Kugler expressed his eagerness to keep their acquaintance low-key to avoid it being compromised before it had time to mature, and the men agreed to keep their friendship from their respective wives.

With the mention of wives, the spy skilfully moved on to the topic of payment. He knew that the MP would baulk at the suggestion of a direct fee but Christmas was coming and he asked his 'friend' what his wife would like as a gift. Stonehouse glibly responded, 'Just send a drink.' The Czech demurred, maintaining, now their friendship had developed, that was no longer sufficient and he would like to indulge him with something more significant. He later reported, 'Of course he "refused" and said that he does not care what he gets,' but Kugler was not to be dissuaded. Using his own wife as an example, he explained that they often exchanged money instead of gifts so that the recipient could be sure to get themselves something they really wanted.

He suggested that he would perhaps give Stonehouse a small sum of cash so his wife could treat herself. Stonehouse was not to be drawn, reiterating that a bottle of brandy would do. The spy wisely pursued the topic no further.

Kugler concluded his report with a request for £50 with which to pay Stonehouse. The memorandum clearly indicated that Kugler considered the situation with Stonehouse encouraging and that he was optimistic that he could develop the arrangement further:

> the recruitment process started. It can be assumed that if I manage to deepen conspiracy at the next meeting we can eventually agree on a system of substitute meetings and agree on continued reward for cooperation, then the first phase of the recruitment will be completed. Obviously, this can only be achieved once he is a Czechoslovak agent. But the decisive step in this direction has already begun.

* * *

The next meeting was on 21 December at Hatchett's of Mayfair. Amid a dull hubbub of diners enjoying pre-Christmas business lunches and office drinks, Kugler was keen to keep the tone light and convivial, feeling that their previous meeting had focused quite heavily on the operational aspects of their activities. Stonehouse seemed relaxed and glad to see Kugler, raising a glass of claret and immediately producing a document for his friend and advisor's appraisal. It turned out to be the written response from Ernest Marples, the controversial minister for transport, to one of the questions the Czech had prepared for his protégé. On 9 December, Stonehouse had asked what would be the minister's 'estimate of the effect on the British shipbuilding industry of the development of nuclear powered ships by the German Federal Republic?' The minister had answered that specific question but could not answer the supplementary question put by Stonehouse as to whether he would 'make a further statement on the provision of nuclear propulsion for British merchant ships?' He had promised to provide Stonehouse with a written response, which Stonehouse now handed to Kugler.

As Kugler studied the papers, Stonehouse gave off an increasingly uneasy air, casting self-conscious glances towards diners at nearby tables. Kugler sought to calm him with some reassuring words, reminding the younger man that any confidential topics could be addressed outside as they were leaving the restaurant. He confided that he had a gift for Stonehouse that he would only hand over when they were in a taxi, to which the MP replied that his car had been ordered to pick him up at 3 p.m. sharp.

They agreed to a further lunch appointment at the Overton on 18 January 1960. In the event that he was unable to attend as planned, Kugler advised Stonehouse to send a letter containing a business prospectus in an envelope addressed to J. V. Koudelka, the name by which Stonehouse knew him. Kugler would know it was from Stonehouse as the J was an abbreviation for John, and the sending of the letter would mean that their meeting was to be postponed for a week. Several such envelopes bearing Stonehouse's writing are contained in the StB files, clearly proving this procedure was used on later occasions.

The clock struck three, signalling that the MP's car had arrived, and the two men left the restaurant. Kugler joined Stonehouse on the back seat of the car, asking for a lift to Trafalgar Square. During that short but pivotal drive Stonehouse handed the Czech a draft of his *Prohibited Immigrant* book. The atmosphere had changed and the luxury car was filled with an air of tense anticipation. Silently, so the chauffeur was unaware of what was happening, Kugler placed an envelope containing £50 inside the book and returned it. Stonehouse slipped the envelope into the inside breast pocket of his suit. Kugler observed, 'He was strained, but his eyes seemed to sparkle with joy.' No doubt Kugler's eyes were gleaming too. He now needed to consolidate the position at their next meeting.

＊　＊　＊

On 18 January, the Czech made his way to the Overton in St James's, an old-fashioned, intimate restaurant which afforded its patrons a degree of anonymity. Kugler was uneasy, unsure how Stonehouse would respond following their Christmas 'gift' transaction. Would the young politician be repulsed by his behaviour? Would he accept the consequences of his actions and embrace his new comrades? Kugler's head was a commotion of possibilities, each one successively jostling for his attention. Unable to guess Stonehouse's attitude, he had taken the precaution of formulating a number of alternative plans to cover any eventuality. There was the distinct potential that Stonehouse could have reported the matter to MI5 and it would be a pair of security officers with whom he would be sharing a bowl of soup. However, if Stonehouse was receptive, he was eager to press forward with his recruitment process.

As Kugler's imagination continued to whirl, the MP arrived and the two men greeted each other warmly. Making small talk about Christmas, Kugler noted that Stonehouse seemed tense, as if there was something on his mind that he was holding back. It was a full three-quarters of an hour and more than one glass of wine later before Kugler managed to coax the politician into relaxing, at which point he thanked Kugler for the 'gifts'. Kugler studied the man sitting opposite him, detecting a loss of ease and confidence in his companion. The younger man's discomfort implied that, having excepted the cash, he felt himself at a disadvantage, subordinate to the Czech, and that this was not a dynamic to which Stonehouse was used. It was interesting for Kugler to observe the psychology of betrayal but he had no wish for Stonehouse to feel on edge as it would hinder the progress of their relationship. What remained of lunch was spent putting the young politician at ease. Kugler himself was encouraged by the MP's positive response to the payment, acutely aware that it had been a watershed moment. The relationship had indeed evolved.

Over the lunch, they discussed the terms of the MP's engagement. Stonehouse agreed to share information with the Czechs on political affairs, not only matters arising in parliament but also providing reports on committee matters and discussions with policy makers. He was utterly adamant, however, that he would not provide any information to Kugler concerning the military, which the Czech accepted.

The conversation turned to the issue of finances. Stonehouse considered that he would require a minimum of £400 a year to achieve his ambitions, anticipating that it would take about ten years, or two electoral terms, to rise to the highest echelons of the party and be in a position to vie for leadership. Bearing in mind the financial and political assistance the Czechs were promising, Kugler insisted that any information should be provided to him personally rather than risk using the post. In addition, he felt that, now that Stonehouse was conspiring with the Czechs, it would not be wise for him to accept invitations to events arranged by other Eastern Bloc countries, including a reception planned at the Hungarian embassy that week. Finally, as the brandies arrived, Kugler confirmed that they would continue to assist the MP with his parliamentary questions.

Within an hour of shaking hands goodbye, a deeply satisfied Kugler submitted a report to his superiors in Prague, in which he concluded, 'In the last report, I assumed the recruitment would drag on longer and that it would take place simultaneously with completing tasks. After today's meeting, Kolon's position as an LP political agent of Czechoslovakia has been established. He agrees with his position, mostly because of reasons concerning his career. I'm assuming that starting today, we can register him as an agent, even though I'm aware that he lacks training in agency work and conspiracy.'

The trap had been sprung. Now compromised, however idealistic his original intentions, Stonehouse was beholden to the Czechs.

* * *

Throughout the next three years Stonehouse continued regularly to meet his Czech handlers at various restaurants across London and was introduced to another operative, Captain Robert Husak, codenamed Hanč. In the event that either side lost connection, a system was set up to help re-establish contact. This involved arranging a meeting at one of two places, either at Beale's restaurant on the Holloway Road or at the Black Horse Inn in Rushey Green. Communication was to be conducted via newspaper clippings on political affairs sent to Stonehouse's home address. If the date on the newspaper was 14 October 1962 then the encounter was scheduled to take place seven days later on 21 October. The rendezvous would be assumed to take place at Beale's unless 'II' was written in the newspaper margin, indicating that it would take place at location two, the Black Horse Inn. In the event of a meeting with a new operative, Stonehouse would be met with the opening words, 'Mr Stonehouse, greetings from Harold Poulter.'

That Stonehouse supplied his handlers with information during this period is not in doubt. File 43075, long buried in the StB archive, contains an abundance of documents in Stonehouse's verified handwriting, including letters, envelopes and a five-page report providing detailed information on members of the African National Congress. In addition are a number of typed letters, reports and minutes of committee and cabinet meetings, for example a detailed description of a Labour shadow cabinet meeting in 1963 concerning the issue of nuclear disarmament and another on the Monckton Commission.

Kugler reported on how the Monckton documents were handed over at Charing Cross train station on 3 June 1960:

Kolon brought the message in an envelope and had a handful of papers in his hand. The meeting took place as a random meeting, when we walked around the corner of the station into a narrow street where no one was, Kolon placed an envelope in my newspaper that I had under my arm and continued my journey. The duration of the meeting is about 3 minutes. The report contains a description of Monckton's mission and provides a background date on its members.

Although the information Stonehouse was imparting was limited, it gave insight into the ethos and organisation of the Labour Party at the time. Recognising that the party was in opposition and that Stonehouse was just an MP, the Czechs were playing the long game. Once Britain was under a Labour government, preferably with Stonehouse in a position of greater power, they would be able to exploit the intelligence they had gathered at this stage, and then their investment would come to fruition.

In return for Stonehouse's information the Czechs continued to make regular payments. A report from 1963 itemised those payments over a three-year period: they totalled just shy of £2,000, a not insubstantial sum, the equivalent of over £30,000 today.

A number of objectives that had been set were achieved. Stonehouse had been elected president of the London Co-operative Society in 1960, and he had developed friendships with significant figures within the parliamentary Labour Party, in particular Jim Callaghan. His stock within the party was rising. However, clearly he did not always jump to the tune of his supervisors, leading to some difficult meetings with Kugler.

The year 1963 was to prove pivotal in British politics. At the beginning of the year Gaitskell died suddenly after a short illness. Despite the huge shock this created throughout the party, Harold Wilson, another prominent figure with whom Stonehouse had begun to nurture a sound working relationship, was quickly elected to replace him. The other significant event was the Profumo affair, which left the Conservative government reeling from the fallout, their reputation with the British electorate in tatters. Stonehouse was also facing issues within the Co-operative Society, in which there had been an attempted takeover by the communists, which he successfully defeated, a move that did not please his Prague paymasters.

An awkward meeting took place at Peppercorns restaurant on Seething Lane on 18 March 1963, where he was quizzed about events within the Co-operative Society. Conscious of his surroundings, the MP maintained a civil tone as he explained that, following his victory, Stonehouse made an effort to work with the communists, only to be faced with relentless attempts to undermine him with populist politics. Giving the example of the pricing policy for goods, Stonehouse outlined how they had tried to force the prices down to the point that the Co-op was operating at a loss. He had been compelled to take active measures to ensure that this did not continue by speaking out against the communists. His handler told him that they did not consider this was at all necessary, adding that, while the Czechs were manoeuvring to advance his political ambitions, they did not expect him to take an active anti-communist stance. He had been warned.

In October 1964, Harold Wilson's Labour Party won the general election with a narrow majority. Stonehouse was appointed a junior minister in the Department of Aviation, which managed both civil and military aircraft. The Czechs would surely now want to cash in on their investment.

4

FLORIAN

London, 1964–1966

Even as London embraced its role as the hub of swinging 1960s culture, Captain Josef Frolík's arrival in the capital coincided with a new phase in the Cold War. The Cuban missile crisis had led the world to the brink of nuclear oblivion, while the construction of the Berlin Wall only served to create a greater divide. Such blatant aggression was unsustainable and would inevitably lead to global conflict, so the combat moved underground. Greater emphasis was placed on counter-espionage and the value of gathering intelligence soared as nations fought to gain an upper hand. For those on the frontline in the secret services, these were times filled with adrenaline and adventure, danger and drama.

Under the codename Florian, the newly installed 'labour attaché' applied himself assiduously to the task in hand. He was briefed on his allocation of contacts and agents, how they should be approached and the type of intelligence that they could provide. Principally he was to deal with members of the trade union movement, though that did not stop him from trying his hand at attempting to recruit susceptible politicians.

All the Eastern Bloc countries actively engaged in the recruitment of those who moved in such circles, specifically aiming to target young or inexperienced MPs considered to be destined for greater things.

Once recruited, an MP could be aided in their ascent to achieve positions, at which point their backers would have achieved their goal of being in a position to manipulate national events. Operating in an atmosphere of gossip and circulating in a well-connected world of politicians, foreign dignitaries, union officials, political lobbyists and campaign groups, MPs were vulnerable targets and, given the right emollient, easy to exploit. So it was with Stonehouse.

It has long since been acknowledged that during those Cold War years the Czechoslovakian StB was more successful than its KGB counterparts in recruiting politicians. It has been suggested there was subconscious residual guilt that Czechoslovakia had been betrayed by Britain when Nazi Germany marched into the country, unchallenged by the world. Neville Chamberlain's policy of appeasement and the Munich agreement with Hitler had rankled with many.

Much time and many resources were spent recruiting within the trade union movement. Proportionally, the Eastern Bloc diplomats achieved greater results in influencing British government policy through the unions than politicians largely because a high proportion of union leaders were communist. The unions exerted a vice-like grip on the Labour Party, providing funding and support, in return for which, at the party conference held each autumn, they were in a position to leverage the policies that the party would follow. This was enabled by the union leadership holding block votes for their members, which easily trumped the individual membership. It is perhaps not surprising that the industrial unrest and subsequent economic paralysis that the country experienced in the 1970s and early 1980s were in part the result of agitation by Eastern Bloc agents.

Frolík, with his receding hairline and deep-set eyes, gave the appearance more of an amiable professor than a spy at the heart of some of the most daring acts of political espionage. There is no suggestion that his two years in London had tempted him to defect. Throughout, he appeared to be nothing less than fully committed to his country's cause. However, appearances, especially at that time, could be deceptive. Frolík was a man already in crisis, but it would have been suicide for him to have confided in anyone about his disillusionment. Frolík had seen that the communist system was not infallible and was riddled with corruption and self-interest. He wanted out.

Frolík managed people who were betraying their country, whether for reasons of ideology, greed, fear of exposure or, as in many cases, a combination of factors. The Czechs had agents inside parliament, the police force, various government departments, including the Treasury and Home Office, several research establishments, trade unions and the City. By Frolík's own calculation they had around thirty agents and a couple of hundred other contacts, more than enough to keep the intelligence staff in the embassy busy.

Stonehouse was already in the paid employ of the Czechs, but by his own admission Frolík had had no dealings with him. Nonetheless he was to play a significant, if not pivotal, role in the politician's fate. Kugler may have recruited and handled Stonehouse initially but from 1961 he was managed by the playboy operative, Captain Robert Husak, who clearly loved his life in London and embraced the Swinging Sixties. Photographs exist in the StB file of Stonehouse strolling through the elegant streets of Mayfair with Husak. The one politician Frolík did deal with was the Labour MP for Morpeth, Will Owen, also referred to as agent Lee. He was paid a retainer of £500 a month and was by all accounts only motivated by money, leading the Czech operatives to nickname him 'greedy bastard'.

Despite his best endeavours, Frolík's time in London was a difficult one. No sooner did he think that he had a politician or trade union official in his pocket than he would discover that the individual concerned was under someone else's control. Whether it was his own StB operatives or the KGB, anything promising seemed always to be scuppered. Nonetheless, he was still a busy man running twenty agents and contacts.

Frolík knew that he was under surveillance from the British security services; in this cat-and-mouse world that was par for the course. As a result, he was scrupulous in taking steps to avoid compromising his position, leaving nothing of a sensitive nature in his family home in Bayswater, and instead retaining documents and information at the embassy. However, in 1965 he began to suspect that he was being watched by his own side. Whether there was any truth in this, and the Czechs had caught a hint of suspicion that he may defect, or he was simply being neurotic is unclear. Far from suggesting any misgivings, Frolík's StB file suggests that his superiors were happy with his work.

No doubt Frolík's paranoia, frustration and disillusionment contributed to the bizarre events of 30 December 1965. Frolík's account of the incident in his 1975 memoir, *The Frolik Defection*, considering his level of intoxication, is remarkably lucid. He described attending a staff party at the embassy. By dusk he was feeling the worse for wear and decided to leave, but his comrades pressed him to stay and, against his better judgement, he agreed. The revelry continued, banter growing louder and coarser, silent waiters winding between the guests, topping up drinks almost unnoticed. As the evening wore on, Frolík's state of intoxication lurched from tipsy to drunk to inebriated. Finally, slurring his farewells, he staggered out of the embassy into the cold winter's night accompanied by a colleague who groggily persuaded him to have a nightcap at a Hungarian restaurant on the Bayswater Road. At the bar, Frolík had complained of having a headache and his drunken companion offered him what he later described as a rather large pink tablet. Having swallowed it, Frolík felt that it worsened the effects of the drink, adding to the mystery of subsequent events. Eventually even his compatriot abandoned him, having teetered off to find the lavatory, never to return.

Frolík reeled on to the frozen, deserted Bayswater Road, gently swaying in the direction of his nearby home. Unfortunately, his unsteady progress attracted the attention of two police officers on foot patrol, one of whom tapped him on the shoulder to ask for his identification. Taken by surprise, Frolík's befuddled instincts sprang into action and, in one swift movement, he spun round and swung a punch that connected solidly with the officer's jaw, causing him to crumple to the floor. His fellow officer swiftly drew his truncheon and, before Frolík could turn on him, his club made contact with the Czech's head and darkness enveloped.

After he awoke from his drunken stupor in a cell in Paddington police station, Frolík was examined by a doctor and informed that he was in the cells not just because of the altercation with the police officers, but for an alleged assault on a prostitute. The allegation prompted him to declare that he was a Czech diplomat and had immunity. The doctor exclaimed, 'You're no diplomat. You're a spy,' spitting the words into the Czech's face with such venom that they hit Frolík like a slap.

The spy quickly gathered his battered wits, abruptly deciding to seize this opportunity. He demanded the doctor contact officials at the American embassy as he wished to speak with them urgently regarding his decision to defect. The doctor stepped out of the room, leaving Frolík to contemplate his options during a lengthy, anxious wait. To his bemusement, and disappointment, when the door eventually opened it was to admit a colleague from the Czechoslovak embassy, who strolled in casually, claiming to have resolved the matter with the police, averting any scent of scandal. A dazed Frolík was ushered into a taxi and whisked home no doubt to ponder events over a large pot of steaming black coffee.

Frolík later wondered whether the vitriolic person who had been introduced as a doctor was in fact a counter-intelligence officer, though he was unable to fathom whether he might be from MI5, his own country or from some other agency. Frolík claimed to have returned to the police station with an MI5 officer after his defection to find the only record of his stay was that he had been there for thirty-five minutes and had claimed diplomatic immunity. The identity of his interrogators was to remain a mystery. The report on his StB files makes reference to the incident:

> At the end of his residence stay, Frolík was involved in a serious incident with London police when he was apprehended in a drunk state in the vicinity of his flat and then taken to a police station by the patrolling guards. During interrogation, Frolík's personal documents as well as a pocket calendar were taken from him. The information contained in this small notebook could not be investigated. He remained at the police station for approximately three hours and was only released after the intervention from our foreign office in London, namely the ambassadorial counsel, comrade Pátcek, who picked him up at the station. Since this constituted another serious breach of his personal promise to the central office that he would abstain from excessive drinking, he was prematurely recalled back to ČSSR from his residence stay.

There is no suggestion that he was under any suspicion from the Czech authorities. It is more likely that the 'interview' was a doctor's examination and that Frolík was still so heavily intoxicated that he had been confused, leading to heightened feelings of paranoia causing him to react erratically.

The incident had compromised Frolík and deeply embarrassed the ambassador, so it came as little surprise that his time in London rapidly came to an end with his recall to Prague in March 1966.

5

TWISTER

Labour's 1964 general election victory brought with it a revitalised and vibrant British economy. The country had thrust off the shackles of 1950s austerity and Cold War gloom and was looking ahead to a time of optimism and prosperity. Harold Wilson had set the tone for his election campaign with his celebrated 'white heat of technology' speech, in which he had set out a vision for Britain as a leader in science and technology. The new cabinet shone with dynamism in stark contrast to the outgoing staid, stale Conservative government, riddled with corruption and scandal.

Stonehouse had drawn favourable attention and was appointed to the Labour front benches as a junior minister. In October 1964 he became parliamentary secretary for aviation, working under the senior minister Tony Benn. Part of the department's remit was to generate sales of British-built aircraft throughout the world at a time when the aircraft industry, having led the world, was on the wane. It was hoped that the Concorde project, the development of the Trident aircraft and work with other European nations to develop the Airbus project would revitalise its fortunes. Stonehouse tackled the tasks in his new post with gusto.

The Czechs had been growing concerned that agent Kolon appeared to have been avoiding them. They had lost contact in 1963

37

and, despite repeated attempts to reconnect with him, Stonehouse had apparently shunned them. A clue as to why this situation may have arisen came from a communiqué to Prague on 16 May 1963. It surmised that two incidents had affected the MP. The first related to the arrest of John Vassall earlier that year. A British civil servant who worked for the naval attaché at the British embassy in Moscow, Vassall had been blackmailed in a KGB homosexual honey trap. Counterbalancing the threat with the lure of money, and the assurance that he would not be compromised, the KGB compelled him to supply copies of thousands of secret documents for which he was subsequently exposed by KGB defector Anatoliy Golitsyn, and received an eighteen-year jail sentence after his trial in September and October of that year. The second was the arrest of Colonel Oleg Penkovsky, a Soviet military intelligence officer who had supplied the British with information on nuclear weapon sites being developed in Cuba. Widely believed to have been executed, with a rumour that he was cremated alive, the Soviets claimed he had committed suicide. Whatever the truth, the colonel had come to an unfortunate end. No doubt both incidents had served to highlight to Stonehouse the stark reality of his activities and the consequences of exposure. The response from Prague was nonetheless sanguine: 'Keep calm, do not attempt to contact. Find an excuse for an official invitation to Czechoslovakia in connection with Kladno. Once in Czechoslovakia discuss another perspective of cooperation and establish a new connection.'

The opportunity would soon arise.

Shortly after Labour's success, Stonehouse visited the Czech embassy in Kensington to attend one of the many cocktail parties that were arranged by the 'diplomatic attachés' hoping to develop contacts in the political and trade union movements. While making small talk over a glass of wine, Stonehouse was approached by Captain Robert Husak. Stonehouse later maintained that he made every effort to avoid the Czech diplomat, but Husak was like a bloodhound scenting his quarry, cornering the errant MP in the embassy's restroom. In the course of an awkward conversation, Stonehouse reluctantly allowed Husak to arrange a lunch meeting between them, during which he suspected that the Czechs were attempting to compromise him, afterwards reporting the matter to MI5. Interestingly, he failed to disclose previous lunches and meetings that had taken place with Kugler and other operatives. His report of this lunch meeting was to hold him in good stead in the years to come.

Stonehouse continued to remain as elusive as ever, much to Husak's frustration: 'I have been calling him . . . either his wife takes the phone or no one gets it. I am determined to call him 11.3. if he doesn't leave a message at home under the name of Robson, I'll call 12.3. at 9.30 in the morning. If K. is out of London in agreement with K.'s wife, I leave a note on the day when Kolon returns.'

The Czechs' hopes of re-engaging Stonehouse had been proving fruitless. They had endeavoured to contact him using the newspaper code, a plan that was thwarted by their failure to update Stonehouse's address in their records. No doubt the new occupants at the address in north-west London had been rather bemused to receive the cryptic newspaper clippings in the post. The London embassy ruefully noted in their regular reports to Prague that the minister continued to avoid them. No doubt, now that Stonehouse had begun to realise his ambitions, he did not consider any further assistance from that quarter was required, having instead become a source of potential embarrassment and political ruin for him. He may have wished to close the chapter, but the story was about to take an unexpected turn.

Around June 1965, Stonehouse suggested to the ministry that he should visit Czechoslovakia to promote British aircraft. The Vickers VC10 especially needed to be promoted as sales were sluggish and the usual markets were considering other options, not least Boeing's latest offerings. Stonehouse judged that Eastern Bloc countries were ripe for developing the UK market. At that time, it was one thing for a government minister to undertake an official visit to a country sympathetic to Western capitalist values but quite another to visit one within the Warsaw Pact, which was regarded as an ideological enemy. Stonehouse considered that the only way to resolve the East–West standoff was to encourage and develop trade links. This was his opportunity. Understandably, the idea was received with some caution within the UK government.

The Czechs, ever keen to promote their man, used other means to encourage the visit. The British industrialist, Rudy Sternberg (later to be knighted Baron Plurenden) was a Labour Party donor and highly influential, paying regular trips to Number 10 and becoming a confidant of the prime minister. Given a free rein to conduct business within the Eastern Bloc, Sternberg was soon in the throes of a passionate affair with a young Czech mistress. It was only a matter of time before he was engaged by the Czechs under the codename 'The Beginner'. Much like Stonehouse, he had met regularly with a Czech handler, Major Pátcek, the man who had the dubious pleasure of rescuing Frolík from Paddington police station. In the summer of 1965 Sternberg was enlisted to encourage the proposed trip to sell the VC10, the principal aim being to boost Stonehouse's profile.

Wilson warmed to the idea and plans for a visit were set in motion. A trade fair was organised in Brno for 21–24 September of that year, and Stonehouse suggested that he should also visit the town of Kladno, which had been twinned with Stonehouse's constituency of Wednesbury. Kladno was near Prague, so it would perhaps be considered a sleight if he didn't.

The minister's itinerary was already a full one so fitting in a visit to this industrial outpost would be a stretch. There were concerns that a formal visit would take up a significant part of the limited time. These fears were exacerbated by the fact that the town was staunchly communist and the Foreign Office worried that residents would use the visit to protest over the escalating war in Vietnam. The minister proposed that, time permitting, he would ask leave to visit for a couple of hours after he had arrived in Czechoslovakia.

The Czechs saw this as an opportunity to re-engage their agent and help enhance his political reputation. Now that he was a minister they planned to do everything they could to assist him to rise through the ministerial ranks. This would afford them an opportunity to obtain valuable information on British government policy in respect of NATO, the European Economic Community (EEC), the colonies and, if possible, military intelligence.

With this level of influence it was of little surprise that the trip was authorised. The trade mission proved to be diplomatically successful: although no planes were sold it provided a basis for further visits and business, and the British ambassador reported in glowing terms how industrious Stonehouse had been, adding that the Czechs wanted to arrange a similar visit, perhaps during the World Cup due to take place in the UK the following year.

At the end of September 1965, Husak attended the Labour Party conference in Blackpool with the intention of initiating further contact with Stonehouse but it proved a frustrating pursuit. Despite regularly glimpsing the minister from the balcony or across the crowded lobby, he could never get close enough to speak to him. Stonehouse then vanished, only to reappear in London, where he had accepted an invitation to lunch at the Czechoslovak embassy, to which Husak had also been invited. The conversation at the dinner table was polite but restrained, politics as ever the hot topic, Husak itching throughout for the opportunity to speak to Stonehouse. He was finally able to snatch his chance when Stonehouse needed to visit the cloakroom. Reminiscent of their clandestine meeting at an embassy cocktail party, the spy followed and 'bumped into' the minister there, managing to engage him in a brief conversation during which Stonehouse asked Husak to call him after the state opening of parliament, which was scheduled to take place the following month. An excited Husak duly reported the matter to his masters and waited impatiently for the rendezvous, but it would not materialise until 29 December.

Stonehouse met the captain at St Ermin's Hotel grill room promptly at 1 p.m. As was the custom, the Czech had taken the precaution of arriving early, having detoured through Turnham Green and Ealing to ensure that he was not under surveillance. Arriving early he found the restaurant busy, ideal cover for the two men to converse. Satisfying himself that he had no unwanted attention he took his seat and waited. It was a curious place to meet as the restaurant was regularly used by the British intelligence services. No doubt with this knowledge, the minister was initially reticent and appeared concerned that they may be observed. Husak tried to put him at ease, casually discussing Christmas and handing the bemused politician gifts: for him, a Schaeffer writing set, and for his wife, a gold pendant.

All the while the politician continued to study his new contact closely, calculating whether he could be trusted. Conscious of his surroundings and the reputation of the place, Stonehouse spoke so quietly that Husak had to strain to hear him above the restaurant's hubbub. The minister mentioned that the Americans' surveillance and wire-tapping equipment was quite effective and expressed his concern that their meetings should remain secret and secure, without risk of discovery and scandal. Despite this Stonehouse was open to 'cooperation', although with his enhanced position there would be a greater price to pay for that assistance. The two men discussed the form such cooperation would take. Stonehouse was clear that it would not consist of any military information, but would involve political negotiations that the British government would have with other countries, with a particular focus on Germany, the EEC and the former British colonies. The Czech accepted this. They agreed that with Stonehouse's recent visit to Czechoslovakia to sell the VC10 was the perfect cover for their future meetings, Husak being the man at the embassy who would be brokering the VC10 deal. The

Czechoslovaks also believed that the promise of a deal would provide further incentive for their man to cooperate. Lunch ended and the two parted company. Husak returned to the embassy excited that contact had been re-established and a cypher was sent to Prague: 'Meeting with Kolon 29.12. Cooperation renewed in its entirety.'

Even with Husak's optimistic assessment, it took time to settle matters between Stonehouse and the Czechs. The issue of payment had to be resolved as his enhanced position demanded more money and this had to be cleared by Prague. The subject was finalised when a letter was sent from the department head in the UK to the Czechoslovak interior minister, Josef Kudrna, to persuade him that Stonehouse was worth it:

> In view of Kolon's high level of discretion, I propose to sell a fee of £1,500. The sale of that amount is justified by the fact that Kolon did not receive any financial remuneration in the last 3 years and is reluctant to support the risk of cooperation without this being adequately balanced by his current position in British political life. By selling this amount, all terms and conditions of the agreement will be met and strong pressure will be put on the full use of its possibilities.

Permission for the payment came from Prague and Stonehouse received his reward. As a precaution the Czechs changed the minister's codename to Katalina. If the StB thought this would encourage further cooperation they were sadly mistaken. The meetings were sporadic, short and ultimately did not produce the desired information. A significant issue was how any intelligence would be passed between them. Stonehouse, perhaps with some justification, did not trust the Czechs. He was concerned that his treachery would be revealed by one of the increasing number of defectors escaping to the West. He also suspected that his meetings were being recorded, whether by the StB or by British intelligence. On one occasion he had asked Husak whether the Czechs were filming him. Naturally Husak denied it, although he had arranged for a colleague to photograph the two of them walking to a restaurant in Belgravia at an earlier meeting in August 1966. The photographs are to this day to be found secreted in the StB files.

Husak complained that Stonehouse would not be drawn into divulging any information in the conversations. The wily minister resorted to providing the intelligence in writing, invariably, when they were travelling in a cab or car. He would afford Husak the opportunity to read his handwritten notes but refused to allow the Czech to take them away with him. Stonehouse was ever conscious that such notes would be fatal were they to be discovered. The nature of the intelligence he provided was disappointing. One of Husak's cyphers expressed their growing dismay, commenting that it could easily be obtained from the newspapers.

Stonehouse's stock continued to rise. In January 1967 he was appointed minister of state for aviation, soon to be followed, in February, with the position of minister of state for technology when the former post was abolished. The huge energy and enthusiasm he put into promoting Britain's aircraft industry did not go unnoticed. He had been actively involved in the development of Concorde, the first supersonic passenger jet, which would become an iconic symbol of that period, and signed an agreement with France and Germany for the development of a European Airbus. However, the minister soon became disillusioned with the effectiveness of his role. When the state-owned British Overseas Airways Corporation (BOAC) made the decision, contrary to his recommendation, to order Boeing aeroplanes as opposed to the British Vickers VC10, he was furious. The arrangement undermined all his work, signalling that a British airline preferred a foreign competitor, eroding overseas confidence in Britain's aircraft industry. While Stonehouse had harboured hopes that his contacts in the Eastern Bloc would bolster the aircraft's flagging sales, salvation came from the Middle East when the Saudis placed a multi-million-pound order. Stonehouse no longer needed the Czechs.

The minister's meetings with Husak were less relaxed than they had been in their early years. As a result of the politician's developing role he now had a far more hectic schedule and there was always the risk that he was under surveillance from MI5. A typical encounter took place on 22 February 1967, when a rendezvous with Husak was arranged to take place on Regent Street. Stonehouse arrived outside the tailor Austin Reed in a black cab and Husak, who had been waiting, quickly jumped in as Stonehouse directed the driver to take them to a restaurant next to Hammersmith tube station. On the journey Stonehouse scrawled out a three-page report, leaning the papers on his briefcase balanced on his lap, and handed it to his contact to read over. Added to this report was a question: was this information useful to them? The minister did not allow Husak to retain the handwritten notes.

Arriving at the restaurant, the two men requested a table in the corner where they settled into conversation while making a show of studying their menus. Husak took the opportunity to answer the politician's query. 'These reports you supply have a very limited life span and value to us,' complained the Czech, waving a hand over his briefcase on the empty seat beside him. 'Given your position, you should be supplying us with better information.'

'You have to understand that I give you information to which I have access. Wilson only calls us into cabinet meetings where there are questions raised specifically in respect of my department, otherwise I am not invited to them,' an exasperated Stonehouse responded.

The Czech frowned and made a mental note to check this against the information they gathered from their other informant, Lee. Moving on to another bone of contention, he expressed his profound displeasure with the manner in which the meeting had been conducted. The back of a London taxi was far from ideal for such affairs and he suggested that future meetings between them should be of shorter duration and take place at official functions. The spy proposed that they arrange a moment in privacy in which Stonehouse could then pass over any written information he had. While Stonehouse concurred with the suggestion of the shorter meetings, he considered it was now only possible to give oral reports.

Recognising the Czech's ominous dissatisfaction, Stonehouse strategically opted to whet his contact's appetite with a tantalising glimpse of some more substantial information. He drew from his pocket a sample of metal about 10 cm in length, which he rolled thoughtfully between his finger and thumb. 'This is a new alloy that's lighter but three times stronger than steel. It's going to be used in the manufacture of new jet turbines.'

His companion momentarily paused, eyes fixed on the silvery metal, dull under the dim lights of the dining room as he absorbed what had just been presented to him. Gathering his wits, he hastily offered to buy the item. Stonehouse seemed to ponder the proposal for a moment before refusing, shrugging his shoulders as he slipped it back into the safety of his pocket, musing that he didn't know why he had brought it along. Husak surmised in his report that the minister knew damned well why he had done that. The dangling carrot was a ruse to extort more money. This would not be the last time the crafty minister would use such tactics; on one occasion, he told Husak of a newly developed transistor for radio communication and tipped him off about his pending promotion to a full cabinet post.

The Czechs did indeed look to their other agents to assess whether Stonehouse was being straight with them. It appeared that he wasn't. Agent Lee, Will Owen, met up with Stonehouse on 1 November 1967 for lunch, at which the conversation centred on the cabinet discussions on NATO. The French had recently withdrawn from the alliance, threatening the very existence of the organisation, but

Stonehouse informed Lee that he had been involved in discussions that demonstrated it was very much alive and kicking. The remaining countries had reorganised at a nuclear planning meeting in Ankara that September and, despite their departure, the French were still cooperating and taking part in essential operations. A recent naval anti-submarine exercise involving forty ships from a number of different countries was considered a success and the US secretary of defence, Robert McNamara, had also reported to them on the strength of the US missile defence system. Add to this the recommendation that the RAF replace their fighter stock with the new American F-111, and it was clear that NATO was as strong and united as ever. He concluded that all NATO member countries were as one in the view that they should maintain their current military strength until agreement could be reached with the Soviets on disarmament. However, the US was anxious to enter into negotiations with the USSR on eliminating strategic nuclear weapons, especially given the recent problems that had arisen with China.

This was precisely the type of information that the Czechs had expected to get from Stonehouse, highlighting their concerns that they were not getting intelligence of any quality from the minister. Add to that his evasiveness and they felt compelled to bring him to heel.

The subsequent meetings continued to expose tensions. The minister wanted more money and assurances that they could not be compromised. Husak continued to point out that the information Stonehouse provided was of limited value and was easily obtained through other sources, making it clear that the StB would not provide any more money until the quality of the material was of the type they expected from someone in Stonehouse's position. The Czech provided the politician with the topics on which they were seeking intelligence: the status of the EEC negotiations; the devaluation of sterling; Anglo-American relations; and events in Rhodesia, where Ian Smith had unilaterally declared independence. With expectations set, the issue of how the information should be provided had to be resolved. Husak did not want to continue with Stonehouse's scribbled notes, all of which the minister retained. He wanted something more tangible to provide to his bosses. Naturally the politician did not want anything he supplied to be traced to him. A compromise was reached: any document would be typed anonymously using an uppercase font.

Stonehouse continued to provide intelligence but the Czechs remained dissatisfied. They concluded that their softly, softly approach was not working. Alternative methods to compromise Stonehouse were considered. At one of the few restaurant meetings Husak managed to persuade the minister to attend, he covertly recorded the conversation, anticipating that such evidence would give them more leverage over Stonehouse should he remain elusive. Unfortunately the noise in the restaurant put paid to any meaningful recording.

Husak's rueful communiqué of 15 June 1967 to Prague perfectly encapsulated the Czech's view of the minister: 'It should be borne in mind that K is an old twister and that there will be some work to do.' In response, Stonehouse's codename was changed to Twister. It was a trait that would resonate in the years to come.

* * *

Twister was to cease to be Husak's problem as the captain's residence in London was to end by the close of 1967. Plans were made to introduce Stonehouse to his new contact, Karel Pravec, codenamed Pelnár, but it proved problematic as a combination of the politician's work commitments as well as a loss of appetite for the games that he had been playing meant that no such meeting could be arranged. However, opportunity soon presented itself again.

Early in 1968, Stonehouse made a formal request to the Czechoslovakian embassy for a business delegation to travel to Czechoslovakia to promote British trade. The plan was for the group to fly into Prague at the end of March. Husak and his team were primed and determined to corner him. Meetings were held in Prague and Bratislava, during which Stonehouse was closely chaperoned by his private secretary and consulate staff, preventing the StB men from speaking to him alone and unnoticed. They used the time to watch, wait and plan; when the opening arose, they would be prepared.

The British delegation took the liberty to break from business and take advantage of some late-season skiing in the Low Tatras, checking into the Hotel Kosodrevina on the slopes of Chopok Mountain. Here the StB men saw there might be an opportunity to catch Stonehouse on his own, either on the slopes or at the hotel. The StB had set up a three-man team, renting rooms at the Kosodrevina: Husak, Pravec and another agent, Fresl, who was acting as one of the Czechoslovak guides to the Stonehouse party and kept his colleagues abreast of the minister's movements.

In his book *Death of an Idealist*, Stonehouse described how he had been approached by the Czechs in what he painted as a bizarre and clumsy attempt to compromise him. The book was written and published in 1975, when, as well as awaiting his trial, the story of his alleged treachery had been resurrected, the Cold War was very much at its height and his account was viewed with some suspicion by the British security services. It transpires that they were right to be sceptical, even without the benefit of access to the StB files, where a different version of those events is recounted.

In the early hours of 30 March 1968, Fresl informed Pravec that Stonehouse had requested breakfast to be served in his room, number 213A. Assuming the rest of his entourage would be taking breakfast in the dining room, Pravec took his chance. At 8 a.m. sharp, he took a tray loaded with baked goods and coffee to the minister's room, where he knocked on the door. Hearing the words 'Come in,' he entered and set the tray down, saying, 'Mr Stonehouse, greetings from Harold Poulter.'

Stonehouse, seated at a small table by the window with a magnificent view of the mountain, wrapped in a hotel robe, knew immediately that this was an StB contact.

'I'm sorry to contact you in this way but we have not had any other opportunity to speak. Robert is here and he would like to meet you. We understand that it is difficult, as you are in company,' Pravec apologised hastily. 'We would like to meet with you for longer. There are three options: we can either meet back here in your room or arrange a rendezvous somewhere outside the hotel, if you think you can get away from your group, or we can meet in my room but it will have to be tonight.' He paused, as if to ensure that Stonehouse was following. If the Englishman had been surprised by the intrusion, he hid it well, appearing relaxed if not a little amused. 'Think about it and let me know when you are out skiing. I will be following your group. I will make an opportunity to meet briefly so you can tell me what would suit.'

Stonehouse nodded and, with that, the agent slipped out.

Having savoured his solitary breakfast overlooking the snowy peaks, the minister joined his companions to enjoy the skiing on the slopes of Mount Chopok. True to his word, Pravec tailed the group, sometimes moving ahead of them to avoid any suspicion that they were being observed. Eventually an opportunity arose and Stonehouse managed to peel away from the group with Pravec discreetly following. As the two men glided to a halt, Stonehouse abruptly thrust a key into the StB man's gloved hand.

'This is the key to the side door of my room. Meet me there at ten tonight. You must understand that we cannot afford to be seen.'

With that brief exchange, the two men parted, Stonehouse to re-join his party while Pravec returned to the hotel to meet with Husak in his room. For five tedious hours the Czechs whiled away the time before they silently crept to Stonehouse's room. It was dark and deserted so they prepared a snack and waited. At 10.30 p.m. the minister returned, appearing comfortable and relaxed in casual wool slacks and a knitted sweater. They made small talk, discussing personal matters and the latest political developments in Czechoslovakia. A more liberal and interesting time seemed in the offing.

Eventually, Husak took control of the conversation. He formally introduced Pravec, advising Stonehouse that this was his deputy at their London embassy and that he would be meeting with him from time to time. He then moved on to the terms of their 'cooperation'.

'The areas of interest for us are Anglo-German and Anglo-American relations. We need as much information about what is happening and the nature of the relationships and, in particular, their attitudes and approach to Czechoslovakia and other Eastern Bloc countries.' Husak paused to check whether Stonehouse had picked up on the back-handed reference to the material they had received via agent Lee late in 1967. The inference was that they were aware that Stonehouse was privy to such information and yet was not feeding them this intelligence. 'This is the most valuable information for us. We need you to use your good relationship with Wilson and encourage more meetings with him.'

Stonehouse nodded. He understood and told them so, adding a caveat. 'I won't be compromised by pursuing irrelevant information. When I get back to London, I anticipate that I will be promoted within the cabinet so the information I can obtain will be far better. With my promotion I will have a greater influence on government policy and will be able to steer them on policies more favourable to you.'

He referred to the recent sale of VC10s to the Czechs, as well as the trade delegation and agreements in respect to closer cooperation between the two countries in science and technology, as examples of how he was influencing government policy in favour of Czechoslovakia. The agents seemed to accept this.

With some level of agreement having been reached, the three men speculated as to how such information should be communicated. The Czechs objected to Stonehouse's use of oral accounts, and Pravec pointed out that providing written reports would mean that they would only need to meet three or four times a year, considerably reducing the risk of being compromised. After some debate they agreed that it was probably the best way to communicate and Pravec undertook to consider in what form the written information should be provided. He would contact Stonehouse once he had this settled.

Husak reported to his superiors that the meeting lasted about an hour and a half and that he considered there was no reason to believe that any problems would arise in Stonehouse and Pravec's working relationship in London.

If the Czechoslovaks thought they had resolved their problem, they were again to be sadly mistaken. They continued to experience problems with Stonehouse's 'cooperation'. Forced to pursue him to the Labour Party conference in Blackpool that October, Pravec managed to corner Stonehouse. There followed an awkward half-hour meeting during which Pravec criticised the minister's clumsy attempts to avoid them. Undoubtedly in an effort to placate the Czech agent's indignation, Stonehouse gave assurances that he was happy to continue to work with them. He insisted that he could only commit to three or four meetings a year, adding that he would not be able to visit Czechoslovakia for at least a year; nor would he convene meetings over the telephone as the calls were likely to be under surveillance. Then Stonehouse sat back and smiled as he dangled another carrot. He confided that the next year was likely to be very promising and again claimed he expected to be stepping into an elevated position within the cabinet. Suitably buoyed by this information, the Czech left, having agreed another meeting back in London on 8 October.

To the Czechoslovaks' continued irritation Stonehouse did not live up to his promise. They were now getting a little impatient with the MP, having invested a great deal of resources in the man. They were not getting value for money and were considering other ways of trying to compromise him, but unexpected events were about to change everything.

6

SPRING IN THE AIR

Prague, 1966–8

The sojourn in London had been an unmitigated disaster for Frolík. He had managed the stable of informants, agents and collaborators well enough but had struggled to recruit foreign agents for the cause. 'His task completion brought minimal results and he was reprimanded for his insufficient initiative and lack of operative wit. That is why he was called off and sent home early. He considered that to be an unfair evaluation of his work,' cited a Czech report written after his defection.

The drunken episode at the end of 1965 was no doubt a symptom of the profound frustration he was feeling at the time. The strain of trying to function naturally and productively, while constantly aware of both the intense scrutiny he was under from all quarters and of all the scheming going on behind the scenes, unquestionably resulted in a pervasive paranoia. A deep sense of resentment grew as he observed many of his colleagues avoiding the censure he had suffered despite indulging in regular antisocial escapades. He complained to his superiors that Husak was frequently arrested for being drunk but, unlike Frolík, he possessed a suave charm that allowed him to shrug off trouble. Tall and darkly good looking, he enjoyed a reputation as a playboy, mixing easily within the diplomatic circles of London, the complete antithesis to Frolík. His sense of injustice and resentment was a cocktail that would eventually poison him.

Returning early from his foreign tour of duty under a cloud had done him no favours, leading to some troubling uncertainty as to how he was going to be employed. His section head curtly informed Frolík that he was no longer welcome on the London desk, and the unfortunate officer was forced to fall back on his resources, managing to secure a place on the Africa desk through his contacts. Applying himself diligently to the mundanities of the role, he eventually became responsible for Beirut and Kabul. He had a point to prove and, in throwing himself into his work, he proved to be highly effective and managed some successful operations.

In spite of this, Frolík recognised that he had been under continual observation since his return from London. The stringency of the state demanded that anyone returning from a tour in the West would attract intensified scrutiny to detect whether they had been seduced by the decadence and freedoms enjoyed in those countries.

It was undoubtedly a time of turmoil for the authorities. Yet, while the reception he had received had irked him, he gave no cause for his superiors to think that he was tempted to turn. His dissatisfaction did not arrive in a dramatic moment of revelation; it was more akin to a dripping tap, but eventually the sink would overflow.

* * *

By the mid-1960s the Czechoslovaks had tired of the communist experiment, the economy had suffered and the Soviet Union's influence had been all-pervasive. A number of feeble attempts to reform by the Antonín Novotný administration had failed. Despite government crackdowns, the clamour for change grew and became irresistible, the nascent buds of the 1968 Prague Spring were beginning to form.

On 5 January 1968, Alexander Dubček was elected first secretary of the Czechoslovakian Communist Party. Immediately there was a noticeable relaxation in the vice-like grip of state security, with citizens embracing the freedom to express their views more openly. There followed a period of liberalisation of the media and the economy, in which censorship and party propaganda were abolished and the abundance and variety of consumer goods increased. By April, Dubček's reform package was being implemented. For the next four months the Prague Spring blossomed.

Frolík revelled in his sudden emancipation, feeling at liberty to be vocally supportive of the Dubček administration and all it had to offer. The weight of surveillance he had been oppressed by lifted as the Cold War, at least for Frolík and Czechoslovakia, seemed to be thawing.

This was reflected by the appraisal of Frolík's work in his personnel file between 1 January and 15 July that year. His impressed superiors reported that 'Frolík has a good knowledge of the issues he is working on and is evaluated as an independent operative worker with a wealth of internal experience and practical experience . . . abroad . . . is an educated, highly versatile comrade, has a perfect overview of the internal political situation in the countries being processed.' With effect from 1 July 1968, the captain would be Major Frolík, and receive a 1,000 koruna bonus.

Nineteen sixty-eight would be remembered as a year of revolution. French students and workers united in protest in Paris, in London similar events erupted in Grosvenor Square, and civil rights activism reached its zenith in the United States, culminating in the assassinations of Martin Luther King Jr and Bobby Kennedy. The world was burning for change, optimism replaced by rebellion and unrest. Czechoslovakia too ignited, the relaxation of central control precipitating greater freedom for the people culturally and for the media. It was not to last.

With the increasing concern a parent would have for a wayward child, the Soviets watched the Prague Spring unfold. Ever conscious of their own security, their unease grew. Longstanding hostility to Soviet oppression spilled on to the television screens and into the newspapers. The Soviets waited for Dubček to act. His response was telling: no arrests; no interrogations; no property confiscated; no trials . . . nothing.

For the first time in a generation, the country was finding a voice and openly questioning their place within the Soviet sphere. The Kremlin's unease quickly turned to alarm as structural reforms took hold. The USSR feared a repetition of the Hungarian uprising of 1956, in which the Hungarians had introduced reforms and threatened to pull out of the Warsaw Pact, the Eastern Bloc's answer to NATO. Then it had responded by sending tanks into Budapest and arresting the president, who was tried in Moscow and hanged. The country had been ruthlessly brought to heel. Despite Dubček's assurances that Czechoslovakia had no intention of quitting the Warsaw Pact, the Kremlin decided that enough was enough. The Prague Spring must be crushed, and the perpetual winter of Soviet communism reimposed.

From his unique position, Frolík noticed the Soviet manoeuvrings. Surveillance of the major had been reinstated, not by the Czechs but by the KGB. Changes were creeping in within the StB. There had always been a pro-Soviet lobby within the organisation and Frolík suspected, correctly, that a number of his colleagues were in the paid employ of the KGB. In the months before the tanks rolled into Prague, the Soviets had already insidiously taken control of the Czechoslovak security system. Anyone suspected of holding even a vaguely anti-Soviet stance was ruthlessly dismissed to be replaced with someone loyal to the Kremlin, while those identified as dissidents and troublemakers were put under observation. Vital parts of the state machinery were manipulated so that Soviet control could be implemented without hesitation or opposition from within.

On 20 August 1968, Czechoslovakia was invaded by half a million Warsaw Pact troops who had been massing along the Czech borders. Unlike in Hungary, there was little in the way of violence. Dubček called on citizens not to offer resistance and instead tanks and troops were met with flowers and questions as to why they were there. The die was cast and the Soviet 'normalisation' of Czechoslovakia had commenced. Dubček and two other leaders were arrested and brought to Moscow, while back in Czechoslovakia further purges of the organs of government were undertaken. During the state of emergency, Frolík was among a number of officers who had absented themselves from the StB headquarters in Prague, which was now under the control of the Soviets. On 21 August, urgent rumours of mass arrests and internments began to circulate, and Frolík was warned that his name was on the list. Though he was not immediately arrested, he sensed it would only be a matter of time.

The treatment Frolík had been subjected to on his return from London and the Prague Spring had a profound effect on him, and his sense of resentment deepened as he witnessed the Soviet invasion of his country. Rather unwisely, given his precarious position, he vented his views to colleagues and friends he considered sympathetic, views that were duly noted.

His conspicuous reluctance to conform and his erratic behaviour led Frolík to speculate that not only his own but his family's lives were in jeopardy, a suspicion that was confirmed when he was detained at the StB offices in Prague. He was not questioned, though, and was eventually able to talk his way out of the building.

A second arrest was more harrowing. A car picked him up from his home and drove him out to a location deep in the woods surrounding the city. The terrifying journey, crushed between two grim-faced security officers on the back seat of the Škoda, provided plenty of time for Frolík to reflect on his continued loyalty to the regime. He was questioned at length, eventually managing to persuade his interrogators that he was faithful to the party and posed no threat to national security. It was with overwhelming relief that he made the return journey, watching the woods retreat from view before he hurriedly climbed out of the cramped back seat and closed his front door behind him.

Nonetheless, the time to make his move was rapidly approaching. A report supplied after his defection noted, 'In the politically tense period in 1968, he expressed significant engagement in the so-called progressive development. He underestimated some negative effects of the development of normalisation and got into conflict with the members of his . . . base organisation, resulting in certain isolation from his co-workers' collective.'

Frolík's frustration boiled over in another drunken incident in which he abused his colleagues and again criticised the regime. On 9 May 1969 he was reprimanded by his superiors and removed from the list of persons to be awarded a medal 'for service and defence of the country'. When notified of this decision, Frolík derisively informed his chief of department that he had no care for medals or commendations.

There was to be no redemption and Frolík understood that dismissal was now inevitable. Once the protection of his post was withdrawn, it would be only a matter of time before he could expect a dawn raid, arrest and, at best, an uncertain future, if there was to be a future.

He resolved to take drastic measures, if not to defend himself then to shield his wife and son from the consequences of his fall from grace. Frolík had a plan.

London, 1968

Nineteen sixty-eight was the year that Stonehouse was to reach the peak of his political career. On 1 July, he was appointed postmaster general, and gained a full place in the Labour government cabinet. When the role was abolished in 1969, Stonehouse became the first minister for post and telecommunications. He was responsible not only for the General Post Office (later to become the Royal Mail) but also all communications whether radio, television or burgeoning satellite technology. He achieved underwhelming renown by introducing first- and second-class postage, as well as the dubious distinction of directing the jamming of pirate radio stations and pursuing TV licence-fee evaders with detector vans. There were highlights too: the opening of the Post Office Museum, where Stonehouse escorted the Queen and was himself presented with a commemorative book of stamps, which, years later, would prove very helpful.

With his elevation to postmaster general and position in the cabinet he was also appointed to the Privy Council, comprising current and former members of the House of Commons or House of Lords whose purpose is to provide advice to the Queen on constitutional and legal matters of state. Unless the appointee chooses to resign or, on the very rare occasion, is expelled, the position is for life, a condition that would prove significant as the events of the next few years unfolded.

With his newly acquired prominence, figures from Stonehouse's past emerged: some, such as the Czechs, to haunt him; some, such as an old RAF chum, Gerald Hastings, to cheer him. On leaving the RAF, Hastings had moved to Europe, sensing that the UK's future lay there. He had done rather well and no doubt his success attracted Stonehouse. After their reacquaintance, the two friends would meet for dinner at least twice a year, during which Stonehouse would confide his ambition to be leader of the Labour Party and become prime minister. Simultaneously, he wished to pursue a parallel career as a businessman. Though sympathetic, Hastings considered that there was little either could do for the other, as his interests lay in Europe and Stonehouse's in Africa.

This was also the year in which an entirely new figure entered Stonehouse's life, one who was to become inextricably entwined with the MP's future. As with most MPs, particularly cabinet ministers, Stonehouse needed administrative support to meet the demands of political life. His advertisement for an assistant led to an attractive, dark-haired, twenty-two-year-old woman perching nervously in the dingy corridor outside the minister's office waiting to be interviewed. She introduced herself as Sheila Buckley, and Stonehouse was struck by the intelligent, vivacious, married woman. He immediately offered her the post as his parliamentary secretary for an annual salary of £1,000.

Undoubtedly, Stonehouse was instantly attracted to her, being as much driven by sex as he was by ambition. In the high-octane environment he occupied, he had developed a reputation for having a roving eye. As a good-looking, suave and powerful man, he had a litany of lovers. This behaviour was starkly at odds with his strong family values. He was devoted to his three children and we all remember at the family gatherings what a fuss he and Barbara would make of us all when we were small. Stonehouse took great pride in his efforts to provide everything his children could want: a comfortable and loving home, a good education and any other support they needed.

Barbara had become aware of her husband's infidelities relatively early on in their marriage. Aged nineteen, they were travelling by train through Sweden with their infant daughter when they were joined by a beautiful Swedish woman with whom her husband had already started an affair, later admitting this to his young wife. It hurt her immensely, but she had learned to accommodate his needs. Barbara later confessed that she had thought many times about leaving him, but his dedication as a father and her recollections of happier times stopped her. Years later, she confided to one newspaper that she felt as if Stonehouse needed to fall in love every two to three years; she also disclosed to a family member how he had been brutally honest with her after the first affair, stating that was simply how he was programmed. Like many men of his type, there appeared to be a symbiosis between career achievement and sex, the two fuelling each other.

There was something different about Sheila Buckley though. From the start she was to prove a highly effective and capable personal assistant. Amenable to the long hours that Stonehouse needed to work, she enjoyed the cut and thrust of Westminster politics. Up to 1970 she was based in Stonehouse's office in the House of Commons, principally dealing with his political career, and the pair grew close, initially as work colleagues. Sheila's relationship with her husband began to suffer, whether because of her commitment to her new employer or the fact that she had been very young when she had tied the knot and was now finding her own identity. Life in politics had opened a whole new world to her, a world in which she was susceptible to falling under the Stonehouse spell. Sheila's marriage ended when she discovered her husband had been having an affair and she left him, starting divorce proceedings that were eventually finalised in 1973. Bitterly heartbroken, Sheila turned to her friend and colleague, and Stonehouse was there to listen and counsel. With her marriage ended, the two soon became lovers.

7

BACO

Prague, Winter 1968–Summer 1969

With his dismissal from the service pending and the prospect of arrest, detention and worse, Frolík set in motion his escape plan.

Encouraged by recent successful defections, Frolík realised that, with meticulous planning, considerable cunning and a whole heap of luck, he stood a chance of extricating himself from what seemed a hopeless position. The KGB grip on the Czechoslovak security apparatus was tightening, gradually throttling any dissent within its ranks. Frolík's desperate position was highlighted by the sudden apparent suicides of a number of Czech agents based in the West. Frolík suspected Soviet skulduggery. The West seemed oblivious to the internal power struggle taking place.

Frolík's first priority was to present himself as a shiny, bright trophy to the CIA. For that he needed to acquire information like a magpie. Not little pebbles of information, but diamond-quality intelligence, rare and valuable, that would deeply wound Czech and Soviet operations for years to come. That would be his currency. To this end, he had to go to the very heart of the StB under the pretence that he was undertaking research into the recent defections. Frolík stepped into the shabby building that housed the central archives.

Throughout that bitter winter of 1968 he spent hours poring over the intelligence contained in those bulging files, committing to memory everything he read, painfully aware that it was far too hazardous to make copies or take notes in the building. His precarious position meant he could be arrested at any moment and evidence of his enterprise would be a death sentence for himself and his entire family.

As darkness fell he would trudge wearily home to the family apartment, his mind heavy with the intelligence that he had gathered. He dared not confide in his wife until he was confident that his plans were in place and they stood a chance of success.

Night after night, Frolík would lock himself away from his wife and son to prepare an exhaustive dossier, the 'gift' with which he needed to impress the CIA. He meticulously recorded every detail he had gleaned from the archives, hoping and trusting that the information he was planning to offer was a legacy of which the CIA could only dream. He took the precaution of translating the document into a code he had himself devised, the key for which was based on Jaroslav Hašek's novel *The Good Soldier Švejk*.

His next cautious step was to cultivate a contact within the CIA; he had to be incredibly careful whom he approached. The StB were well aware of the CIA operatives hiding behind the title of 'diplomats' in the US embassy. Some were young, rash and indiscreet; others, older and more cynical, would, with the right inducement, betray their own grandmother. Frolík gave the matter much attention, eventually settling on someone who appeared to have slipped under the radar. It had taken a little research, but Frolík's years of training and intuition assured him that he had the right candidate. Contact was made and a meeting was arranged to take place at a small garage deep in the Prague suburbs.

Perpetually conscious that he was under surveillance and anything out of the ordinary would be considered suspicious, Frolík staged an accident. Running his 'company' Škoda into a wall, he had the perfect excuse to take the vehicle to the garage to be repaired. While the mechanics busied themselves with the repairs, he met his contact.

In the cobbled alley behind the workshop, their hushed conversation was disguised by the clunk of tools. The discussions focused on two main issues: what Frolík had to offer and how to get him out of the country. The first of these was readily accepted and the operative was duly impressed by the quality of the information Frolík had gathered. In order to establish trust, Frolík had taken the risk of giving the contact his real name. For the CIA, being involved with such a high-profile defection was a coup. The second matter was a conundrum: how to get Frolík out of the country without alerting the suspicions of the authorities? A scheme was devised.

Fortune favours the brave, and Frolík was struck by the most incredible piece of luck on discovering that the Czech security services had recently agreed with their Bulgarian counterparts to set up a training camp in Byala on the coast of the Black Sea. Frolík had visited Bulgaria on a number of occasions and arranged to give a couple of lectures to his colleagues about the country, with the intention of diverting any suspicion from his superiors when he put the next phase of his plan into operation.

Inevitably, the circumstances were taking their toll on Frolík. The strain of devising his escape while trying to maintain a facade of 'business as usual' intensified his bitterness at the treatment he felt he was receiving and the repression of the Prague Spring. He harboured a festering resentment towards those colleagues who appeared to support the Soviet takeover and seemed to be working with them. In an ill-timed incident, he yet again allowed alcohol to fuel a drunken rant against them when he should have been keeping a low profile. It was the final straw and his employers confirmed that his dismissal was inevitable.

On 28 May 1969 he put in his usual request for four weeks' annual leave. Whereas he usually requested Yugoslavia as his destination, on this occasion he applied to attend the Luna training camp in Bulgaria. This was to ensure that any suspicion that he may defect across the Yugoslav border would be removed.

Having completed his 'research' in the directorate, the dossier he had spent so many nights filling with secrets was encased in concrete and fixed underneath his car, ready to be smuggled out of the country.

With the arrangements in place, the time had come for him to bring his wife in on his plans to defect. This was not a conversation he could broach at home, which he knew was bugged, so only the most mundane of topics could be discussed. So it was that on a beautifully sunny June day he took his wife for a trip into the countryside where he broke the news of his plans. Faced with little option, Mrs Frolík accepted their fate.

The date of 23 June had been fixed for the family to depart for Bulgaria, but before they could leave Frolík had to obtain a permit to allow him to travel, which had to be signed off by the directorate chief. To Frolík's concern, despite having put in his request some weeks earlier, the necessary permit had still not materialised.

Counting down the days to departure felt interminable as tension mounted, but there was nothing to do other than wait. The suspense escalated when Frolík was summoned to his section chief's office on 15 June, with only a week to go before they intended to flee, and was informed that he was to be dismissed from the service for his anti-Russian sentiments with effect from 1 August. Frolík knew that with his dismissal he would be precluded from leaving the country for a minimum of five years so it was absolutely vital to get away on 23 June to avoid being forced to abandon his plans.

Over those final days in Prague, the Frolíks paid visits to their extended family. Mrs Frolík called on her father, who was in hospital awaiting an operation, for the last time, where she was unable to help herself from lingering over a farewell kiss and hug, committing to memory his beloved face, his familiar smell and warmth, unbearably aware that she would never experience them again.

Frolík was up early on 23 June. He still did not have the permit. He had deliberately stopped himself from pushing the matter with his section chief in case it alerted him to his plans. The Škoda was packed up and he donned his casual holiday clothes before making his way to the StB offices where he found that neither the directorate chief nor his department head were in to sign off the permit. Disaster. Feeling his heart start to race and his head swimming, his years of training kicked in and he forced himself to breathe deeply until he had quelled the panic and could think clearly again. If the directorate chief was not available, he needed to think of an alternative. Then it struck him that the head of personnel had the authority to sign him off.

Filled with renewed purpose, he strode into the personnel offices, explaining to the secretary at the desk his urgent need for the permit and why he was there. His earlier groundwork paid dividends when she heard that he was going to Bulgaria. As she handed him a fresh application form she commented that was a natural destination for the 'expert' to be going to for his holidays. He completed the application in a flash and she disappeared to get the permit signed off by her department head. Frolík felt a bead of sweat trickle between his shoulder blades and roll down his back as the minutes ticked by.

After an unbearable wait the door to the office swung open and, with a smile and a flourish, she handed the signed permit to Frolík. Barely able to contain his relief and excitement, he struggled to check his impulse to run out of the offices. Had he realised that his letter of 28 May had merely been sitting on a colleague's desk with a handwritten note authorising the trip he might have found the morning a little less stressful.

Within the hour, the Frolík family were on their way to Bulgaria and the next step on the path towards a new and uncertain future. There were many hurdles still to overcome and Frolík had no choice but to depend on the word of the CIA. If they let him down then he would have to rely on his own wits to find a way out or abandon all hope and surrender to his fate back in Prague. Arriving in the camp, mingling with many of their compatriots, they settled into the daily holiday routine, spending the days on the beach, dinner in the evening, going through the motions of socialising with colleagues. With the end of their month's holiday fast approaching, Frolík was now waiting for his CIA contact to reach out to them and Frolík and his wife were becoming uneasy and a little fretful. It was hard not to linger on the sand, wistfully gazing across the water towards the Turkish coast.

The details of Frolík's exact route to freedom were covered up by everyone concerned – Frolík himself, the CIA and the StB – as the information was highly sensitive and would compromise agents on both sides. Frolík described a meeting with a CIA operative in a stinking toilet at the Bulgarian coastal resort as the start of his road to freedom. The StB undertook a thorough investigation, providing a preliminary report in early 1970 and a more comprehensive one in November of that year; in both, Frolík's codename had been changed from Florian to Baco. The reports stated that the family left Camp Luna on 12 July, from where they had driven through Yugoslavia, slipping across the border into Austria. This route was based on information they had gleaned from postcards, photographs and press reports, including a postcard sent to relatives in Czechoslovakia dated 18 July and postmarked Maribor in former Yugoslavia, now Slovenia. Frolík notes in his memoir that he and his wife sent postcards from the border when they were travelling to Bulgaria. The StB reports concluded that the family had reached Austria by 22 July and it was there that Frolík claimed asylum.

At the time, the StB remained entirely oblivious to unfolding events. It was noted that Frolík had failed to return to the office as required on 22 July. On 23 July the Bratislava office was asked to enquire whether Frolík might have crossed the border. By 25 July the suspicion was that Frolík had 'emigrated' and an encrypted circular was sent to all their intelligence agencies abroad, informing them of his suspected treachery and requesting them to undertake 'safety evaluations' to ascertain any potential damage such a disappearance may have. On 28 July the minister of interior was informed of Frolík's 'desertion' and, between 26 July and 26 September, twenty-three of Frolík's colleagues were interrogated in an effort to ascertain what had motivated the defection and what information he may have possessed. On 16 August the Frolíks' Prague apartment was searched.

One aspect that was absent from Frolík's account was that, after he had arrived in the US, the intelligence he provided to the CIA was of such importance to the British that he was flown to London to be debriefed by MI5. The StB 1970 report describes in some detail Frolík's attempts to make contact with his fellow agents in London. Several days after the Maribor postcard, another postcard was received by his wife's parents, originating from the United Kingdom and dated 8 August; it explained that he had extended his family vacation abroad.

Frolík attempted to contact the Czechoslovak ambassador in London, sending a letter through another contact of his, Kratochvíl, which included photographs of Frolík and his family in Austria, a signpost in German clearly visible in the background. The letter suggested a meeting, which the Czechs ignored. A second attempt was made to contact the ambassador on 19 August by British counter-intelligence and, though the ambassador took steps to avoid them, the letter was eventually thrown into his car. In it Frolík stated, 'I heard about your reaction to my letter, which was delivered to you through Mr Kratochvíl. I understand your actions after you have read the letter because it is the normal reaction of someone working in our type of service. However, I do not understand your reaction to my request for a meeting with you.' The Czechs chose not to respond.

A third letter followed, in which he allowed himself to give vent to his feelings: 'I know that according to our law, I have committed treason, and that the Moscow protocols do not apply in my case, unlike with KGB agents, but I will much rather work with the devil than with an invader. I am not writing this letter to justify my actions, but because I know that you are in serious danger and right now it's everyone's duty to help anyone who is put in danger by the invaders and their agency back home.'

Conscious of the risks that Kratochvíl and others were taking through their involvement, he added, 'The people who deliver this letter to you don't intend to harm you even though you have worked against this country, just like me. They want to help you secure your peaceful future, provided you help them in matters relating to the safety of this country.'

He signed off in more ominous tones, 'That is probably all that I wanted to say to you. If you notify Prague of this letter, make sure to add that as long as I can stand on my two feet and breathe, I will do everything in my power to go against them, and they know very well that I am good at that.'

True to his words, Frolík's work was not yet complete. Once he had handed over the dossier to his new masters there followed hours, days, weeks and months of interviews. The debrief was to cover not only the information Frolík had supplied but also to establish how genuine he was, whether he could be trusted and that this was not all an StB ruse to get one of their men to infiltrate the CIA. Finally, there came a point when the CIA interrogators were satisfied with all that they had heard, having exhaustively checked, double-checked and triple-checked the information they had been given.

After assimilating the intelligence, they were now faced with the question of how best to make use of it. A significant portion of the data concerned a number of figures in British politics and trade unions. One of the names Frolík had collated before he left his old life was Stonehouse.

As NATO partners, there was a regular exchange of information between MI5 and the CIA. Of great concern to the Americans was that, according to Frolík's intelligence, there appeared to be a group of informants and spies at the very heart of the British political establishment. The information concerning Stonehouse, among others, was shared with the British.

As the CIA received the intelligence with delight, the StB were taking stock of their former operative's treachery. Late in 1970, a comprehensive thirty-plus-page report was submitted to the Czechoslovak minister of interior, listing the names of all those who may have been compromised by the defection, which numbered scores of agents and informants who were now directly threatened. Focusing on those whom Frolík would have come into immediate contact with in his various posts, as well as his knowledge of the operational structure of their activities, they set about withdrawing large numbers of agents from the field. Operations were cancelled and embassy 'diplomats' across the globe had to be replaced as the Czechs considered that they would now be susceptible to 'turning' by foreign counter-intelligence services, their vulnerability emphasised by recent political upheaval. In the UK, Lee and another agent, known as 'Marconi', were compromised, Frolík having first-hand knowledge of those men. However, what the Czechs had not accounted for were the months that Frolík had spent in their archives during that cold winter, memorising names of those with whom he had not even come into contact. Names such as agent Kolon. Little was said as to how the damage could be repaired in respect of the foreign agents.

Stonehouse was about to suffer the consequences.

8

SPY?

Downing Street, 1969

Stonehouse had reached a period in his life where he felt comfortable and fulfilled. His smooth rise through the party ranks had seen him progress from junior minister roles to member of the cabinet and privy council. His post as minister of telecommunications reflected the advances in technology for the average household in Britain. The business of telecommunications was relatively straightforward as the post and telephone system both fell under the state-owned monopoly of the General Post Office. With no rivals for commerce, the public relied entirely on the GPO unless they wished to communicate via smoke signal or carrier pigeon. As far as Stonehouse's duties were concerned, while he was now a cabinet minister, he would only be required to attend if there was business directly relating to his department to discuss.

It came as a surprise to Stonehouse when he was summoned to Number 10 by the prime minister. With a significant majority of ninety-six seats, Wilson's position within the Labour Party appeared unassailable, but the prime minister suffered from a sense of insecurity and was suspicious of anyone in his party who might threaten his leadership. Stonehouse had drawn attention as someone to watch, with his youth, good looks and dynamism. Wilson kept a very close circle of advisors, principally yes-men and -women, preferring to surround himself with people who helped relieve his neurotic tendencies.

Stonehouse describes the confrontation with the prime minister in *Death of an Idealist*. Much of that book is permeated by lies, half-truths and self-validation, but the description of the meeting and its effects appear to offer a rare glimpse of honesty. He describes arriving at Downing Street in the late morning, where he automatically walked through to the cabinet meeting room on the ground floor, only to be advised that he should go up to the sitting room on the first floor. There he was met by the prime minister and his private secretary, Michael Halls, who introduced a third person as Elwell, of counter-intelligence. Charles Elwell had a formidable reputation as a communist hunter and his career at MI5 had been propelled to new heights through his unmasking of the Portland spy ring and later, John Vassall, the admiralty's KGB spy. Stonehouse noted the man's smart military bearing, ingrained from his years in the Royal Navy.

Inviting Stonehouse to take a seat, Wilson immediately came to the point. Notifying Stonehouse that a Czech defector had named him as an informer, the prime minister then gave the floor to Elwell who proceeded to provide a little more detail. The individual concerned was a member of the Czechoslovak StB who had recently been debriefed by the US security services, at which time he had named the minister.

Startled, Stonehouse instantly denied any wrongdoing, referring to the occasion on which he had reported a lunch meeting with the Czech spy, Robert Husak. Elwell acknowledged that he was aware of the episode but felt compelled to ask the MP whether there had been contact with any other Czech agents. Hoping that his alarm did not show outwardly, Stonehouse strongly denied any such involvement, the memories of all those meetings with Kugler, Husak and others swirling through his head. Even as he spoke, he wondered if he was falling into a trap if MI5 was already aware of the information he had exchanged with the Czechs but, for the time-being, Elwell seemed to accept his rebuttal.

Wilson interjected, emphasising how vital it was for Stonehouse to assist in the enquiries, and brought the ten-minute meeting to a close. For Stonehouse, as for many others, Josef Frolík's allegations were to resonate for years to come. It was with no small sense of relief that the MP discerned that, while the matter had to be investigated, there was a presumption that it was untrue. Self-reporting the meeting with Husak had clearly helped considerably to assuage concerns and, while checks of Stonehouse's bank accounts and lifestyle were no doubt undertaken, nothing suspicious was uncovered. Fortunately for Stonehouse, all payments had been made in cash.

According to cabinet meeting minutes from October 1980, the attorney general, Michael Havers, reported that Stonehouse 'was interviewed twice in the late 1960s and he vehemently denied allegations that he was a spy and said that his meetings with representatives of the Czechoslovak government were "no more than the usual contacts which any minister would have with an East European embassy".'

Stonehouse claimed that there were meetings with Elwell at various locations around London, most frequently in the basement at the RAC Club on Pall Mall, where he was a member, apparently disclosing further information concerning Stonehouse's Czech associations, though mysteriously the meetings with Kugler in restaurants in west London seem not to have been mentioned.

The investigation's findings were inconclusive. There was nothing to corroborate Frolík's information as the defector had never dealt directly with Stonehouse and merely copied information from records apparently held by the StB. In the absence of anything conclusive, Stonehouse was given the benefit of the doubt, the British establishment being content to conclude that he was a trusted and respected minister of state, while his accuser was of questionable character, having betrayed his country.

Wilson received the report with some relief that he could now close the matter. However, he could not have anticipated what would follow from Frolík.

That wasn't the end of the matter for Stonehouse; he still had to manage the expectations of the Czechs. After the meeting at the Hotel Kosodrevina in the spring of 1968, Stonehouse had failed to attend any further meetings. Karel Pravec had needed to resort to attending that year's Labour Party conference, but again he was thwarted by Stonehouse who, when confronted, told Pravec that the conference was not a suitable place to have their discussion. He suggested that they arrange another meeting, perhaps at the Polish embassy where he was due to attend a function. That meeting did not take place. Pravec attempted to contact Stonehouse at his apartment. He later reported that he had called on no less than twenty occasions, leaving messages with his wife to return his calls. The Czechs contemplated something more drastic.

The episode was a rude awakening for Stonehouse. The exposure that he had feared, and which had been a topic of anxious discussion in those early exchanges with Kugler and recent months with Husak and Pravec, had come to pass, even though he had successfully convinced MI5 that he was not working as a spy and probably considered in his own mind that he was not an agent of the StB, as he had given away nothing of any significance. Frolík's revelations had, however, irreparably damaged his political aspirations and would lead to a change in career focus, and with it his ultimate downfall.

While Stonehouse remained a cabinet minister for the remaining period of Wilson's tenure in Number 10, the spying allegations undoubtedly sullied his political career. Any further hint of suspicion would have been very damaging, prompting Stonehouse to reflect on just how tenuous a political life was. Evaluating his position, he could not deny his political achievements but was bound to admit that financially his circumstances were very weak. He could not escape the reality that he had a family and lifestyle to support and, despite drawing a cabinet minister's salary, he lived to the limit of his means, privately funding his children's schooling and ensuring he always furnished them with the best he could afford. This experience demonstrated that he needed to make better financial provision for himself and his family. During the course of his career he had seen others achieving similar cabinet rank successfully transitioning to a life in business using the contacts and skills they had developed. He had been highly critical of such practices at the time, regarding those colleagues as hypocrites. The Labour Party nurtured a natural mistrust and disdain for successful businesspeople, and in particular anyone within the party itself who prospered personally from such conduct.

Now, however, Stonehouse was confronted with the uncomfortable truth that he needed to plan for a rainy day.

9

A NEW BUSINESS

December 1969

On a crisp winter's day, under a clear sky, the frosted fields whizzed past as I pressed my nose against the window of the train and watched the exposed trees slide by, silhouetted against the sun.

My father, Michael Hayes, sat opposite and, when I turned my gaze, I was able to watch him unobserved, his head buried between the pages of a broadsheet newspaper, swaying gently with the rhythm of the carriage. I was excited to be making this trip all the way from our busy home in Sunderland to visit our beloved uncle and aunt, happy to be spending time with my father while my younger siblings stayed behind with our mother, Patti.

We had recently returned to England from Africa, where Michael had spent three years on a teaching placement in Zambia. My parents had made the most of our time living in Lusaka, exploring all that the country had to offer. During the same period, they had expanded their small family, providing a little sister and brother for their inquisitive and mischievous first-born son.

In the late summer of 1969, Michael and Patti packed up our belongings and set off with the three young children on a thrilling train journey from Zambia to Durban in South Africa, where we boarded a ship for Southampton. There we stayed briefly with Michael's parents before settling in Whitley Bay, on the north-east coast.

Michael had decided, encouraged by his wife, to pursue a career in law and found a position as an articled clerk with a firm in Sunderland. It was there that they bought a modest three-bedroom house in the Tunstall Hills area.

Stonehouse had contacted Michael on his return, with a view to discussing his plans for the future with his nephew. Doubtless he was keen to profit from his nephew's position to assist with a number of projects in which he was proposing to invest.

Several long hours later, punctuated by packets of homemade sandwiches provided by my mother, our train eventually pulled into the station at Andover where we were met by Barbara Stonehouse, John's wife, who drove us the final few miles to his family's country home, a large, comfortable Georgian farmhouse deep in the Hampshire countryside.

I was installed in their son Matthew's bedroom, as he was away at boarding school, a happy turn of events for an active, curious child. I felt as if I had landed in paradise, surrounded by every toy imaginable, from a Dinky Toys replica of James Bond's Aston Martin, replete with ejector seat, which I used to re-enact my favourite scenes from the films, to beautiful painted Wild West figurines with which I planned complex campaigns marching across the plains of the blankets, ambushed from the bookshelves.

With me contentedly occupied in Matthew's bedroom, the two men began to plan Stonehouse's future over the course of a critical couple of days.

The series of discussions continued during country walks wrapped in heavy coats and scarves, over piping-hot casseroles around the kitchen table and while sipping scotch and soda in Stonehouse's study. Stonehouse was candid with his nephew about the prospect of a Labour victory in the general election due the following year. He knew that, if defeated, he would lose his ministerial post and salary. Life in opposition, either as a shadow minister or a backbencher, would be hard politically and financially.

As a precaution, Stonehouse intended to capitalise on the contacts and influence he had developed to pursue his own business interests, explaining to Michael that he felt his talents lay in selling British interests abroad, specifically promoting exports of UK goods.

With that in mind, he planned to set up a small group of companies of which he would be a director with the controlling influence. Stonehouse was frustrated with the disdain with which those in the Labour Party viewed anyone who wished to pursue private business interests, considering that to be a betrayal of socialist values. Stonehouse disagreed with the philosophy and considered that pursuing business ventures, making money and enjoying the benefits should be encouraged.

Michael was instructed to set up three companies, to be bought off the shelf for £100 each in early 1970 in preparation for the general election. In the event of a Labour defeat, Stonehouse would be ready to make the seamless transition into business while still maintaining his job as an MP.

By the time Michael and I departed the cosy confines of the farmhouse, a plan of action had been firmly established. The hedonistic days of the 1960s were shortly to be replaced by the turbulent 1970s.

1970

The start of a new decade invites reflection on times past and planning for the future.

The free-spirited hedonism that had defined the mid-sixties had given way to a more cynical and contentious society by the decade's end, as people were spurred to challenge traditional values and disrupt the status quo.

Neither communism nor capitalism were immune from the waves of dissension sweeping society worldwide. Cobbles had been ripped from the streets of Paris by rioting students and workers, party leaders were ousted by disenfranchised Czechoslovaks in Prague, the United States was divided rather than united by demands for civil rights and the unpopularity of the Vietnam War. Tensions that had been fermenting below the surface of society in Northern Ireland erupted in violence on the streets of Belfast. All the while, the spectre of a nuclear attack, triggered by the Cold War, loomed over a globe in turmoil, leading many to greet the unfolding decade with foreboding rather than fervour.

On a chilly, cloudy morning on 15 January 1970, police and MI5 officers raided the Carshalton home of the Labour MP Will Owen, who had been unmasked as agent Lee in the information supplied by Frolík. Owen was charged with 'communicating information useful to an enemy' and held in custody until his trial at the Old Bailey that April. The case was front-page news, which Stonehouse would have followed meticulously, having met and worked with Owen on many occasions as Co-operative colleagues. Frolík's allegations against Owen were that he had supplied information to the Czechs, meeting with Captain Robert Husak on numerous occasions in order to exchange sensitive government intelligence in return for money. Owen admitted that he had received small sums of cash from the Czechs, stating in his defence that both the data he had supplied and the financial rewards had been trivial, involving general political information but nothing concerning matters of national security. During the course of their investigation the police were easily able to establish that Owen's bank accounts betrayed a very different version of events. 'Greedy bastard' had lived up to his name.

Frolík had confirmed that, throughout his time in London from 1964 to 1966, he had been agent Lee's handler. The prosecution suggested that, during his many years as a member of the parliamentary estimates committee, Owen would have been privy to secret information but, despite a thorough probe into his affairs, the police were unable to provide solid evidence to support such treachery and the MP was acquitted at the beginning of May. Years later, the Owen and Stonehouse files were to suggest the two men had been involved far more deeply than was able to be proven at the time.

The case must have preyed on Stonehouse's mind, anxiously awaiting the outcome of the trial, no doubt reflecting that, if Owen were convicted, it might only be a matter of time before the police came knocking on his door.

In the meantime, with the assistance of his wife Patti, preparations were in motion as Michael set about putting into place Stonehouse's grand design. Sitting at the dining-room table of their modest Sunderland home, Michael guided his wife as she rattled out the applications on her portable Silver Reed typewriter. In March 1970 three companies were set up. Export Promotion and Consultancy Services Limited (EPACS), Connoisseurs of Claret Limited and Systems and Consultancy Services Limited were all established for £100 each. Michael was named as one of the directors, although the plan was that he would not have much to do with the day-to-day running of the companies and later that year he handed all books and paperwork to Stonehouse.

Back on the political stage, Harold Wilson called the general election in late spring of that year, possibly hoping to capitalise on the World Cup celebrations, having previously benefited from the England triumph of 1966 and hoping for a similar result in the finals in Mexico.

Sadly, Wilson's faith in the England squad was misplaced and the country went to the polls the day after England's elimination in the quarter-final against West Germany, a humiliation mirrored by Labour's defeat and the election of Ted Heath's Conservative government.

Stonehouse lost his cabinet post and Wilson opted not to appoint him to the shadow cabinet, later claiming he had based his decision on Stonehouse's handling of charitable donations for an organisation he had been working for. It seems likely, nonetheless, that the shadow of the allegations made by Czech defector, Frolík, was significant in

Wilson's judgement. Either way, Stonehouse was consigned to the obscurity of the backbenches.

With fewer political commitments, Stonehouse threw himself into his new enterprises with gusto, taking full advantage of his political and economic contacts. His aim was to make as much money as possible, considering it a retirement plan of sorts.

* * *

While Stonehouse applied himself to his new ventures, in Czechoslovakia the StB were giving consideration to the problem of what to do about agent Twister. He had not conformed to expectation and, despite advancing him in excess of £5,000 (equivalent to over £76,000 today), the Czechs had received scant return on their investment. Pravec undertook a comprehensive evaluation, submitting a report to his superiors in Prague on 20 January 1970 describing in detail how Stonehouse had gone to considerable lengths to evade their advances and listing the numerous attempts they had made to re-engage with him, to no avail.

Before the election, the Czechs considered Stonehouse to be an important asset, having held on to his ministerial position in the aftermath of the Frolík defection. Endeavouring to find a way to persuade him to cooperate, Pravec outlined what evidence they possessed with which to compromise him. This included the photographs of him strolling through Mayfair with Husak. The rakish Husak, however, had suffered a reversal in fortunes, having been withdrawn from London in the aftermath of the defection and then dismissed from the StB for apparently expressing views critical of the repression of the Prague Spring and Soviet interference. Pravec conceded that on their own the photos would now have little impact.

They also possessed the tape recording of a luncheon meeting between Husak and Stonehouse on 9 August 1966, but the quality was poor. While Husak could be heard making comments that had the potential to compromise the minister, Stonehouse's responses were obscured, leading Pravec to query whether the background noise could be reduced. Otherwise the recording was of little use.

The most compelling evidence in discrediting Stonehouse was the money he had accepted. As Pravec observed, 'The money was received by Twister willingly, without the slightest restraint, even by himself. This was also obviously the main reason why, after the first interruption, he resumed cooperation. He'd basically been going to the agreed appointments for as long as he could hope to get more money.'

Notably absent from the report was any reference to any record or film of the fabled 'honey trap' which supposedly took place during his visit to Czechoslovakia in 1957, begging the question as to whether any such event ever occurred.

The prospects of cooperation and compromise dwindled as the events of 1970 unfolded, with Labour's defeat, Stonehouse's demotion and Owen's prosecution all acting as contributory factors. By November a final decision had been made following a further review:

> In the last 1968/69 period, Twister began to consciously evade any contact, and the R[esident] O[fficer] could be denied even though threats against him [Stonehouse] were used. When evaluating the whole development of the case, it is obvious that Twister was primarily interested in obtaining money. Twister will not be in contact with us after the Lee case because of concerns that his career might be jeopardised. Given that the use of compromising material against him is questionable, I suggest that the Twister file be permanently stored in the . . . archive.

Although he could not know it, the jeopardy of exposure directly by the StB had dissipated and Stonehouse was safe from disclosure from that quarter. In typically devious fashion, though, fate had another plan for Stonehouse.

10

BANGLADESH

1971

By the start of 1971, Stonehouse's companies had begun to pay dividends as business started coming in, bringing with it the money he craved. His focus having shifted from the world of politics to that of commerce, he required suitable office accommodation, which he found in Dover Street, where he installed Sheila to administer his business affairs. In addition, Stonehouse asked her to become a director of his companies, in particular EPACS. She agreed, although, like Michael, her understanding was that she would not have any influence on the running of those businesses.

On the world stage, the troubles of the seventies continued to mount. A bloody civil war broke out in East Pakistan, an area that had been given over to the Pakistani state as part of the 1947 partition of India with little thought as to how to integrate the indigenous Bengali population.

Over the intervening years this part of Pakistan had been the subject of ethnic and linguistic discrimination, leading, with ever-increasing volume, to calls for independence from Pakistan. These demands rose to a crescendo in the aftermath of a devastating cyclone that killed up to 500,000 in 1970 to which the Pakistani central government failed to respond adequately. In the general election that took place in December that year, the Awami League, the Bengali nationalist party, won all but two of the seats for East Pakistan on the national assembly. With a landslide majority, the party considered that this gave them a mandate to set up an independent state, a proposal to which the Pakistani military were hostile.

A period of civil disobedience and protests followed, rapidly escalating in response to the heavy-handed manner in which the Pakistani army reacted, coming to a head when the prime minister elect of Bangladesh, Sheikh Mujibur Rahman, declared independence at the beginning of March 1971. On 25 March the Pakistani military launched Operation Searchlight, attacking strategic sites in Bangladesh, declaring the election results void, and arresting Rahman and flying him to the East Pakistan capital, Dhaka.

Conflict erupted, giving rise to horrific atrocities including numerous massacres. In the first stage of the war, young men, Hindus, Awami League members, intellectuals, students and academics were slaughtered; during the second stage, tens of thousands of women were raped, with evidence of rape camps set up by the Pakistani military subsequently emerging. The third and final stage arose a matter of days before the end of the war in December 1971, when it was clear the writing was on the wall for Pakistan. In a desperate bid to eliminate their opposition, lists of potential political leaders and intellectuals were drawn up and used to carry out a series of assassinations and executions.

The war was short but bloody. While there remains no officially accepted figure on the numbers of those who were butchered, estimates range from 300,000 to 3 million. Whatever the numbers, it was a truly horrific and brutal conflict.

The crisis had caught Stonehouse's attention and he closely followed events as they unfolded. In the midst of the conflict, the MP decided to visit the country to witness the hostilities in person, travelling to Bangladesh in April 1971, where he met his friend and fellow MP, Bruce Douglas-Mann. The experience was to have a profound and lasting impact on the two men. Visiting refugee camps, towns and villages they were confronted with the bloody and psychological consequences of the conflict, an ordeal that caused them to be visibly moved. They were disturbed by the utter devastation they saw and the accounts they heard of the genocide perpetrated by the Pakistani armed forces.

The MPs met and spoke with the Bangladeshi leadership, finding them in a dispirited state, which was greatly lifted by the knowledge that their cause was being followed and supported by the international community. Stonehouse returned to the UK resolved to help the Bangladeshi call for independence.

He identified two key ways in which he could assist. The first was to raise money for the cause, even going so far as to make enquiries to purchase weapons to supply to the rebel fighters. His old RAF chum, Gerald Hastings, later described at Stonehouse's trial how he had been approached by the MP to explore the options of purchasing arms, an operation referred to as the 'Shangri La Project' in the correspondence between them. It transpired that, by the time Hastings had contacted an American company that manufactured bazookas, political events had taken a turn and the project proceeded no further.

The second, and perhaps most effective, way he could help was to drum up support in parliament. He put forward several early-day motions – formal requests for a debate – about the plight of the Bangladeshis, obtaining over a hundred signatures in July of that year in support of his most popular motion, asking for the British government to recognise Bangladesh as a sovereign state. There is no doubt that the Pakistani determination to cling on to the disputed territory was weakened by the international condemnation of their conduct, and the pressure brought to bear by Stonehouse's contribution should not be underestimated. By the year's end the war had reached its bitter conclusion and Bangladesh was recognised in its own right.

In 1972, as a direct result of his involvement in their emancipation, Stonehouse was approached by a group of Bangladeshi businessmen to facilitate the financing of the fledgling state. With this aim the British Bangladesh Trust was set up, with Stonehouse as chairman, to help subsidise and promote trade and industry there. The trust was a secondary bank, created to supply banking services and investment opportunities in Bangladesh. The Crown Agents for Overseas Governments and Administrations, set up to help investment in the former British colonies, contributed £350,000 (£4.38 million today) to the bank's available funds. The enterprise was soon to prove a millstone around Stonehouse's neck. A downturn in the UK housing market in the early to mid-1970s led to a crisis in the secondary banking sector but his troubles were exacerbated by his own mismanagement of the trust. It was to prove one of many burdens that Stonehouse was desperate to escape by the middle of the decade.

* * *

A new source of unease surfaced when another casualty of Frolík's defection was apprehended and brought to justice. Nicholas Prager appeared to be a mild-mannered electrical engineer but agent Marconi, as he was known to his StB handlers, hid a dark secret. His father had originally come from Czechoslovakia, settling in the UK where he successfully applied to become a British citizen, which in turn allowed his son the benefit of citizenship. Prager spent a brief time in the RAF, after which he took up civilian employment as an electrical engineer at the RAF Research and Development Institute. With a predisposition towards communism, he made a trip to Czechoslovakia, where he caught Husak's attention. With the intention of recruiting him to the StB, Husak introduced Prager to a young Czech woman, Jana, apparently also involved in the plan. The combination of Husak's persuasiveness, Jana's charms and Prager's communist leanings, expedited by the added incentive of cash, convinced him to supply classified information to the Czechs under the codename Marconi.

The most significant secret he sold was the anti-radar jamming device fitted to the RAF V-bombers. In a farcical episode, Marconi had managed to smuggle a Polaroid camera into work and had taken photographs of the plans.

With Frolík's defection, Marconi's Bramley home was raided by police and evidence of his activities uncovered. In 1971 he went on trial at Leeds Crown Court where he was convicted and sentenced to twelve years in prison.

The trial was a sensation and Stonehouse would have followed it on tenterhooks, painfully aware of his entanglement in the net, agonising as to whether Twister would come to suffer the same fate as Lee and Marconi.

11

THE TROUBLES

1972–4

While Stonehouse's businesses, apart from the British Bangladesh Trust, were proving satisfactorily prosperous, they demanded his constant attention to generate the work and bring in the money. This exacerbated a fundamental issue, which was that the businesses were not particularly well managed, with Stonehouse running things as he thought best, irrespective of the other directors. The accountants he had employed, and he went through a few, complained that the books showed irregularities; a mysterious 'miscellaneous' account, involving unexplained withdrawals and transactions, was flagged up. Stonehouse chose to ignore the overtures. His behaviour could be domineering, even outright arrogant at times, making him incredibly difficult to work with let alone stand up to.

His nephew Michael had ceased to be engaged with the companies in 1971, having surrendered all the relevant paperwork to his uncle, but, to his eternal regret, he remained a director. Over those years Michael would attend Stonehouse's Dover street offices whenever he was in London. He never formally discussed the businesses affairs, although he did on occasions ask Sheila or one of the other officers of the companies for information but never received it. Michael's involvement was such that by the beginning of 1974 he had contemplated resigning his directorship but to his eternal regret did nothing further about it. The nephew trusted his uncle to run the company honestly and efficiently and did not feel the need to attend any of the directors' meetings, so had no suspicions that anything untoward might be going on.

While Stonehouse gave the impression he was enjoying life as a successful businessman and family man, those closest to him began to detect some worrying characteristics. His daughter Jane became concerned in the early 1970s: 'I noticed he was shutting himself off a great deal and becoming more difficult to communicate with and relate to. He had always had time for me and my problems, but as time went on he had less time.' He was prone to angry outbursts, shouting and slamming doors, leaving his family troubled.

He hosted the extended family at his Andover home for Christmas, 1972. I was there with my parents and siblings, and vividly remember the thrill of the bustling household as I paraded proudly in my newly acquired cowboy outfit, replete with six-shooters. We all gathered together for the obligatory photo in the generous living room next to the splendid tree, no one, not even Stonehouse, being aware that this would be our last family Christmas together. We had been regular visitors, whether for Sunday lunches in the country or tea at his London house. His home always seemed to be full of activity, courtesy of his own adult children and friends.

Though his family were oblivious, Stonehouse was suffering critical business and financial difficulties, largely stemming from the failing British Bangladesh Trust. In 1972, a share subscription of £1 million had been issued but only half of it had been taken up. It was unlikely that the remainder would be bought as a result of a hugely damaging article that had appeared in the *Sunday Times* business section immediately before the subscription was issued. The column alleged that the Bengali version of the prospectus had made false claims, which may have amounted to fraud. Despite Stonehouse's best efforts to halt the article, visiting the chief editor to discuss the matter, and then to respond to the accusations, the damage had been done. Stonehouse was becoming quietly desperate. This exacerbated damage already inflicted by one man who had apparently been insulted when the Trust decided not to take him on as a Director. He proceeded to organise meetings to actively discourage the Bangladeshi community from investing in the bank.

In a reckless attempt to prevent the immediate collapse of the bank, arrangements were made for a number of companies to take out loans to buy the remaining shares, with Stonehouse later also approaching various individuals to take over the shares as nominees. Some of the companies and individuals were later surprised to receive demands for the repayment of overdrafts to which they had unwittingly put their names. Even his sister Elizabeth, my grandmother, was unwittingly recruited to buy shares.

Ex-RAF colleague Gerald Hastings was one friend who became embroiled in the dubious business when Stonehouse arranged for him to purchase £12,000 worth of shares in the bank, now named London Capital Securities. Hastings, a Canadian businessman based in Belgium, had initially not been interested when it had been the British Bangladesh Trust. 'I was not keen on the name of the bank or its affiliations with Bangladesh. Later, the bank changed its name to the London Capital Group and my attitude changed towards it.'

In June 1974, Stonehouse invited Hastings to dinner at the House of Commons where they discussed the prospect of Hastings becoming an investor. After his initial reticence, he was convinced of the venture's respectability when Stonehouse confided in him that Sir Charles Forte and the Crown Agents had already contributed substantially to the enterprise. Hastings did not have the money to hand to endow but Stonehouse told him not to worry, the bank would lend him the cash, arranging a loan in Hastings's name of £12,000 within days. The appropriate documents were prepared which, by Hastings own admission, he signed without reading. Second thoughts promptly arose, but when he tried to reduce his investment, Stonehouse informed him that it was too late. It was to Hastings's immense relief when, in September that year, he was notified that the investment had been cancelled. He later told the Old Bailey jury that he was so pleased he cracked open a bottle of champagne.

A few months later Hastings received a letter from the bank advising that he owed £17,000, a problem which would not be resolved until the spring of 1975. Inspectors from the Department of Trade and Industry (DTI) had opened an investigation into Stonehouse's business affairs, during the course of which Stonehouse had informed them that he had loaned his friend £5,000. Hastings denied knowledge of the loan, or that the £12,000 worth of shares that he had purchased had been sold for £17,000, at a profit of £5,000, which had apparently been transferred to Export Promotion and Consultancy Services. Hastings declared absolute ignorance of signing over £5,000 to the company, though he did recall signing a blank piece of paper for Stonehouse at one of their meetings in what would become a familiar theme of boozy lunches facilitating the signature of documents valuable to Stonehouse's enterprise.

Stonehouse did not confine this behaviour to his colleagues, regarding his wife, children, family and friends all as fair game. In one incident, which apparently took place in December 1973, he approached Susan Hill, a friend of one of his daughters, who was living on benefits in very modest accommodation in west London. Ms Hill later gave evidence explaining how Stonehouse had involved her in a £20,000 transaction as a share nominee, urging her to advise auditors that the investment came from her own private means. 'I told him they would be surprised if they came around to my address and saw my two grotty rooms in Ladbroke Grove.'

Stonehouse assured her that she would not be involved in any liability and she was persuaded to sign forms that in reality meant that she had borrowed £20,000 from the bank to buy the shares, and that the shares were security for the loan that she had taken out.

When she voiced misgivings at this, Stonehouse allayed her fears by using the example of another investor who had been provided with a letter stating that he was acting as a nominee as a favour and, when she asked him to prepare a similar document for her, Stonehouse duly obliged. This letter was later adduced as evidence by her and read to the court:

Dear Susan,

In consideration of your acting as nominee in holding shares in BBT (British Bangladesh Trust) to the value of £20,000 for which BBT is advancing facilities for a like amount. I undertake to arrange for the interest payment to be paid and also to arrange the purchase of shares at par at any time you wish.

When questioned at trial about her understanding of the process, she retorted, 'I didn't realise that British Bangladesh Trust was lending me £20,000, so I was surprised when I received a statement from the bank saying that I had an overdraft of £20,000.'

If Stonehouse thought that he had sidestepped his troubles, he was to be sadly mistaken. The *Sunday Times* article had attracted the attention of the Department of Trade and Industry, which focused on the prospectus that had been issued in Bengali, suggesting that it had made some misleading claims. A department investigator conducted a brief interview with Stonehouse and, returning a week later, informed him that the department had received an anonymous handwritten report. When he showed Stonehouse the documents, the MP instantly recognised the handwriting as that of an acquaintance who was bent on causing him as much trouble as possible. The matter was consequently considered closed, but that proved not to be the case.

Several weeks later an Inspector Grant from Scotland Yard contacted Stonehouse to advise him that the police were conducting their own investigation independent of the DTI. There followed a series of interviews conducted under caution at the bank's offices. The investigation centred on the allegation that the Bengali prospectus contained deliberately false claims with the intention to induce people to invest in the bank. In other words, fraud, a charge that filled Stonehouse with dread.

The inspector spent months investigating the matter, visiting Bangladeshi shareholders at their homes and obtaining statements. Arrangements were made to translate the 'offending' document but using multiple translators confused matters further as each version differed. Having concluded his enquiries, Inspector Grant submitted a report to the director of public prosecutions (DPP). It later transpired that a separate report had gone to the DPP from the Department of Trade and Industry investigator recommending that no action be taken.

Stonehouse approached Peter Walker, the minister for trade and industry, who had been unaware that there had been any investigation and immediately made enquiries, indignant at the breach of protocol by which he should have been advised of the matter. Stonehouse also appealed to the former attorney general, Elwyn Jones, for advice but he was unable to give Stonehouse any reassurance.

Stonehouse instructed counsel for guidance, and in accordance with that the bank commissioned and produced its own report, which was sent to the DPP to consider alongside the police report.

Finally, Stonehouse turned to the Bangladeshi high commissioner, Abdus Sultan, who, horrified to hear of the predicament the MP found himself in, intervened with phone calls on behalf of his friend. With that, Stonehouse had exhausted his resources.

Within days, the case was formally dropped by the DPP but the investigation had taken its toll on Stonehouse, whose business reputation and political future were at stake. No doubt he may have also been concerned that the DTI and Scotland Yard might uncover other irregularities. Further, while he had managed to convince the external investigators there was nothing untoward going on, it was to prove more difficult for him to keep control of the internal audits.

Alan Le Fort had been employed by Stonehouse in 1972, taking on responsibility for managing the accounts of three of his companies, Global Index, Connoisseurs of Claret and EPACS. He began to have concerns regarding the money drawn out of EPACS by Stonehouse and the transfer of funds between the companies, forming the view that the payments contravened the 1948 Companies Act. He was unhappy that loans received by the companies were used to pay Stonehouse's consultancy fees.

In fact, Stonehouse was using his own money to keep the British Bangladesh Trust afloat, as Le Fort reluctantly admitted later.

In regular morning meetings with Stonehouse, Le Fort would present thirty-five to forty accounts and Stonehouse would direct how and where the monies should be transferred between them. Le Fort's disquiet with the businesses' management grew, with him considering that, by 1973, four of Stonehouse's companies had solvency problems. The pressure took its toll and, rather than blow the whistle, Le Fort chose to resign.

By mid-1974, the company auditors of the British Bangladesh Trust, now renamed the London Capital Securities, began to question the accounts held by the nominees. In order to manage the concerns raised, the shares held by the nominees were sold to a subsidiary business of the bank, Dover Street Nominees, which bought the shares for a hugely inflated price. To cover this cost, the account held by Dover Street at the bank was overdrawn to the tune of £340,000. The original nominees' accounts had their overdrafts paid off and, in some cases, put into credit, as was the case with EPACS: the shares that it held were sold for £188,000 (£1.9 million today) and the money was used to pay off a £150,000 overdraft, leaving a surplus of £38,000 (£393,000 today), a sum that Stonehouse syphoned off to fund himself. The company auditors were asking some very awkward questions and it was only a matter of time before the whole ruse would unravel.

Further anomalies arose with the administration of the bank

which, in fairness to Stonehouse, were not of his making. One of the bank's directors, a Mr Ahmed, had been loaned money by the British Bangladesh Trust in a very dubious transaction that Ahmed chose to cover up by devising for another company, Ambulant Finance, to appear to borrow the money he had received and arranging for the bank not to pursue Ambulant Finance should the director default on repayments. When the loan was discovered, the bank's manager, a man named Broad, wrote to Ambulant Finance demanding the funds, to which the outraged company responded denying responsibility for the loan, pointing to Mr Ahmed as the true borrower. The deal had been done by the time Stonehouse discovered the transaction and, when he confronted Ahmed, the culprit resigned as director. Further to this, another one of the bank's directors, named Jim Charlton, had been loaned money to purchase shares in the bank by Hanover Barclay, which was now demanding repayment.

Threats were made by both Ambulant Finance and Hanover Barclay, not only to raise matters with their shareholders but also with the DTI. Stonehouse received an unpleasantly aggressive telephone call from a solicitor director of Hanover Barclay by the name of Mr Gorman: 'Unless something is done about the shares, I will report the bank for improper activities and, as you are an MP, there will have to be an inquiry. I don't suppose you'll profit from the sort of publicity *that* will bring,' Gorman said darkly, adding in a spiteful tone, 'Don't forget what happened to Jeffrey Archer. Bankrupted, disgraced and forced to resign from parliament.'

The threats had the desired effect, as Stonehouse later confessed, 'I was absolutely staggered and shocked and went absolutely cold with these sort of threats. I suppose I was terribly frightened and a sick man. As a result, I lost my judgement . . . as a result of this blackmail I signed an agreement to buy £30,000 worth of shares from Hanover Barclay. It was a great mistake because I didn't want the shares. I was trying to get a blackmailer off my back.'

No money was ever paid by Stonehouse, who instead issued a promissory note with a view to payment in December 1974. He had no intention of honouring it. With the accountant's audit looming and the losses of the bank likely to be exposed, on top of the sinking share price, Stonehouse needed to buy time and to give the bank a facade of prosperity. Arrangements were made for shares to be sold to a Miss Black, which just happened to be Sheila's maiden name, but the ploy failed and the bank's share value continued to tumble. The money loaned to Miss Black by the bank was not secured by the value of the shares, prompting the auditors to ask problematic questions about Miss Black. Desperate to conceal the truth, the MP arranged for money to be paid into Miss Black's account to cover the value and part of the loan, temporarily throwing the auditor off the scent.

In the midst of this dire situation, a financial crisis rocked the secondary-bank industry, adding to his woes. Many of these banks had invested heavily in the property market and when the bubble had burst several faced disaster. Stonehouse was critical of the government, who had been quick to bolster many of the secondary banks' flagging fortunes but had refused to assist the trust. The bank limped on, but the suspicion of business irregularities paralysed its development, consigning it to the portfolio of catastrophic Stonehouse companies.

That portfolio had been created in order to finance the MP's ostentatious lifestyle. As well as renting the country house near Andover he also leased a number of properties in London, but he harboured a long-held dream to buy the perfect family home. After exhaustive searching, he located the ideal property, commissioning improvement works as soon as it was purchased. Sadly, Stonehouse's folly, as it was coined by the press, would forever remain a fantasy.

Failing businesses, financial irregularities, a faltering political career, spying allegations and trials: it was a toxic cocktail. It was only a matter of time before the poison would take effect, killing all Stonehouse's ardent political, business and personal ambitions.

12

THE JACKAL

June–November 1974

The MP was in turmoil, desperately dodging the company auditors' awkward questions, living in dread of a knock on the door from the police and the DTI, and facing the horror of bankruptcy and ruin looming. He couldn't stop his imagination from conjuring up newspaper headlines gleefully broadcasting his arrest and prosecution. He was gripped by the urge to escape but trapped by the practicalities. Stonehouse started obsessively to create mental lists of all the steps he would need to put in place to escape: creating a new identity with credible paperwork; financing his flight and new life; making provision for his family, and his mistress.

Frederick Forsyth's bestselling novel *The Day of the Jackal*, published in 1971 and made into a film in 1973, contains a description of a fictitious attempt made by a hired hitman to assassinate the French president, Charles de Gaulle. In the process of planning the hit, the 'Jackal' arranges alternative identities to allow him to slip in and out of various European countries as, in those days, passports were needed to travel anywhere on the continent. To this end the Jackal visits a churchyard, identifies the grave of a child who would have been roughly his age if he had lived and uses this information to apply for a British passport.

Stonehouse set about replicating the plot in real life. A plan began to germinate to stage his own death and establish a new identity or identities. The purpose of establishing new identities was twofold. Firstly, it would allow him to travel and settle overseas incognito; secondly, he would be able to set up bank accounts under those new names, where he would be able to deposit funds in advance of Stonehouse's 'death'.

He needed to select a couple of likely candidates, but loitering around local graveyards was not for him, so, after some thought, he contacted the Manor Hospital in Walsall. Once put through to the right department he explained to one of the officials there that, as the local MP, he was seeking the names and addresses of women whose husbands had recently died, claiming that he was the custodian of money to be distributed to the widows. No doubt encouraged by this apparent philanthropic act, the information was duly provided by the hospital.

From the list of names supplied to Stonehouse, two of his constituents proved to be ideal candidates, being of a similar age. So it was that Joseph Markham and Donald Clive Mildoon were resurrected from the dead. Now, Stonehouse needed to glean some personal information in order to complete applications for the paperwork he would require.

Joe Markham had died in April 1974 and his widow Jean had certainly not been expecting to find Stonehouse on the doorstep of her family home in Branfield, Staffordshire, a couple of months later. Charming his way in, the smartly dressed, smooth-talking MP informed her that he was conducting a survey of widows' pensions and taxes to assist him with his quest to help people such as her to improve and maximise the financial benefits they should receive from the state. Beguiled by his charisma and cover story, Mrs Markham promptly provided the MP with all the data he required to assist in making a passport application.

In early July 1974, Elsie Mildoon received a visit at her home in Darlaston, near Wednesbury, where again the silver-tongued Stonehouse teased the information he needed from her.

For the next phase of his plan, Stonehouse needed to identify a person of public standing who was in some way incapacitated, making it difficult for the passport office to approach for verification as the countersignatory to the applications. His thoughts naturally turned to his colleague Neil McBride, the MP for Swansea East who had been chief whip for the Wilson government. He had been returned as MP in the February general election but had not been able to take his seat due to ill health and sadly, by the summer, Stonehouse was aware that the illness was likely terminal. Tragically, McBride died in September 1974.

Applications for copies of birth certificates were made for Markham and Mildoon in July 1974, which were both issued promptly, and later the same month a passport application was submitted for Joseph Markham, countersigned by Neil McBride, confirming that he had known Markham for at least a period of three years prior. The signature was, of course, forged by Stonehouse. The passports were processed and soon fell into his possession, bearing the photograph of a smiling, bespectacled, dark-haired man in his forties.

Simultaneously, Stonehouse set up an address for Markham, using the Astoria Hotel in Pimlico, not far from the Houses of Parliament, for postal deliveries in that name. He stayed at the hotel as Markham on no fewer than four occasions between July and October. He made a point, after his final stay, to phone the manager to thank her for her assistance in a calculated effort to cement his Markham persona in her consciousness should she ever be asked.

Stonehouse recognised that Markham and Mildoon would need finances to support themselves in their new lives and determined that this was the time for his businesses to transform from a burden to a blessing. Money passed between the parts of the Stonehouse company group as if they were one entity, with fees that had been paid to one company transferred to another. From a business point of view it was a mess, but one that he could use to his advantage. Amid the chaos he would rinse as much money from the businesses as he could through authorised overdrafts and loans, and from the fees that he generated from his consultancy work.

Stonehouse needed his business group to generate as much money as possible as quickly as possible in order to establish the life he envisioned, which he planned to achieve in two ways. Firstly, by arranging for the businesses to secure bank loans, and secondly, by increasing his salary, both steps requiring the agreement of the directors of the company. Alongside himself, Sheila and Michael there was a fourth man, an accountant named John McGrath. Records seemed to show that both Michael and McGrath were present at a series of directors' meetings, over the course of which the minutes state that the directors agreed to both courses of action. Stonehouse quickly raised the loans and overdrafts necessary and the monies held in those accounts, amounting to £25,000 (around £250,000 today), were transferred to a covert account in the name of Markham.

The capital Stonehouse was appropriating from the companies needed a discreet home so new bank accounts were opened in the Markham name at the Midland Bank on Vauxhall Bridge Road, the Bank of New South Wales on Threadneedle Street, and the Australia and New Zealand Banking Group on the Strand.

The loans were boosted by the funds that Stonehouse had obtained from the British Bangladesh Trust and deposited into the EPACS accounts at the bank. He withdrew money from the EPACS bank accounts and, in at least one instance, Sheila made out a cheque payable to him for an amount far beyond his legitimate salary.

In addition to this, he continued to earn fees for the consultancy work that he was undertaking through EPACS, such as a cheque for $12,500 received in August from the Garrett Corporation of America payable to EPACS which, with Sheila's assistance, was converted into a banker's draft. This enabled Stonehouse to pay it into his personal account as money from other consultancy work done for Aeromaritime

Ltd, a US company registered in the UK, for which he earned £2,400 a year. Meanwhile, a lawyer in Lichtenstein, Oswald Buhler, had formed a company named Victa International with a bank account in New York. In a deft move, Stonehouse arranged for the fees that he earned through Aeromaritime Ltd to be paid into the Victa International bank account. That October, Stonehouse contacted Buhler requesting the payment of three cheques to cover expenses, which were to be paid into Sheila's bank and converted from dollars to sterling at the same time. The implication is that Sheila was complicit, a notion supported by a letter Stonehouse wrote to Buhler: 'I enclose a cheque for 5,000 dollars which would you please pay into the Victa Swiss bank account? As the mail is not reliable please do not write to me anymore. You may telephone me on any of the following numbers in normal office hours UK time, 9.30 a.m. to 6 p.m. and speak to either myself or Mrs Buckley but to no other person.'

By the time Stonehouse was ready to put his plan into action in November 1974, the series of loans, overdrafts, fees and other payments amassed via his businesses and personal accounts amounted to well over £1 million (£10 million today).

Stonehouse had resolved that he would make a fresh start in Australia for a number of reasons, not least because geographically it was as far away from the UK as he could get. The culture was very similar, emigration from Britain was common and he felt confident in his ability to seamlessly assimilate into Australian life. Finally, he had an admiration for the Australians; their brusque, no-nonsense, practical approach to life appealed to a man who was tired of the intrigue, intricacies and nuances of political life.

In September, he flew to Zurich and opened two Swiss bank accounts in Markham's name, depositing £90,000 (£930,000 today) and informing bank officials that he was a self-employed export consultant shortly due to be married. In the same month he advised the Bank of New South Wales that he was considering emigrating to

Australia and wished to set up an account in Melbourne. Once this had been organised, he transferred funds held in the Midland account into the Bank of New South Wales's Threadneedle Street branch and from there he moved £14,000 into the new account in Melbourne. A letter dated 24 September, written and signed in the name of Markham, putting the arrangement into effect would subsequently return to haunt him. It stated, 'As you know, I shall be leaving next week for the United States and Canada where I shall be spending about five weeks before going on to Australia. Could you kindly let me have the letter of introduction to the Melbourne Stock Exchange branch?' There followed a signed declaration to the effect that he would be residing in Australia for the next three years. The name used was J. A. Markham.

Credit cards in the Markham name were acquired. In the days before ATMs and electronic banking this was as fluid as cash could get. He would later use both his Stonehouse and Markham cards on a huge spending spree.

* * *

Though much of his conduct at that time seemed to suggest otherwise, Stonehouse always remained conscious of his responsibilities to his wife and children. While his plan meant that they would be left emotionally bereft, he had no desire to leave them financially destitute and passed many anguished hours contemplating how to ensure that they would be financially provided for in the event of his demise. He had no savings as such, other than the reserves he was hoarding, and his businesses could not be sold as going concerns and would no doubt be wound up after his death. The only option he could perceive was to take out life insurance policies, calculating that he would need more than one to sustain their standard of living, with his son attending private school and Barbara fully engaged with managing the household. She was not in a position to find employment easily, having devoted years of her life to the care of her husband and children.

This resolution placed him in a quandary. Taking out policies was easy enough but he must avoid alerting anyone to his evolving scheme, fearing any sudden change in his behaviour and habits could tip off his wife, the police and authorities to delve beneath the surface. The problem was that he was fit and healthy with thriving business concerns and an established political career in a relatively safe seat. With his disappearance and presumed death, suspicions would arise as to why he had taken out policies only a few months beforehand. Barbara might fall under suspicion of killing him or, worse still, doubts could arise as to whether in fact he was really dead, with the subsequent nullification of the policies. He restlessly brooded over the conundrum.

In a serendipitous turn of fate, a perfect pretext for taking out life insurance policies presented itself in the early months of 1974. That May, Stonehouse had to make a short business trip abroad, driving himself to Heathrow airport on Friday 18 May, where he parked his Rover on the third floor of the Terminal 1 car park. On Saturday, the press received a telephone call from a purported representative of the provisional IRA giving a coded warning that a bomb was shortly to explode on the airport site. Having been immediately alerted, the police scrambled to react to a five-minute warning, racing to clear the area. The car bomb detonated at 11.15 a.m. damaging at least fifty-eight vehicles, one of which happened to be Stonehouse's Rover. Stonehouse returned to find his car written off amid an urgent police investigation. That the IRA was responsible was never in doubt, with the attack bearing all their hallmarks.

Having been fortuitously delivered the perfect solution to his dilemma, Stonehouse pounced on the opportunity. Returning home, he dramatically relayed the incident to his wife and, linking it with the increasing number of bomb attacks and shootings of prominent public and political figures, proposed the wisdom of having his life insured. No fewer than five life assurance policies were taken out to a total value of £119,000 (£1.2 million today), the beneficiary of which would be Barbara.

*   *   *

In August, Stonehouse sent a trunk to Melbourne containing some personal effects and clothing, including some items belonging to Sheila, a detail that was to prove significant to the case against her, as it suggested that she had prior awareness of Stonehouse's plans before he disappeared.

The extent of Sheila's involvement in the conspiracy is unclear as she has never spoken of the business since. Examination of their activities during those fateful months, as his lover, confidante and support, suggests she knew of the plans for his disappearance, a view supported by their correspondence. On 23 October, Stonehouse arranged for a valuable stamp collection to be auctioned, requesting that the auctioneers not advertise the fact and to organise for the proceeds to be paid to Sheila. It was later suggested this was to provide the money to tide her over until she could join her lover in Australia, as her current source of income, EPACS, would cease trading with the MP's disappearance. Further events hint at her entanglement in the subterfuge such as an occasion on 24 October when she accompanied Stonehouse to the Highfield House Hotel in Hampstead where he requested a room for his 'wife' while he was away. This was later taken to indicate that the couple had arranged for Stonehouse to contact her by telephoning the hotel following his disappearance in order to avoid detection. Had Sheila remained in her flat, which belonged to Stonehouse, any such telephone calls would have been easily traceable.

Throughout these months, Stonehouse continued to function as a loyal backbench MP, fighting and winning his new Walsall North seat at the snap election called by the Heath Conservative government in February of that year, following which Heath tried and failed to form a coalition government with Jeremy Thorpe's Liberal Party and the Ulster Unionists. With four more seats than the Conservatives and, in light of Heath's failure to establish a coalition, Harold Wilson was asked to form a minority Labour government, resulting in a hung parliament, creating considerable difficulties for any government to put policies in place. Wilson called a second general election in October, which saw Labour increase its share of the vote, managing to obtain an overall majority in parliament of just three seats. With such a narrow margin, Labour could ill afford the loss of any seats, whether through sickness, death or misconduct. Stonehouse's plans would have a devastating effect on that delicate balance of power.

13

FAREWELLS

November 1974

With the October election victory, Stonehouse could now concentrate on his own plans. The compulsion to flee was intensifying, his anxiety over increasing financial pressures competing for attention with his apprehension about the imminent publication of Josef Frolík's book recounting his defection. While the account did not explicitly name him, it nonetheless made a brief and critical reference to a senior politician who had spied for them, and Stonehouse was possessed by the uneasy feeling that further speculation about his involvement as a Czech spy would arise in the press and security services.

His foresight and months of manoeuvring at least meant that everything was now in place. He had at his disposal two false identities, substantial reserves of cash, several secret bank accounts, a desirable destination, even a trunk full of personal effects and clothing waiting for him in Melbourne. The issue now was timing. He had been winding down over the previous months, summoning up enough enthusiasm to fight the second general election of the year and had found the campaign a welcome respite from his tribulations. Now that it was over he felt the weight of the millstone around his neck once more. He had taken as much as he could bear and concluded that November would be the time to bow out.

Only Stonehouse was alert to the poignancy of the final meetings and farewells with his family. We all gathered together at a birthday celebration he held for his mother Rosina at his country home in Andover around bonfire night. My mother noted that Stonehouse was not his usual sociable and avuncular self. He had withdrawn to his study with her husband, Michael, where they remained for most of that evening playing backgammon. It would to be the last time that my father and his uncle ever spoke face to face outside the confines of a courtroom.

On one of the rare occasions Stonehouse emerged to socialise, he announced to the excited throng of children that there would be fireworks, adding to the mounting clamour that he had decided that there should also be a bonfire. He then galvanised us to help him clear the basement of cardboard boxes, wood and other items to build the pyre. I distinctly remember him in his yellow pullover and cravat, the epitome of the country squire, directing us to shadowy corners of the cellar to plunder fuel for the blaze. I have since also wondered what secrets we unwittingly helped him to dispose of.

Gathered around, we watched as Stonehouse lit the bonfire, returning to his mother's side to gaze at the inferno and admire the firework display. For a moment he seemed lost in the flickering flames while, in contrast, his mother looked on impassively, never a woman to show her emotions. She was regarded by some as a cold, stubborn woman and it was hard to tell if she enjoyed the spectacle laid on by her son. If Stonehouse aspired to her approval he must have known that the course he was planning would only serve to hurt and disappoint her. Yet for the moment the family drew together enjoying the extravaganza, little realising the tumult to come.

* * *

Within days, Stonehouse was on his way to catch a flight to Miami from Heathrow. Parking his new Rover in the multi-storey car park at Heathrow, he checked in and obtained his boarding card for his BOAC flight. Travelling alone he was, surely, full of excitement and trepidation. Clutched on his lap was his briefcase containing his new identity, Joseph Markham.

Miami airport was typically busy, tourists milling about on their way to catch a bit of winter sun before Christmas, businessmen arriving or departing for conferences and meetings. The immigration official barely glanced up as he checked Stonehouse's visa and passport and, wishing him a good day, ushered him on.

Stonehouse loitered nearby for a while until he judged sufficient time had passed to ensure that the next stage of his plan would avoid detection. Had anyone been paying attention they would have noticed the same gentleman join another queue awaiting passport and visa checks. He retrieved a passport from his briefcase and, arriving at the immigration kiosk, answered the usual questions. He was travelling for business and was only in the country for a few days. The officer stamped the passport. 'Thank you, Mr Markham, have a good stay.' With that, Joseph Markham entered the United States.

Stonehouse arrived at the luxurious Fontainebleau Hotel and was shown to his room, where he tipped the porter for delivering his luggage before gathering himself for the task at hand. The first duty on his list was to attend a meeting with some bankers, with a view to securing much-needed investment for the British Bangladesh Trust, but Stonehouse's attention was elsewhere and he was unable to convince them of the benefits. The parties agreed to schedule a further meeting and they went their separate ways.

Stonehouse returned to the hotel, where he changed into his swimming shorts and donned a shirt before wandering through the tasteful corridors to the private beach. Swimming away from the beach, he returned to shore and picked up the spare set of clothes he had covertly deposited at the hotel next door. Not long after that, he was on a flight to Houston. From there he would take a connecting flight to Mexico

City, where he would board a further flight to take him to Australia in a series of long, tortuous journeys with innumerable changes that were to become a feature of this whole saga.

Everything was going as planned. However, as the Robert Burns poem 'To a Mouse' makes clear, 'The best laid schemes o' mice an' men, Gang aft a-gley'. Often the smallest margins produce the difference between success and failure, and when the journey between Houston and Mexico City was delayed by ten minutes he missed the flight to Sydney. The next flight was not for another week but he was reluctant to wait, being eager to reach his refuge in Australia before his disappearance was discovered. After a restless night in a nondescript local airport hotel he boarded a plane to Los Angeles, figuring that it would be easier to get a connection to Australia from there.

Once in LA he checked into the Marriott Hotel close to the airport, a place he was very familiar with, having stayed there on a number of occasions. Whether it was weariness, a craving for the familiar or the long hours of solitary contemplation while gazing out over vast vistas, which may have cast his enterprise in a rather insignificant light, Stonehouse's nerve seemed to falter and he hesitated on the brink.

A good friend and business associate from the Garrett Corporation lived locally. In a sudden change of heart he reached for the phone in his room and dialled his friend's secretary, making arrangements to meet for lunch and effectively ending his adventure. He could hardly continue the charade having surfaced for a sociable lunch date and, with relief or regret, he phoned Barbara to let her know that he planned to be back for the Remembrance Day service in his constituency. Another disturbed night was followed by a convoluted return flight via Atlanta and, as he stepped off the plane back in Miami, he was filled with misgivings that he would have some explaining to do, having inexplicably vanished for a couple of days and his absence very likely to have been remarked on.

To his consolation or chagrin, he was surprised to realise that no one at the Fontainebleau had noticed he had disappeared. He slipped back to the beach to retrieve his clothes with resignation. Reluctant to abandon his elaborate scheme, he was once more gripped by a change of heart, embarking on another excruciating attempt to return to the West Coast, this time via Chicago, where he was seized by a crisis of conscience as he gazed at his reflection in the plane's lavatory, contritely returning to London and Barbara.

*   *   *

While he had not achieved his objective, Stonehouse had gained valuable insight into how to progress more successfully. It was imperative that there be witnesses and for him to make his presence known at key moments. During the following tense days he arranged the follow-up luncheon meeting with the bankers in Miami for 20 November, using this pretext to invite another business associate, Jim Charlton, to accompany him. He had his witness. By all appearances it was a routine business trip, on which, according to Charlton, his companion seemed normal, if not a little 'ebullient'.

After an uneventful passage through US customs and passport control, they picked up a hire car, a Plymouth, from Hertz, and Stonehouse drove them to the Fontainebleau Hotel.

The Fontainebleau is a classic of the high-rise, glitzy hotels which sprang up in the 1950s along the Miami beachfront in a reflection of brash American post-war optimism. It features in the opening scenes of *Goldfinger*, where Bond first encounters the villain and an unfortunate young woman comes to an untimely end coated in gold. It was typical of Stonehouse to have selected such an ostentatious location for this most dramatic of acts. Perhaps he imagined himself as the hero in his own film, or as the director, manipulating the plot, the rest of the cast oblivious to the melodrama that was playing out.

Checking into the hotel, he and Charlton were lodged in rooms in an annex some 150 yards from the main building. That evening the two dined together and retired early as the jetlag began to set in, making arrangements to go swimming at around ten the next morning. According to Charlton, Stonehouse telephoned his room at about 9 a.m. and they agreed to go to the beach earlier. Fifteen minutes later Charlton knocked on Stonehouse's room door and they made their way to the hotel's private section of beach, where Stonehouse quickly undressed while entertaining Charlton with a tale of his previous experience at the hotel in which his unattended belongings had been stolen. Neatly folding his clothes, he approached the woman at the hotel's beach kiosk, asking if he could leave his clothes there, to which she agreed while Charlton made the informed decision not to go for a swim.

The beach was busy as the two men strolled across the warm sand to where the crystal-clear waters lapped the shore. As Stonehouse waded into the water, Charlton stretched out on a breakwater, savouring the warmth of the sun on his face. Stonehouse enjoyed swimming and caused his colleague some concern when he swam so far out that he almost disappeared from sight, eventually returning to shore some way down the beach and jogging back to join his companion. For the next few hours the two sat soaking up the rays and discussing the MP's future plans. He told Charlton that he planned to remain politically dormant for the next four years, by which time he fully intended to have made his fortune with a view to returning to a more active role in politics. Nothing in Stonehouse's tone or behaviour caused Charlton to suspect that anything was amiss.

At midday the pair attended the meeting with the representatives of the Miami bank. They were politely received by their American hosts although Charlton had the impression that it would prove a fruitless enterprise. As Stonehouse drove them back to the Fontainebleau he appeared to be filled with a renewed optimism that Charlton did not share.

Upon their return to the hotel, as they collected their room keys, Stonehouse turned to his companion. 'Jim, I think I'm going to go for another swim and then possibly do a spot of shopping for the wife and children,' he commented casually.

'That's fine, John, I think I'm going for a lie down. Shall we meet in the hotel bar for a pre-dinner drink? Seven-thirty?'

'I'll see you at seven-thirty.' Stonehouse turned on his heel and strode off down the corridor.

Charlton remained in his room, although he didn't sleep as planned. Propped up on the bed reading, he noticed that the weather had turned a little squally and he was distracted by the rain pattering against the window.

At 7 p.m. he got ready, went to the hotel bar and waited. And waited. Stonehouse did not materialise. Mildly irritated, he thought that his colleague may have overslept so he placed a call to Stonehouse's room, receiving no reply. Annoyed rather than alarmed, he chose to pass the time exploring the hotel and its grounds, returning to the bar at 8 p.m., where he ordered a drink and fell into conversation with a group of insurance brokers who were there for a convention. As time wore on, Charlton's concern at his colleague's absence began to manifest. He contacted housekeeping and arranged to meet a maid at Stonehouse's room to check in on him, fearing that he could have collapsed or had an accident.

Entering the room, the evidence was clear that Stonehouse had gone to the beach, having left his watch and other personal effects 'strewn' around. Charlton noted that the clothing that Stonehouse had worn to the beach that morning was not there and, after a quick check that the hire car was still in the hotel garage, he called security. Recalling the episode that morning when Stonehouse had taken great pains to leave his clothing in the kiosk, he enlisted a member of staff and together they hastened down to the beach area. Unable to gain access to the kiosk, they used the security officer's torch to look inside the little office. The flashlight beam flitted about until it paused, illuminating a shelf on which rested a neat pile of clothes. Panicking that his friend may have got into difficulties while swimming, poor Charlton cut a forlorn figure as he paced the deserted beach searching for his friend. He contacted Miami Beach Police Department and visited their offices that evening, where he was told there was little they could do until daylight and warning him that under no circumstances should he contact Stonehouse's wife, as there was still a chance he could return.

As next day dawned and Stonehouse had failed to return, Charlton entered his missing companion's room a second time, accompanied by police officers. Cautiously snapping open his briefcase, they found nothing to suggest anything other than he had gone missing while swimming. Charlton hesitantly began the agonising process of informing his colleague's wife, family and business associates.

Having finally seized his opportunity, Stonehouse was long gone, and on a flight to San Francisco and a new beginning.

14

DEATH OF AN IDEALIST

November–December 1974

Dazed disbelief, gradually to be replaced by profound shock and sorrow, was the effect of Stonehouse's death on the family he left behind. As they struggled to adjust to all the implications of his demise, Barbara realised that, in addition to coping with the burden of her grief, she would also have to deal with a daunting list of practicalities, including managing her late husband's business and financial affairs. Unable to handle the task single-handed, Barbara turned to her nephew, Michael, for help, a natural choice as he had not only been involved with some of John's business concerns but had assisted with some of their affairs in his capacity as a solicitor while his uncle was alive.

Michael had held his uncle in high esteem, considering him a fine example to emulate, and had been left reeling by the news of his disappearance and presumed death.

Like his uncle, he had been raised as a socialist and had been a keen activist in his days at Newcastle University, marching to support the Campaign for Nuclear Disarmament in the early 1960s, looking every inch the typical student in his donkey jacket, desert boots and a fetching goatee beard. Hanging out as part of the beatnik scene he could be found in the smoke-filled pubs and clubs of Newcastle, a bottle of brown ale leaving a ring on the table top, using the roll-up stuck between his fingers to emphasise his point as he discussed how to put the world to rights, shouting to be heard over the live band on stage. He took pride in the achievement of being arrested on one CND march and banged up in police cells.

Having graduated and married, he travelled to Zambia with his wife, Patti, and infant son in 1965 to teach English and, though the career didn't suit him, the family embraced the lifestyle. Returning to England in 1969, Michael chose to pursue a new path and took up training as a solicitor in Sunderland, qualifying in 1974 after moving to Wiltshire with his family, by which time he and Patti had four children.

Throughout these years he had followed his uncle's career with admiration as his political career blossomed. On his return to the UK, Michael would often spend time with his uncle, sometimes staying at Stonehouse's family farmhouse in north Hampshire or at his place in London, visits the young man regarded fondly, especially those occasions when, as a proud, card-carrying member of the Labour Party, he would help canvass for his uncle and the party at election time.

With Michael training as a lawyer, Stonehouse would occasionally quiz him during these visits about setting up companies or request his help to complete paperwork, which Michael was eager to undertake.

During 1974, Michael qualified as a solicitor and found a position with an established firm on the High Street in Winchester, though the family were still based in Corsham in the heart of Wiltshire, resulting in a long daily commute between home and the office. He and Patti planned to move the whole family to Southampton once he was properly established in his new job and had time to look around for a new home.

With the new qualification and job, Michael's advice became much sought after by the family and he later recalled regular boozy meals with his uncle, during which they would chat about their ambitions and aspirations. He also recalled that, more often than not as he was hopping into a cab to get to the station for the long train journey home, his uncle would thrust a document or two under his nose to sign in his capacity as a director of Stonehouse's companies. The combination of alcohol and blinding trust caused him to sign without scrutiny or question.

It seemed apt then that Barbara appealed to Michael to take on the task of trying to unpick her husband's tangled affairs, a process Michael began by travelling to Stonehouse's Dover Street office in London. While examining his uncle's papers he discovered the life insurance policies and, as any solicitor acting in the administration of an estate should, he wrote to the insurance companies concerned, notifying them of Stonehouse's death to begin the long process of realising those policies. Unwittingly, Michael was assisting his uncle with his plans.

With that done, he set about looking into Stonehouse's business affairs and the web of companies that he had set up with Michael's assistance and of which Michael remained a director, most significantly EPACS.

Michael spent a week poring over the documents and correspondence contained in his uncle's office, meticulous work would have been supplemented with requests for further documents, company bank statements and audited accounts, invoices and client enquiries. Examining the information filtering through, Michael was filled with horror as it became clear that his uncle appeared to have removed large sums of money from the company bank accounts and that at least one of the companies was insolvent. Michael was wounded that his uncle, a figure he so admired, could act so callously and irresponsibly.

It was not only the personal damage that Michael had to consider but the implication that he could be professionally compromised, and he was painfully aware that Barbara would be devastated to discover the betrayal and deceit. As he contemplated his discovery, Michael uneasily recalled Patti's theory that Stonehouse would have staged his disappearance, an idea that Michael had dismissed but suddenly seemed horribly credible.

He picked up the phone on the desk and dialled his wife. In the course of the ensuing conversation, Michael confided to Patti that he now suspected that, with the raft of financial discrepancies and mess that he had discovered, his uncle may have been up to something and could explain his disappearance. The awful magnitude of the circumstances they found themselves trapped in, through no fault of their own, was almost too much to comprehend.

On 27 November Michael received a telephone call from a journalist at the *Daily Mail* notifying him that they had it on good authority that the political editor of the *Daily Mirror* had reason to believe that Stonehouse had not drowned off Miami but was alive and well, living somewhere in the United States, and that the *Daily Mirror* had informed 10 Downing Street of this 'fact'.

Michael declined to comment but immediately phoned Downing Street to establish whether there was any truth to the matter. When he was eventually put through to a Mr Butler, he explained his connection as Stonehouse's nephew and family solicitor, and repeated the information he had received. Butler promised Michael that he would look into it.

Butler's enquiries revealed that there had been contact from a *Daily Mirror* correspondent to another Downing Street aide asking if he had seen the 'Stonehouse story'. It emerged that a Reverend Michael Scott of the Global Minorities Group had written to the prime minister on 24 November and had later gone to the *Daily Mirror*'s offices to regale journalists with damning allegations of Stonehouse's misconduct with the British Bangladesh Trust. Not only that but he also brought to their attention the news that a scandalous book was about to be published by the Czechoslovakian defector, Josef Frolík, asserting that Stonehouse had been involved with the Czech intelligence service. Harold Wilson remembered the claims when they had first been brought to his attention, recalling that there had been an investigation at the time and the security services had considered them to be unfounded. He told his staff that they could formally deny any such allegation, and Butler was to inform Michael that there was no story.

Michael received the news with a flood of relief, which would have rapidly dissipated when a story about the British Bangladesh Trust appeared in the *Mirror* the next day under the headline, 'Plea to Wilson over lost MP'.

The long, miserable weeks that followed, with ever more distressing revelations in the press given support by his own research, shattered Michael's political beliefs and affiliations and would cause him to rue his blinding trust in his uncle. He was brought to a state of profound disillusionment and bitterness. The idealist had died.

15

ENEMIES

December 1974

The old admonition never to speak ill of the dead did not seem to apply to Stonehouse. Inflammatory articles appeared in the newspapers recounting assorted crimes and misdemeanours, mostly relating to the numerous financial irregularities that appeared to be a feature of his business transactions involving the British Bangladesh Trust, EPACS and Connoisseurs of Wine. Every aspect of his life, and the lives of everyone connected to him, including his family and friends, was minutely examined.

On 2 December 1974 the Foreign Office received a visit from William Molloy, MP for North Ealing, who had been Stonehouse's staunchly loyal parliamentary private secretary. He urgently requested to speak to the under secretary of state, Lord Goronwy-Roberts. A minute of the meeting was taken, recording the time as 4.15 p.m.

'I'm concerned about Mr Stonehouse. He has many enemies. It's a fact that his car was blown up in the incident at Heathrow airport a few months back. The IRA were blamed for it . . . ' Goronwy-Roberts nodded as Molloy recounted his concerns, ' . . . whilst I was his private secretary. I wasn't involved in any of Mr Stonehouse's business enterprises,' Molloy added hastily.

Goronwy-Roberts acknowledged this with another solemn nod.

Molloy continued, 'I received a call from Mrs Stonehouse. She told me that she was worried that she hadn't heard anything from the Foreign Office or from her close friends or anything substantial from the police for that matter. The only person she has heard from is a middle-ranking police officer.' He paused, intently studying the two men facing him, looking for some reaction, but their faces remained impassive. Clearing his throat, he continued. 'I'm just wondering if this whole story of John's drowning is fabricated? You know that he was a very powerful swimmer and he'd often swim a long way out to sea, so I doubt he's drowned. I did speak to the PM's private secretary, who suggested I speak to a Foreign Office minister. So here I am. The other thing is that the BBC want to interview me again, but I am unsure what to say.'

Lord Goronwy-Roberts frowned at the very idea of the MP communicating with the media about a matter that was proving hugely embarrassing to the government, which was resolved to operate a strict damage-limitation exercise.

Goronwy-Roberts explained to Molloy that they had experienced difficulties in communicating with the Miami police. 'The ambassador in Washington has been taking a personal interest in the matter and he sent a personal message to Mrs Stonehouse which we were about to pass on to her.' He added that there had been no public announcements as they had no confirmation one way or another that Stonehouse was dead.

Thanking him, Molloy assured him that he would try to 'dampen down' any media speculation.

Following the meeting, Downing Street made discreet enquiries at the Home Office about the alleged bomb attack.

9 December 1974

The Prime Minister has heard of the allegation that a car belonging to Mr John Stonehouse was blown up at Heathrow airport some months ago, on an occasion when the IRA were at first blamed.

The Prime Minister has asked whether the Police confirmed on that occasion that the car belonged to Mr Stonehouse, and whether they had any discussion with him about it. If so, did Mr Stonehouse on that occasion mention enemies who might possibly have been responsible?

A response was received some ten days later from Mr Hayden Phillips at the Home Office.

Dear Robin,

This is in reply to your letter of the 9th December about a car belonging to Mr Stonehouse which was blown up at Heathrow. We have been in touch with the police and what follows is based on what they have told us.

The explosion which involved Mr Stonehouse's Rover (one of 58 vehicles which were damaged) took place at 11.15 a.m. on Sunday, 19th May, on the third floor of the car park at No. 1 Terminal. There is not much doubt that the Provisional I.R.A. were responsible. A coded message, as often used by them, was received by the press a few minutes before the explosion and as a result of subsequent investigation an Irishman was arrested in connection with the offence.

The police interviewed Mr Stonehouse when he came back to this country on 20th May. He told them he had left the car in the car park at 8.30 a.m. on Friday, 18th May, and he gave the police no indication that he believed himself to be any sort of target. It seems pretty clear that the explosion was not particularly aimed at Mr Stonehouse or his car and that the fact that the car was damaged was no more than coincidence.

Yours ever
Hayden Phillips

While these enquiries were being made, issues surrounding the British Bangladesh Trust/London Capital Securities were gathering momentum. Accusations made by the Reverend Michael Scott regarding the misuse of funds had heightened concerns, added to which the resignation of four company directors over the previous twelve months suggested that the bank was battling significant problems, with one of the directors on the verge of issuing proceedings against Stonehouse.

An increasingly vexed government was buckling under the pressure to make an announcement about the accusations and to call for an inquiry, as revealed in correspondence exchanged between the private secretaries at the Home Office and Downing Street. The dilemma was succinctly summed up in a letter of 13 December from Tony Hutton to Hayden Phillips, stating that the bank had

> substantial resources from Bangladesh sources and a £350,000 deposit from the Crown Agents. Information which has come into the possession of this Department in the last few days suggests that the company may be hopelessly illiquid and also that there may have been serious irregularities in its management. The Department proposes to put in its own inspectors in order to carry out confidential enquiries . . . In light of what those reveal we shall have to consider whether there is a case for the formal appointment of outside Inspectors to carry out a formal investigation . . .
>
> It is the normal practice not to disclose that . . . enquiries are being made, in order to avoid damaging a company when the result of the enquiries may be to reveal nothing amiss. This is particularly important in the case of a banking company like London Capital Securities where public knowledge of Department of Trade enquiries would be likely to start a run by depositors which would almost certainly bring the company down. I must therefore ask that nothing should be said about our enquiries in the reply to the Rev. Michael Scott.

This policy would soon change.

16

MAN HUNT

November 1974

A week had passed since the MP's disappearance. Surveying the rapidly multiplying pile of reports, the grizzled detective, Lieutenant Jack Webb of the Miami Beach Police Department, was perplexed. If the man had drowned, he would have expected some evidence of a body by now, his usual experience being that the sea surrendered its dead within a couple of days. Even in the case of a shark-attack victim, some remains would be found. In this case, despite an extensive investigation, not a trace had been recovered.

The Miami Beach detectives were nothing if not thorough, having conducted a comprehensive search, circulating Stonehouse's photograph to shipping offices, bus stations, rail terminals and airports as well as checking out all car-hire companies. Oceanographers were consulted about sea currents in the area to determine where a body would be likely to wash up while the coastguards undertook exhaustive searches of the coast and sea, and yet their collective efforts revealed nothing.

The police knew the politician had checked into the $70-a-day Fontainebleau Hotel with a business associate, James Charlton, where he had been allocated room 2425 in the spa wing on 19 November. By now the detectives had pieced together Stonehouse's movements on 20 November.

10.45 a.m. Stonehouse took a morning swim. His companion Charlton had reported that 'he was a strong swimmer and often swam three miles at a time'.

12.45 p.m. He and Charlton had had a working lunch with representatives of the First National Bank to discuss expanding his banking business.

3.50 p.m. Stonehouse and Charlton had by this time returned to the Fontainebleau Hotel and, during the course of a conversation with Charlton, Stonehouse apparently told him that he was planning another swim followed by some shopping. The pair parted having arranged to rendezvous for dinner later that evening.

4 p.m. The MP arrived at the hotel beach where he deposited his clothes with the beach kiosk attendant, Helen Fleming, who described him as being in a good mood and commenting on how good the water looked, and reminding her that there had been a previous episode where his clothes had been stolen.

4.05 p.m. The last person he spoke to was another guest on the beach, telling them that he was going for a jog, seemingly confirmed by sightings of him running on the deserted shore. That was the last anyone saw of him. The lifeguard had not seen anyone entering the water and had described the sea as being calm.

7.30 p.m. Mr Charlton had by this time expected to meet with Stonehouse for dinner and had become concerned when the MP failed to appear, firstly checking with the hotel's beach attendant and then calling for hotel security.

7.45 p.m. Mr Charlton and a security guard accessed the MP's hotel suite where they could find no sign of Stonehouse or of anything in the room having been disturbed.

8 p.m. Miami police department was advised of the disappearance and was entered in their records as 'missing presumed drowned'.

Nothing about the case stacked up for Lieutenant Webb, and now he was hearing stories that the politician had been experiencing some business and financial difficulties. It had been reported that Scotland Yard were preparing a dossier to pass to the FBI on Stonehouse's business affairs, while the British press were unearthing all sorts of financial and banking irregularities.

Rumours were also filtering through about some shady business dealings that had taken place between Stonehouse and a Nigerian businessman who had been found mysteriously drowned in the Thames, apparently relating to a cement business with suggested mafia connections, though nothing could be substantiated. Lieutenant Webb and his team contemplated the possibility of Stonehouse having been the victim of a kidnapping.

A breakthrough arrived in the form of a body, not washed up on the beach but found encased in concrete, indicating a feasible mafia connection. The police in Florida contacted their colleagues in London requesting blood and hair samples of the missing MP. Disappointingly, the lead proved fruitless, as tests showed the body wasn't that of Stonehouse.

Not only the British but the world's press were swarming all over the resort and the exasperated lieutenant had been constantly harassed by journalists, relentlessly phoning his office or mobbing him every time he stepped out of the police precinct, desperate to glean any titbit of information. A BBC news crew had even managed to access his office and film him at his desk. On being quizzed yet again about the progress of his enquiry, he commented, 'I cannot rule out the possibility that the disappearance could be something of a voluntary nature.'

Webb snatched up the phone on his desk, dialled and drummed his fingers on the desk as he waited impatiently for his call to connect. As soon as a voice answered he said, 'Get me the FBI.'

17

THE ODYSSEY

November–December 1974

Having generated a storm of chaos and controversy on both sides of the Atlantic, Stonehouse continued to pursue his bizarre personal odyssey, which he described in some detail in *Death of an Idealist*.

Having learned his lesson from his earlier 'dry run', he had decided to fly to Sydney via San Francisco. Arriving in 'Frisco', he took a cab to the Fairmont Hotel, high up on Nob Hill, where he spent a disturbed night contemplating his next move, finally resolving that, rather than travel directly to Australia, he would make a diversion to Honolulu.

Landing in Hawaii, Stonehouse spent five days in the Sheraton Waikiki Hotel, enjoying swimming and visiting the local tourist attractions. Whether his predicament left him prey to loneliness or the couple had prearranged it, Stonehouse surrendered to temptation and telephoned Sheila, who was now ensconced in the Highfield House Hotel in London. Telephone records retrieved by the police from the hotel show that there were two calls, on 22 and 25 November, making Sheila the only other person in the world to know that he was alive. Stonehouse and Sheila claimed that the calls came out of the blue, a cry for help from a tormented man, while cynics would suggest that he was phoning to confirm his disappearance had been noticed and to learn how the news had been received. Possibly imagining he would be able to fade imperceptibly into the background, the wild conjecture that had broken out in the British press took him aback. The story of his disappearance was not a minor paragraph on the fourth page of the newspapers but headline news, meaning any plan for Sheila to fly out to join him was wrecked, it being far too suspicious for her to slip away so soon after his supposed drowning.

Caroline Gay, the wife of Stonehouse's personal assistant, Philip Gay, had felt sympathy for Sheila, having suspected that her relationship with the missing MP was more than that of his secretary. She also appeared to have been largely ignored in the maelstrom that had followed the disappearance. Whilst her husband was in Miami sorting out his missing employers affairs she invited Sheila to her home for dinner on the 25 November. During the course of the evening they spoke of her lovers demise. 'She did not seem as upset over his presumed death as I thought she would have been,' the astute housewife later observed in her police statement. When discussing her future Gay noted, 'she thought that she might go to Australia as she had friends over there who had been pressing her to go for sometime.'

After his tropical sojourn, Stonehouse flew from Honolulu, briefly stopping at Nouméa, New Caledonia, before continuing on to Sydney. While there he found himself again unable to resist temptation and, checking the newspaper stands, was disappointed not to find any reports on his disappearance. With no news, he was left in an agony of suspense. A week after striding into the Atlantic Ocean, Stonehouse arrived at Melbourne on 27 November 1974. He entered unhindered through immigration control on his Joseph Markham passport, pleasantly surprised at how straightforward it had all been.

After all the emotional and mental strain, the burden of his perilous position, the months of planning, the false start and the arduous journey, Stonehouse no doubt relished the thought of retreating into obscurity. Any hopes that news of his disappearance would have subsided were sadly dashed by a feeding frenzy among the sharks of

Fleet Street, chewing over salacious stories of financial irregularities and spewing out headlines of extramarital affairs.

Stonehouse had booked two rooms at a hotel in Melbourne, one in the name of Markham, the other Mildoon, but by the time he arrived there he had already determined that he would not be staying long. He needed to talk to Sheila to plan the next move but it was too dangerous to write and certainly too risky to phone. He asked the clerk if he could simply leave his luggage at the hotel, which consisted solely of a light-brown leather case, as he planned to go away for a few days and would return to collect it. For a fee, the hotel agreed and the luggage was signed off in the name of Mildoon, the pseudonym he had decided to employ once in Australia. Concerned that investigators would conclude that he had travelled using a different name and discover the Markham identity and the route that this character had taken, Stonehouse hoped that the cunning ploy of assuming the third identity would help to throw them off the scent.

The media frenzy in the UK had not quite filtered through to Australia and both curiosity and the need to develop a contingency plan for Sheila to join him got the better of him. Agreeing a rendezvous with Sheila in Copenhagen, Stonehouse jumped on a flight to Singapore, via Perth, using his Markham persona. After an overnight stopover, he flew to Copenhagen, stopping briefly in Soviet-controlled Tashkent, arriving in the Danish capital on 29 November. He checked in to the Grand Hotel near the central railway station.

In *Death of an Idealist*, Stonehouse was less than candid about the purpose of his trip. Conscious that he was facing a trial at the time of the book's publication in October 1975, he did not wish to damage Sheila's defence by suggesting she was with him in Copenhagen and, by implication, involved in the fraud so, leaving that 'small' detail out of the book, he claimed that his sole purpose for travelling there was to elicit more information of his disappearance from the British newspapers. Apparently, they were more readily available in Scandinavia than Australia.

At seven in the morning, from the comparative anonymity of his Copenhagen hotel, Stonehouse telephoned Sheila at the Highfield House Hotel, informing her of his arrival. The prosecution would later assert this demonstrated Sheila's complicity in her lover's crimes, an accusation compounded when she immediately booked a flight to Copenhagen under an alias of Mrs Morgan, enabling her to slip out of the UK unnoticed by the press and authorities on 6 December. The lovers savoured two deliciously illicit days together in a welcome, if brief, respite from the vicissitudes of their respective recent experiences.

Stonehouse studied all the British newspapers that he could gather, flabbergasted by the lurid headlines and venomous columns. He had been vilified, with doubt cast on the veracity of his death, some quarters of the press going so far as to suggest that he had staged his demise to evade the consequences of his crumbling business empire. The Department of Trade and Industry had set in motion its own investigation in respect of London Capital Securities in the wake of four directors resigning from the company board shortly before the Stonehouse disappearance, scenting the decay of a rotten company.

Further revelations were released about his apparent mismanagement of other businesses in the Stonehouse portfolio, particularly EPACS and Connoisseurs of Wine. The intricate web that Stonehouse had woven was unravelling but, no matter his indignation, there was little he could do without exposing his deceit. He was relying on people assuming that he was dead, which allowed the press to publish anything about the missing MP without fear of libel action.

Inevitably, the lovers had to part and, with tearful farewells, Sheila returned to London and Stonehouse began his journey back to Australia. Setting off on 8 December, the return trip was as tortuous as his journey there. The first leg took him from Copenhagen to Moscow, where he stopped for a few hours before catching a connecting flight to Delhi, at which point he endured another transfer, boarding a flight to Bangkok, where he took the opportunity to freshen up and shave in the airport restroom. A couple of hours later he was gazing wearily down on the South China Sea on his way to Perth before finally embarking on the four-hour flight to Melbourne. It was with considerable relief that he eventually arrived in his adopted home on 10 December, ready for a fresh start.

Stonehouse located suitable accommodation at Suite 411, 500 Flinders Street, approaching the landlords, who seemed pleased to be renting the property to an apparently respectable English gentleman, Donald Clive Mildoon. Stonehouse was dead in Miami, Markham consigned to endless air travel.

The fugitive needed to ensure that his financial affairs were in order with his banks. To withdraw cash, deposit cheques and conduct any other transaction, physical attendance was a necessity in those pre-digital days. Making his way to his new bank he was irritated to discover a construction site. With further enquiries Stonehouse located an alternative branch to which he found that the Markham account he had opened in London had been transferred.

Withdrawing the bulk of the money from the Markham account in the Bank of New South Wales, he strolled a few doors down to the Bank of New Zealand where he proceeded to open a new account in the name of Donald Mildoon. Money-laundering checks were unheard of for banks at that time, yet Stonehouse's careless indiscretion was to cost him dearly.

Brian King, a bank teller with the Bank of New Zealand, later described in a statement made to the police how Mildoon had arrived at his counter to enquire about opening an account. Having completed the initial application, 'Mildoon' had produced a brown leather satchel from which he retrieved several neat stacks of banknotes amounting to $22,000. It was at this point that King was asked to assist a colleague to count the money. Once completed, Stonehouse disappeared with one of the bank's managers to complete the remaining paperwork and identity checks. It would seem that Stonehouse's inability to produce identification in this process had begun to raise suspicions. King went on his lunchbreak and, being a creature of habit, followed his usual routine, eating his sandwiches in the staff canteen before heading out for his regular walk. As the bank teller strolled through the summer sunshine, he passed the premises of the Bank of New South Wales on Collins Street. His attention was drawn to the same 'Mildoon' exiting that bank and the two men met with Mildoon, having to step around him as they passed each other on the pavement. King completed his walk and as he returned to his branch he again saw Mildoon and followed him into the bank. King suspected something was amiss and reported the matter to his manager. It would seem that this, coupled with the lack of identification, caused the bank to consider something sinister was afoot, informing the Melbourne police and marking the Mildoon file 'Treat with extreme caution'. Subsequent enquiries revealed that the staff at the Bank of New South Wales knew this man by another name, Markham.

In his attempts discreetly to cover his tracks, Stonehouse had displayed a careless lack of judgement. He was to draw further unwanted scrutiny when he wrote to his Zurich bank providing instructions for the money to be transferred from his Markham account to his Mildoon account in Australia with the specific instructions: 'Do not inform the receiving bank of your client's identity.'

The house of cards was teetering.

18

THE BOLTHOLE

December 1974

The press were hungry for information, regularly hounding Michael at home or in the office and even Patti had come to regard the telephone with hostility. But the journalists' greed was greatest for a quote from Barbara or Sheila.

Suggestions were made that the Stonehouse marriage had been on the rocks, implying that this may have been the motive for something sinister. The family were outraged and Barbara was provoked to make a statement through Michael. At the end of November he gave an interview to a *Daily Mirror* journalist and insisted that Barbara and her husband were 'absolutely devoted' and that 'there was no other woman. No other man. There are no money worries.' He confirmed that the family were convinced of Stonehouse's death and, in a quote that would no doubt come to haunt him, added, 'He is not the sort of person who would cause his family anguish.'

Michael was then quizzed about the Bangladesh Relief Fund (a charitable organisation quite distinct to the British Bangladesh Trust that had been set up to help provide relief to the victims of the war and famine), of which Stonehouse was a trustee, in the light of claims made by the Global Minorities Group that donation funds had disappeared and that, of the million pounds donated, only just over £400,000 had been accounted for. Michael pointed out that there were two other trustees, stating that the accounts were properly 'kept and audited'.

When the press discovered that Stonehouse had taken out three insurance policies amounting to £119,000, with his wife as beneficiary, speculation surged that she could be complicit in his murder. Despite being reassured by friends and family that the theory was absurd, Barbara felt driven to respond and, on this occasion, directly addressed journalists from the *Mirror*. She stated that it was she who had taken out the policies after her husband had been caught up in two recent bomb attacks, events which were corroborated by an enquiry made by the prime minister in the brief police report confirming that Stonehouse's vehicle had been damaged in a bomb attack at Heathrow airport.

If the feeding frenzy of the press was not enough for the family to bear, a further crisis rocked them. Stonehouse's mother, Rosina, my great-grandmother, collapsed, suffering a suspected heart attack. She had taken her favourite son's disappearance very hard, although she did not show it outwardly. Its impact, exacerbated by the stories besmirching the Stonehouse name, had an adverse effect on her health. It was touch and go as members of the family took up a vigil at her bedside in Southampton General Hospital. Stonehouse was oblivious to his mother's plight. He would only be informed through letters from Sheila after the crisis had passed and Rosina was on the road to recovery.

Further stories circulated speculating on Stonehouse's relationship with Sheila. On 11 December the *Daily Mirror* reported that they had located a flat that the MP had rented in Pimlico, to which they had despatched journalists armed with photographs of Sheila to speak to the neighbours, who identified her as the occupier. Barbara came to her defence, explaining that the flat functioned as a convenient second residence-cum-office, close to Parliament, where Sheila would stay and work, adding that she also paid rent for the property.

Privately, the truth was that the rumours that Sheila was her husband's mistress had caused Barbara to wonder. Throughout her marriage she had been aware of her husband's many infidelities but had tolerated them, taking the view that Stonehouse needed to pursue these liaisons as a pressure release. She felt secure in her marriage despite her husband's indiscretions, reminding herself that he told her every day that he loved her, that he was a good and devoted father to their three children and, above all, she loved him.

In an interview with the *News of the World* in the immediate aftermath of Stonehouse's trial, Barbara described the sickening suspicion that if her husband was having an affair this somehow seemed different and she needed to know. Filled with the mad adrenaline of the betrayed, Barbara sought to locate Sheila and confront her about her suspicions. Initially Barbara contacted the Dover Street office only to be told that Sheila was absent. Unknown to Barbara, the mistress was in Copenhagen with her Stonehouse.

Eventually, Barbara tracked Sheila down, subsequently meeting her at a friend's home in south London. Through tear-stained mascara Sheila confessed to the affair and disclosed that she believed she was pregnant. Understandably Barbara was incandescent with rage but realised that the fault lay not with the mistress but with her absent husband. Calming down, Barbara dropped Sheila at the tube station. She confided in the article that she felt pity as the younger woman disappeared into the Underground, blaming her husband for the mess that he had left behind.

Finding life under the microscope of the media unbearable, Sheila needed a bolthole to escape the attention and turned to Michael, who suggested that she stay with friends close to our home in Wiltshire. When Sheila arrived, Patti immediately took her under her wing, showing her the prettiest walks in the countryside, joining her on shopping expeditions to Devizes and inviting her to meals with the family. I remember, after one such retail adventure, her bursting through the front door of our home shaking the rain from her umbrella with my mother close behind. Despite seeming to form a close bond with Patti, Sheila managed to hold on to her dark secret, and we remained completely ignorant to the fact that not only was Stonehouse alive, but she had been with him recently. We only became aware of the significance of the timing of her visit when, shortly after Stonehouse's discovery, Sheila's visits to our home were revealed and we saw our front door flash across the TV screen on the national news.

Patti recalls that while on one of their shopping excursions, Sheila mentioned that she needed to send a letter to a friend in Australia. It transpired that she had written two letters to Stonehouse, both of which would subsequently form part of the evidence against them, and in particular Sheila.

It seemed that Sheila had more than Stonehouse's deception on her mind. As she had divulged to Barbara, she was concerned that she may have been pregnant. In her first letter, composed in a Corsham coffee shop, she wrote:

> I don't know about my boyfriend and as for junior well couldn't bear to produce a chip off the block I've been hearing about . . . I don't recognise him as the same man at all. Two entirely different personalities and I'm frightened to death . . . Can't get to a doctor re you know but I'm pretty sure think I'm going to lose it . . . My boyfriend is away at the moment and I've heard the most dreadful things about him from his former wife . . . He had an affair with Aimi M on holiday which nearly drove his wife to suicide . . .

In the second of her letters she elaborated on her fears.

> The dilemma with my man still exists and he has not yet returned . . . The thing that confused me mainly was the double life – so completely unnatural and hurtful . . . I asked many times

136

for him to leave me alone and in peace but he always convinced me that he couldn't do without me . . . You can imagine my shock to discover that he had said the same thing to his Mrs for nearly thirty years.

Sheila left the relative tranquillity of Wiltshire and four days later was visiting Brighton, where she revealed the emotional turmoil she was suffering in a third letter reflecting the awful dilemma she found herself in, alone with the burden of her knowledge and guilt: 'Junior is still around, mainly because the option to get him out of the way seems impossible. I'm at a complete loss on that one cos it will soon be too late to send him elsewhere.' Paradoxically, she signed this letter off with the poignant phrase, 'Shall wait for you forever.'

On 20 December, the fourth and final letter in the series testified to the contradictory emotions coursing through her: 'My Dearest Darling . . . things are bad, almost as ever . . . George must keep okay – it would break her heart if he wasn't. She loves him more than life . . . The worst problem so far is the Aimi M let down and also Miss Smith . . . I am shaking with rage.' As a postscript she added, 'Junior makes me feel so tired and drawn – wish I could lose him. He has been with me eight weeks. I think and I must do something about finding him a new place. Brings tears to my eyes. Love XXX.

Everyone, it seems, who had been in contact with Stonehouse was affected by his actions. Some would never quite recover.

19

REVELATIONS

17 December 1974

Over the five years that Josef Frolík had been in the States life had settled into a routine. When he had first arrived in the country he had been fêted by the CIA, who were delighted that the information he supplied had not only been of considerable help to them but also put back StB operations for years. Agents in which they had invested years targeting and nurturing 'behind the lines' in the West were now lost to them.

Frolík's intelligence on Stonehouse had been substantiated with the defection of another Czech operative, codename August, in late 1969, who had also seen records referring to Stonehouse in the StB archive. Like Frolík, he had not 'handled' Stonehouse directly, so this hearsay evidence had to be treated carefully. In the ensuing MI5 investigation Stonehouse had been interviewed on a number of occasions, during the course of which he had managed to convince the authorities that he was not, in fact, a spy.

With the passage of time, the intelligence provided by Frolík had staled but he was approached by a publisher, and together they condensed his work and experiences – carefully redacted to avoid compromising anyone from the intelligence services – into a volume entitled *The Frolík Defection*, published in autumn 1974. This was the book to which the Reverend Scott had referred on his visit to the *Daily Mirror* offices.

The timing of the publication was ideal for the opposition to put Wilson and his government on the back foot. Conservative MP Norman Tebbit planned to take advantage by tabling a question for the prime minister on the subject. The government's tiny majority had been reduced to two with the loss of Stonehouse, and the resulting press allegations, now aggravated by the publication of Frolík's book, put the prime minister under increasing pressure to comment. The media hummed with speculation surrounding Stonehouse's disappearance, whether it could be connected with the book's publication, whether he really was a Czech spy, and if he had been under surveillance at the time of his disappearance.

The matter irritated Harold Wilson immensely. He considered that the issue had been laid to rest back in 1969. Recognising that the matter of Frolík's book and Stonehouse's disappearance had to be dealt with, discussions were held between the Wilson and members of the cabinet, and agreement was reached that he should specifically address parliament about the matter.

On 17 December Harold Wilson stepped up to the dispatch box. 'With permission, Mr Speaker, I should like to make a statement on a security matter.'

The speaker nodded and the prime minister continued:

> Publicity has recently been given to allegations that my Right Honourable Friend for Walsall North was spying for the Czechoslovak Intelligence Service at the time he held ministerial office. These allegations were first made by a Czechoslovak defector in 1969. With my approval, the Security Service investigated these allegations fully at the time. In the course of their enquiries they interviewed the defector, and they questioned my Right Honourable Friend about his contacts. Following their investigations, the Security Service advised me that there was no evidence to support the allegations. I am today advised that no evidence to

support the allegations has come to light at any time since then. There is no truth whatever in reports that my Right Honourable Friend was being kept under investigation or surveillance by the Security Service at the time of his disappearance.

A flurry of supplementary questions followed, easily rebuffed with quick, concise responses and, so far as the prime minister was concerned, the matter was laid to rest. Unfortunately for him, it refused to remain buried and his statement to the Commons was to have ramifications later. Frolík's personal response to Wilson's comments was to demand a meeting with a representative from Her Majesty's Government.

The mystery deepened when it was reported to Downing Street that an unidentified caller had contacted the *Daily Telegraph* on 20 December, making claims to have knowledge of Stonehouse's movements. He had, according to Wilson's private secretary's note, 'flown, under an assumed name, from Havana to Moscow and from Moscow to East Germany on two dates in November. The caller did not give the name under which Mr Stonehouse was supposed to have flown, or the precise details of the flights; but flights between Havana and Moscow are not all that frequent, and there was a flight on the date in question.'

The note added, 'Our people do not regard this as very hard: they have been expecting a number of episodes of this kind following your statement. But there is a certain verisimilitude about the story, which makes one wonder. I suggest that we should see if discreet sources in East Germany have any information to offer.'

In fact, the mysterious caller was not far from the mark. Stonehouse's travel odyssey had indeed taken him into the Soviet Union on two occasions, firstly to Tashkent on his way to Copenhagen and again to Moscow on his way back to Australia. The enigmatic informant was never identified; nonetheless, within days, the net was to close.

* * *

The missing person investigation was still underway. On 23 December, Detective Chief Inspector Barbara Tilley, accompanied by Detective Sergeant George Crook, attended Stonehouse's business address at 26 Dover Street to interview Sheila. They reported that she appeared amiable and open, describing her employer as having been preoccupied with business affairs and experiencing health issues, in particular suffering with pains in his left arm. In answer to their enquiries she confirmed that he was a strong swimmer, but both officers noted separately that, unprompted and out of context, she had declared, 'He is dead.' It struck them both as an odd thing to say. According to Sheila, the last time she had spoken to Stonehouse was on 20 November, recalling that he was in good spirits and looking forward to the meeting with the American bankers. Satisfied for the time being, the officers left. The significance of Sheila's declaration would shortly become apparent.

20

THE ARREST

Melbourne, Christmas Eve 1974

Relishing the subterfuge of the masquerade, Stonehouse had begun to settle into his adopted persona as the distinguished English gentleman. He became a familiar figure, attending various social events, barbecues, house parties and even making plans to attend an upcoming jazz festival, having joined the local jazz club.

His first task each day was to walk to a local newsagent to buy a copy of *The Times*. He was still keen to keep track of any developments in the UK concerning his disappearance. The unfolding of the Czech spy story in the world press, including Australian newspapers, featuring clear, recent photographs of him, caused him considerable alarm, fearing he could be recognised at any moment.

He pored over accounts of Harold Wilson's address to the House of Commons in response to these allegations, his apprehension eased to learn that the prime minister had categorically stated that the Security Services were satisfied that there was no foundation to the claims. Describing these events in *Death of an Idealist*, he admitted to having suffered terrible anxiety over the spying charges, a hint that it was not only his catastrophic financial problems that had led to his breakdown and disappearance. Stonehouse had been aware of the Czechoslovak allegations since 1969 and was painfully alert to Major

Frolík's disclosures as two of those identified by him, agents Lee and Marconi, had been arrested and tried for spying.

Meandering through the Melbourne streets he was unaware of the undercover detective in blue bell-bottomed jeans and denim jacket. He had been under observation for some time, following a report made by the manager of a branch of the Bank of New Zealand, whose eagle-eyed bank teller had noticed a distinguished-looking gentleman, conspicuous in his trilby and thick dark spectacles, visiting different banks, making peculiar cash withdrawals, deposits and transfers under two different names.

Detective Sergeant John Coffey of the Victoria State Police was tasked with investigating whether a fraud was being perpetrated, either on the local banks in Melbourne or on a larger scale. On 12 December, Coffey, with eight other officers, commenced a surveillance operation. For the next twelve days the 'dog squad', so called for their propensity to hunt their quarry in a pack, had Stonehouse under intensive observation.

The information from the bank had provided the names Markham and Mildoon and an address at Suite 411, 500 Flinders Street. Enquiries were made of the apartment landlords who reported that the Englishman had been a model tenant and they had no complaints. An observation post was hastily set up in a flat adjacent, from which officers took turns following the mystery man through downtown Melbourne. Coffey's suspicions were raised when he observed the Englishman sitting in his apartment watching television still wearing his hat and glasses, but he was not living an extravagant lifestyle, he did not hang out in the city's flashy bars and clubs, and he kept himself to himself. This is direct contradiction of opening paragraph in this chapter which details house parties, jazz festivals, popular figure, etc. Suggest delete just 'and he kept himself to himself'. They trailed him as he went about his daily routine, leaving his flat in the morning with his hat jammed down around his ears, peering out from behind thick, dark-rimmed glasses. After picking up his morning newspaper he would often stop at the post office to collect and send post, and the officers were able to establish in one instance that he posted a letter to a 'Ms Black'.

Disregarding protests from the managers of the two banks, there were three occasions when Coffey took possession of unopened letters, without the authorisation of a warrant, two addressed to Mildoon, the other to J. Markham. He carefully steamed open the correspondence, copying the contents, and covertly returned the documents to the bank, seemingly untouched.

At Stonehouse's trial Coffey described the events: 'We were trying to establish whether a fraud was about to be perpetrated on our banks in Melbourne or had been perpetrated on some other country. We searched through English newspapers looking for some reference to Mildoon or Markham, but couldn't find anything. We then looked for some other fugitives from British justice. We first of all came up with the name of Lord Lucan, who at that stage was front-page news,' he reasoned. Lord Lucan had vanished from London after the brutal murder of his children's nanny at his estranged wife's home. 'Then we found a reference to John Stonehouse, the MP missing off Miami Beach. We kept both files running, trying to establish whether Markham/Mildoon was Lord Lucan or Mr Stonehouse.

'In the course of our investigation we obtained a search warrant for the apartment we had observed him coming from. When we searched that apartment, we discovered a pile of match books. One of those books of matches had the name of the Fontainebleau Hotel, Miami. We were aware that Mr Stonehouse had disappeared from that hotel.'

That clue finally convinced them that they had almost certainly located the enigmatic MP.

'A photograph of Mr Stonehouse was received from London. It showed similarities between Mr Markham and Mr Stonehouse.'

The temperature of the investigation rose as each piece of incendiary information was uncovered, building towards a blistering climax on Christmas Eve. The detectives trailed their prey as he paid his usual visits to the post office, banks, apartment and newsagent but scented danger when he took a detour into the then less-than-salubrious St Kilda area of Melbourne. As he made his way to the St Kilda train station and purchased a ticket, his pursuers became concerned that their target may 'do a runner' and, as the Englishman ran for a train, the shout went up and the three detectives pounced.

The man they sought was quickly cornered among the bemused St Kilda commuters as he took his seat in the carriage. Bewildered, he asked who they were, and the officers flashed their identifications before bundling him off the train and escorting him to a station office where he was informed that he was under arrest as a suspected illegal immigrant and placed in handcuffs. An unmarked car pulled up and he was placed into the back of the vehicle with officers, still hot from the chase, pressed on either side.

As the car sped towards the police station one of the officers spoke. 'Sir, can you please pull up your right trouser leg?'

Without protest the Englishman complied, revealing a pasty white knee bearing a scar.

'Ah, I thought so. Thank you.'

The rest of the journey passed in silence as the car slipped through the morning traffic until they reached the Victoria State police headquarters, where the prisoner was booked in with the custody sergeant. The contents of his emptied pockets testified to the multiple lives the Englishman had been leading.

He was led into an interview room where three detectives, including the denim-clad undercover officer, encircled the now dishevelled, slumped figure. The ensuing interrogation was secretly recorded but, during the fifty-one minutes for which the man maintained his silence, the investigators confessed that the interview was being taped. The recording was subsequently produced at the magistrates' court committal proceedings the following October, but has long since disappeared. What follows was gleaned from the court records, government cyphers and Stonehouse's own account in *Death of an Idealist*.

In exasperation one of the suited officers produced a file, slapping it unopened on the table at which the man mutely sat. 'Who are you?'

The man stared at him soundlessly.

'Do you know who you are?'

Again, no response.

'Are you Mr Joseph Arthur Markham?'

No reply.

'Where do you live?'

Nothing.

'We saw you looking at Suite 411 . . .' showing him the keys. 'Do you admit that you live there?'

The man continued to watch them wordlessly.

Flipping open the file on the table, the officer withdrew some of the enclosed documents. 'Perhaps we can help you.' Laying out a couple of sheets, one a tenancy application in the name of Donald Mildoon for 500 Flinders Street, the other, details of a bank account in the name of John Markham, he asked, 'Are these yours?' Waiting a beat, he exchanged glances with his colleagues. 'We believe that you're John Stonehouse.'

A pause swelled to fill the room as they let that sink in.

'Is that true?'

The figure in front of them seemed to deflate as the word 'yes' escaped his lips.

A moment later he straightened up in his chair, revitalised, as he repeated, 'Yes, I am John Stonehouse.'

The tension that had gripped the room was in that instant released, as the officer leaned across the table and, taking Stonehouse's hand, shook it warmly, a gesture repeated by each of the two other detectives. Having scored a victory, they relaxed into a much more friendly disposition.

The weeks of solitary subterfuge had taken their toll on Stonehouse and he seemed relieved to unburden himself to the officers about the lengths he had gone to in his efforts to escape to Australia. A Chinese meal was ordered for lunch and the dialogue continued on into the afternoon as he divulged how he had created the alternative personas, taking pains to explain his motives. He described the unbearable pressure oppressing him at every turn in the UK and how he had felt compelled to kill off his identity as John Stonehouse MP in order to regain his freedom by assuming the identities of his alter egos and start afresh.

At 5.30 p.m., Detective Inspector John Sullivan attended the Victoria State Police Headquarters in Melbourne to transfer Stonehouse to the Commonwealth police headquarters in the city. Accompanying them on the short journey was a black briefcase found at the Flinders Street flat, containing proof of the duplicitous life that the politician had been leading. On arrival an 'official' interview was conducted by DI Sullivan, during which a statement was drawn up and signed by the now exhausted MP, who would later rely on the document to mount part of his defence.

> In order to escape from exceptional political and business pressures which I suffered in England, I wished to establish a new identity and live and work in a more congenial country. Hence, I decided to represent myself as a prospective migrant to Australia, a country which I had visited and for which I had formed an admiration. Accordingly, I obtained the birth certificate of one Joseph Arthur Markham, deceased, and obtained a passport in his name. After visiting the United States, I arrived in Melbourne on 27th November 1974 and presented the false passport to the Immigration Officer and was admitted as a migrant to Australia. On 28th November 1974 I left for Europe as I was very concerned about the reported reactions to my disappearance. I returned to Australia on 10th December 1974 and presented the same passport

in the name of Markham to the Immigration Officer at Perth and was again admitted as a migrant. Despite all the circumstances I still wish to apply to remain in the Commonwealth of Australia as a migrant and to establish a new life as a citizen here.

Stonehouse later told the police that he had decided to go abroad in July of that year, confiding that he didn't know anyone in Australia, although this latter fact was untrue.

By the time they had concluded their interviews, the detectives who had listened to his sorry tale were inclined to regard him with some sympathy. Nonetheless, he was charged and held for having entered Australia on a false passport and was due to be produced before the magistrates' court in Melbourne on Boxing Day. The interviews had been conducted without the benefit of a solicitor and, realising that Stonehouse was in need of a decent lawyer, DI Sullivan suggested he contact a former police officer, James Patterson, on Stonehouse's behalf. The counsellor was a gamekeeper-cum-poacher, who had the begrudging respect of police officers throughout the city and had, some years before, acted for Charmian Biggs, the wife of the Great Train Robber, Ronnie Biggs, with great success. The lawyer attended the station immediately and spent the rest of the evening diligently listening to his client. Stonehouse spoke of him in glowing terms as someone with infinite patience and understanding, who put his clients' interests before those of himself or his firm.

A press conference was promptly held at which the Australian authorities formally announced that they had arrested and detained Stonehouse, news that rapidly seeped through to the UK, where his shocked wife and children, his bewildered extended family and a horrified Downing Street were now faced with the consequences.

21

THE PANTOMIME

Christmas 1974

The jangle of the phone stole along the dark hallway and into the bedrooms above, where it crept through the synapses of Michael Hayes's slumbering brain, causing him to stir. He might have sunk back into his dreams but his wife Patti nudged him insistently, rousing him enough to register the ringing. Reluctantly lowering each weary leg to the floor, he sat up and rubbed a hand over his face.

'Who on earth could be phoning at this time?' he grumbled uneasily.

It was the early hours of Christmas Eve morning and the country was poised for the seasonal festivities; work and routines were on hold for last-minute shopping, present wrapping and preparations for family celebrations. Michael's sluggish brain slowly processed the thought that only an emergency would prompt a call at such a time. Fearing news of an accident or worse, his heartrate quickened.

Stumbling down the stairs and along the hallway, he fumbled the receiver from its cradle and held it apprehensively to his ear. 'Hello?'

For a moment there was silence, then Michael heard an unfamiliar voice. 'Is that Michael Hayes?'

'Yes. Who is this?'

As Michael's wits rapidly recovered, he listened intently as a *Daily Express* reporter proceeded to inform him that his uncle had been discovered alive and well in Melbourne, Australia. The newsman was undoubtedly fishing for more information. A comment from the Stonehouse family lawyer and nephew would be the perfect place to start. What comments could be given save for the obvious relief that his uncle was alive and well?

Michael stood with the receiver in his hand for a moment before replacing it and cutting off the impertinent voice, wrestling with the enormity of what he had heard.

He trudged back upstairs and, as he padded across the room, Patti rolled over to face him.

'Is everything OK?' she asked anxiously, studying his stupefied face.

'They've found John. He's alive and well and living under an assumed name in Australia.'

'What? Really?' she gasped.

'Yes . . .' Michael trailed off pensively. Climbing into bed he added, 'It would probably have been better for him if he had never been found alive.'

Pulling the covers up to his chin and drawing his wife into his arms, he managed to fall asleep again. Peace and goodwill would soon be a blessed memory.

* * *

The political ramifications of Stonehouse's reappearance and arrest were immense and complex. A cypher was received by Downing Street from the British Consulate in Canberra notifying them of the MP's discovery within an hour of the police interview being concluded.

1. Following are facts as known to us so far. Because of Press enquiries seeking confirmation that Mr Stonehouse had been arrested in Melbourne, Consulate General Melbourne made enquiries and was told by Victoria soon after that –

A. On basis of Interpol circular message Victoria State police had yesterday detained a man using name Markham and questioned him on suspicion of being Stonehouse.

B. Within previous hour Markham had admitted to being Mr Stonehouse and police now virtually though not completely satisfied of his identity.

C. Police had no basis on which to hold him.

D. Consul General or his representative was welcome to see him.

E. Police would be holding press conference about Mr Stonehouse.

2. We are arranging for Consul General to see Mr Stonehouse as soon as possible but not yet revealing this to press. We are taking line in answer to press enquiries that we know no more than what Victoria police have told us and cannot comment. We are informing Attorney General's Department, DFA and Australian Security Authorities.

3. Grateful for earliest guidance (by flash telegram or telephone) on following points;

    i.   Will there be a request from British (or American) authorities to Australian authorities to hold Mr Stonehouse pending charges or extradition proceedings? If not I assume we should seek his immediate release and offer any help he may need, but please confirm?

    ii. What were nature and origin of Interpol message?

    iii. Is there any message for Consul General to deliver to Mr Stonehouse?

    iv. What if anything should we say to the press?

The response from James Callaghan, the foreign secretary, was swift. There was to be no preferential treatment for the MP and authorities should proceed 'strictly in accordance with the normal consular practice for any United Kingdom citizen facing charges in Australia'. They had no knowledge regarding Interpol and the British government had no message to convey to Stonehouse.

> In answer to press enquiries news department are saying on the record that Mr Stonehouse's presence in Melbourne has been reported to us by the Consulate General. That we have been in touch with Mrs Stonehouse and that a member of the Consulate General in Melbourne has visited Mr Stonehouse. No. 10 have released the text of Mr Stonehouse's message to the Prime Minister. The Home Office in answer to enquiries about extradition are saying unattributably that the question of extradition has not arisen. In answer to questions about any alleged offences which Mr Stonehouse may have committed in Australia No. 10 and news department are saying that this is entirely a matter for the Australian Authorities.

The Labour government was clinging to power with the slimmest of majorities, and was acutely aware that this situation would need to be handled very carefully. The lurid press speculation concerning Stonehouse's business enterprises and extramarital relations led the party to distance themselves as much as possible in an effort to limit the damage caused by his association. They were terrified that the fallout would result in, at best, the loss of their narrow lead, at worst long-lasting damage at the polls in any subsequent election.

The newspapers and television companies were rapacious in their pursuit of the story, embellishing every mundane detail in a bid to create ever more sensational headlines.

On receiving a visit from the British Consulate, who were tasked with checking on his welfare, Stonehouse, ever the politician, asked for the following message to be relayed to the prime minister:

> Please convey to the prime minister my regrets that I have created this problem. And to all concerned. The Prime Minister's statement in the House was correct. My wish was to release myself from the incredible pressures being put on me. Particularly in my business activities and various attempts at blackmail. I considered, clearly wrongly, that the best action I could take was to create a new identity and attempt to live a new life away from these pressures. I suppose this can be summed up as a brainstorm, or a mental breakdown. I can only apologise to you and all the others who have been troubled by this business. Again, thank you for your kind statement in the House.

When arrested, Stonehouse had been allowed to make a phone call to his wife Barbara. This was recorded and transcripts later played at his trial.

'Hello Barbara, it's me . . . John.' A pause. 'Hello, Barbara, I'm fine and in good heart.'

'Is that you, John?' Her voice was faint, her tone incredulous.

'You'll realise from all this that I have been deceiving you. I'm sorry I was deceiving you so much. I'll tell you the full story one day. I think there is a chance I can apply to stay in Australia.'

He groped for the words as he laboured to explain to his bewildered wife the circumstances and reasoning behind his disappearance and the position he now found himself in.

'I decided I would drop out of my identity in Miami. Pressures became far too great. It was just impossible. Everyone was on to me. They all wanted me to be the scapegoat for everything. There was no way in which one could survive. I thought I'd be like lightning and thunder. I'd drop out in Miami. All I can say is that I'm sorry that

I misled you. Everyone has been hugely helpful and understanding here. I understand that your situation has been far worse than mine because I hadn't told you the truth. I hoped that it would be a clean break. I would go away and set up a new life with a new identity.'

As the initial upwelling of emotion subsided, Stonehouse gathered his wits, making a robust effort to reassure his wife. 'The charge on which the Australian police are holding me is not extraditable. I've done nothing criminal. They can't pin anything on me, but what they will make up I don't know. I just hope that what I have done will solve it all and lift all the pressure from me. Can you please telephone Sheila and both of you come out as soon as you can? I would truly love to have someone I can talk to. Do come out and bring Sheila.'

The insensitivity of the request, given the torrent of emotions flooding through Barbara at the time, appeared to have been lost on Stonehouse. Barbara, of course, was to ignore the request.

His wife passed the phone to their son, and it was only then that Stonehouse choked up with emotion as the impact of his actions fully dawned on him, no doubt gripped by the realisation that, no matter his reasons and justifications, the effects on his family would be profound and lasting.

Barbara was approached by the *Daily Express*, which offered to pay for the flights on the condition that she agreed to be accompanied by one of its journalists. In bewildered gratitude, her mind consumed by ceaseless questions, she accepted, immediately packing her bags to leave for Australia.

In the Downing Street cyphers news continued to arrive; 'Mrs Stonehouse arrives Melbourne at 10.25 a.m. on 26 December by flight TN 493. Her journey is at the expense of the *Daily Express* and she will be accompanied by one of their reporters. They are travelling under the names of Mrs Church and Mr Paulson. Please ask Melbourne to offer her every assistance and courtesy with the formalities on arrival and with visiting Mr Stonehouse whom she has asked to be informed of her impending arrival.'

Under her newly acquired pseudonym, Barbara's Christmas Day was spent on a long, tedious flight, her thoughts in turmoil, plagued with conflicting emotions of relief, fury and pain.

Meanwhile, at 3.30 p.m. Chief Superintendent Paterson of the Victoria State Police held a press conference at which he formally announced that at 11.15 that morning a gentleman suspected by the CID of being an illegal immigrant had been interviewed and confessed that he was the missing MP John Stonehouse and had further admitted that he had entered Australia using a false passport. He went on to confirm that there were ongoing enquiries in England about other offences he may have committed but, in the meantime, he would be held in custody as an illegal immigrant. He concluded his statement by confirming that Stonehouse had been seen by the Consulate General and was in good health.

The chief superintendent, having completed his statement, faced a barrage of questions from the throng of journalists.

Yes, Mr Stonehouse had spoken to his wife on the telephone, was his response to the first and most pressing query.

'Where had he been staying?'

'Mr Stonehouse had been staying in Flinders Street, although we cannot disclose the precise location,' answered the officer.

'Where was he arrested?'

'In the St Kilda's area of Melbourne.'

'How did you find him?'

'Mr Stonehouse had been under surveillance for about a fortnight.'

'What is going to happen to him next?'

'He will be appearing before the court on the next available date, probably Boxing Day.'

'How was Mr Stonehouse when he was arrested?'

'Mr Stonehouse appeared to have plenty of money. He wasn't in disguise. He had been frequenting the Melbourne Post Office where we would receive information from England.'

The chief superintendent confirmed that Stonehouse appeared to be in good mental health, going on to describe how and when the MP had travelled in and out of Australia and confirming that he had been in Melbourne since 10 December.

The final question he took was whether Stonehouse had offered any explanation of his actions to the police.

'He told us that he felt under a great deal of pressure and was unable to cope with the strain so he decided to create a new personality, to forget his past and start afresh in Australia.'

The clamouring press would have prolonged the conference for hours, but the officer was mindful of his own Christmas arrangements and brought it to a swift close in the face of shouted protests from the assembled journalists.

22

CAPTIVE

December 1974–January 1975

Stonehouse spent a joyless Christmas Day in the cells of Melbourne police station. On Boxing Day he was produced before a magistrate in chambers charged with an immigration offence where he set the tone for the following proceedings and reporting by announcing to all assembled, 'I am not a criminal in the accepted sense of the word.' The bemused magistrate remanded him in custody to appear in Melbourne Magistrates' Court in seven days.

Although Barbara had arrived earlier that day and had been picked up at the airport by consular officials, the extraordinary events of the past hours had taken their toll on her. She was suffering from an excruciating migraine, obliging her to retire to her hotel room to recover, so she was not present at the hearing.

To Downing Street's dismay, the following day they were advised by the Australian minister of labour and immigration, Clyde Cameron, that the Australian authorities had reluctantly concluded that Stonehouse had in fact not committed any offence, as his status as a member of parliament from a commonwealth country allowed him to enter Australia without any travel documents. Stonehouse's lawyers successfully applied for his release on 28 December. Once freed, he immediately wrote to the Australian minister to appeal for residency.

A short statement released by Cameron explained the position:

> Mr Stonehouse has applied to remain in Australia and has written to me at length giving a personal explanation for his actions. I wish to examine this carefully, along with other reports which have been received. I am expecting further reports during the week. Mr Stonehouse has committed no offence since his arrival in Australia. At his point of entry he presented a passport in a name other than his own. However, as a member of the British House of Commons, Mr Stonehouse has a right to enter Australia without an entry permit. This derives from an order made by me to continue the exemption from entry permits granted to Members of Commonwealth Parliaments by my predecessors. In these circumstances I did not consider his continued detention was warranted while I studied the reports put to me. Mr Stonehouse agreed as a condition of his release to report to an officer of the Department of Labor and Immigration in Melbourne once a week.

This presented an unexpected and unwelcome twist for members of the British government, who had been working on the assumption that Stonehouse's detention would allow them time to develop a strategy and arrange for the repatriation of their runaway MP. Wishing to avoid any diplomatic embarrassment with the Australians they needed to hurriedly explore their options, suspecting that with Stonehouse's release he would try to evade British justice.

Encouraged by his treatment by the Australian authorities, Stonehouse expressed a keen desire to stay, unsurprising given the reception facing him if he were to return to the UK. If he wasn't already aware during that Christmas period, he was to find out shortly that the Department of Trade and Industry had decided to undertake a formal investigation, not just regarding the bank, London

Capital Securities, but all of his companies, including EPACS and the remaining companies that Michael had set up for him back in early 1970. An initial report had been prepared raising a number of areas of concern, the first of which was that he had secured a loan of £150,000 (£1.5 million today), for London Capital Securities and had then paid the loan into three of his other companies, which was then repaid by means of a 'circular cheque' transaction leaving a group of shareholders owing £150,000 to London Capital Securities. Apparently, this had been arranged through another company, Dover Street (Nominees) Ltd, which held these shares on behalf of a number of people but was also connected to Stonehouse. The department needed to establish a clear understanding as to who was connected and their involvement with these companies as directors and shareholders.

A second aspect that was concerning the DTI was evidence of a number of unexplained transactions, one of which involved Stonehouse withdrawing in excess of £44,000 from his company EPACS between 1 April and the time of his disappearance. The preliminary report stated, 'The information which has been provided to date provides grounds for the appointment of Inspectors . . . and I recommend that this should be done as soon as possible.'

The report acknowledged that escalating the matter to a full-blown inquiry, with the resulting public announcement, could lead to a run on the bank with depositors withdrawing their investments. However, as the significant investors were the Crown Agents, who had indicated that they would not be withdrawing their money at this stage, the bank had sufficient funds to meet the withdrawals of the smaller investors, though in the event the Crown Agents were to withdraw support, the bank would have to be liquidated. The report concluded, 'I invite the Secretary of State's agreement to the appointment of Inspectors into the London Capital Group Ltd and other Stonehouse companies.'

On 30 December the secretary of state concurred, and the names of Michael Sherrard, QC, and Ian Hay Davison were appointed as inspectors.

The same day an urgent cypher was sent to the British consulate in Canberra:

> Please pass the following to appropriate Australian Authorities at a suitable level and in the strictest of confidence.
>
> Begin. Urgent enquiries are proceeding into allegations of very serious offences and all the indications are that when evidence has been collected charges will be preferred. Indeed there are strong indications that an application for extradition in respect of one of the serious allegations could be made within about ten days. Ends.

Downing Street was anxious to distance itself from Stonehouse as quickly as possible in an effort to avoid further embarrassment, determining that in order to do so they needed to have Stonehouse removed from his seat in parliament. While technically unable to resign, there are occasions where an MP cannot continue to sit. For the purpose of stepping down, a constitutional legal fiction had been created, devising a rule whereby an MP cannot hold an office of profit under the Crown and by taking up such an office they are disqualified from their position in parliament; the two posts commonly used were the 'Steward of the Manor of Northstead' and the 'Steward of the Chiltern Hundreds'. That was the mechanism that Downing Street wanted to use, with Stonehouse's agreement, tentatively confident that he would not be resistant to such an idea, given that it would allow him to extricate himself from the mess he had gone to such lengths to escape.

The consulate provided Downing Street with the Australians' response on 31 December. They intimated that, while they did not wish to rush the British government, they were eager to know what was planned as soon as possible so they could publicly announce how matters were proceeding. Stonehouse was due back before Melbourne magistrates on 2 January and, adding to the difficulties because the matter involved the Foreign Office, the minister responsible was James Callaghan who was at that time in the Zambian capital, Lusaka.

The communiqué went further:

> There were legal difficulties in relation to possible holding charge under Australian Migration Act (apparently the only Act under which Mr Stonehouse could be held) which further necessitated in lodging a charge for issue of provisional warrant. Situation was complicated because Mr Cameron, Minister for Labour and Immigration, had reputation of being 'difficult' until request was made for extradition, Mr Cameron had discretion as to whether or not Mr Stonehouse was prosecuted for offences committed in Australia. If Mr Stonehouse decided to leave Australia only a decision by Mr Cameron to prosecute him could prevent him. Once extradition proceedings began, matter became the responsibility of Attorney General who had recently had dispute with Mr Cameron on another case.

Despite the desire to refrain from politicising the case, it was very clear that the matter was inextricably bound up with politics. As the communiqué concluded: 'For organizational and political reasons, Australians would prefer extradition to deportation, should that possibility arise.'

In the meantime, a meeting between the UK's director of public prosecutions and the attorney general had taken place to discuss the investigation into the Stonehouse business affairs with the result that two senior Scotland Yard police officers, Detective Chief Superintendent Kenneth Etheridge assisted by Detective Inspector Townley, were dispatched to Australia. The British authorities stated their belief to their Australian counterparts that there was evidence of significant fraud, which would result in charges being preferred against the elusive MP, and they were sending detectives to trace money they believed Stonehouse had stolen from his companies and was now using to fund his life in the Antipodes.

Etheridge was to lead the criminal investigation into Stonehouse. At just forty-eight, he was an old school detective, with an attitude very much of his time, as portrayed in popular TV dramas such as *The Sweeney*. He adopted the stance of being tough on crime, tough on the causes of crime, and using whatever methods obtained results. He had no interest in administration, only in collaring criminals, throwing himself into long hours at work matched by time spent in the pub. He featured large in Dick Kirby's book, *The Scourge of Soho*, on his fellow officer, Harry Challenor, with whom he had a close working and social relationship. Indeed, in 1964, when Challenor faced charges for planting a brick in the possessions of the cartoonist Donald Rooum, it was Etheridge who appeared at his prosecution to give evidence as to his concerns over his colleague's mental health.

Born and bred in London, Etheridge served in the Royal Navy before joining the police force in 1946. Throughout the 1960s and early 1970s he was stationed at West End Central police station, which at that time covered Mayfair and Soho, where he rose through the ranks to become deputy head of Scotland Yard's fraud squad and the go-to man for high-profile cases.

Soho was notorious for being the centre of the capital's vice trade and the police were reliant on local criminals to provide intelligence in a furtive arrangement by which officers would receive payoffs or 'favours' in return for turning a blind eye to criminal activities. In 1971 Etheridge was exposed in the *Sunday Times* for having accepted a holiday in Cypress from a local nightclub owner and, although he was cleared after an internal investigation, he could never quite rid himself of the taint of scandal. Nonetheless, he was considered a very effective detective and developed a reputation for getting results, particularly having been significant in assisting with the investigation into the architect, John Poulson, and the Newcastle politician, T. Dan Smith, uncovering a web of corruption reaching to the very highest echelons, even, it was suspected, as far as the then Conservative home secretary, Reginald Maudling. Etheridge was not cowed by rank or station and was dogged in his pursuit of any miscreant. His involvement was to be significant in the events that were unfolding.

If the British government had hoped that they would resolve the whole affair quickly they were to be disabused of that notion with Stonehouse's release from custody. Political and constitutional ramifications were to cause the administration a colossal headache. The circus was about to begin.

23

LIQUIDATION

December 1974–July 1975

Christmas had been purgatory for Michael. Despite the Sisyphean task of entertaining, feeding and pacifying what were by now five children under eight, not to mention his in-laws who were joining them for the festivities, he was constantly distracted by the events surrounding his uncle. He would drift away from the family festivities to scan the limited TV news bulletins for any developments. On Boxing Day he dashed out as soon as the local shop opened to buy copies of all the national newspapers. Although my parents did their best to shield us, the story had caused a furore and the phone seemed to ring incessantly as journalists desperately sought quotes or, the greatest prize, an inside scoop. I remember picking up the phone in our hallway and a voice asking if they could speak to my 'daddy' and my feeling of indignation as I had long since stopped using such baby talk and addressed him instead as 'dad', as befitted my mature years.

With the family duties of Christmas and New Year fulfilled, Michael arranged to take some leave from his new practice in Winchester, the senior partner acknowledging that this matter required the young solicitor's undivided attention.

One of Michael's most pressing priorities was to establish what was to be done with EPACS and the other companies of which Stonehouse had appointed him director, and to this end he arranged a meeting with

John McGrath, who acted both as the company accountant and joint director, in order to consider the financial state of the businesses. Their dismay on discovering the extent of the loans and overdraft facilities taken out by those companies turned to alarm on realising the huge sums of money that had been paid out of the company bank accounts, the beneficiary being Stonehouse. But their alarm turned to outrage when they found that the minutes of the directors' meetings appeared to have been doctored to give the impression that they had been present at crucial meetings, authorising loans and overdraft facilities as well as sanctioning an increase in salary payments to Stonehouse.

To exacerbate the impending crisis, they had now been informed that the DTI was undertaking a comprehensive investigation into all of Stonehouse's business activities, which would encompass the three companies with which Michael and McGrath were involved.

The directors' meeting was, of course, held without Stonehouse or Sheila present. It was relatively short, as they simply had to determine if the businesses were viable; their discussions focused on the money that had been removed and the fact that the businesses were solely reliant on Stonehouse to generate the work and, without him, there would be no income. Both directors were of the view that EPACS was hopelessly insolvent and passed the resolution that the company should be wound up. A minute was taken and entered into the company books.

In February 1975 an insolvency administrator, Michael Francis, was instructed to manage EPACS's liquidation. Francis soon discovered that were some unrealised assets in the company. The first was £34,300 due from Stonehouse on a loan account. The second was $12,500 that Stonehouse had received from the Garrett Corporation in the US. Neither had been recorded in the company books. This was to be merely a taster of further revelations to come.

With the DTI involved, everything connected with the Stonehouse group of companies was frozen. The Dover Street offices were searched, documents, bank accounts and other records were seized, and both Michael and McGrath, among others, were interviewed by the department inspectors and police, giving statements that were ultimately to form part of the criminal case against the truant MP. The DTI quickly formed the view that Michael, and many others connected with the company, had been used by Stonehouse so that he could pursue his own ends and that, while they were directors in name, they had little, if any, control over how the companies were run. That was Stonehouse's domain. Unfortunately, Michael's professional and personal future had been put into grave jeopardy by his uncle's behaviour.

24

RELEASE

January–February 1975

Detective Inspector Sullivan of the Commonwealth Police arranged for Stonehouse to be released in the early hours of the morning in order to allow the MP to evade press attention. As he stepped into the cool night air, Stonehouse's instinct was to seek solace in the arms of his wife. Barbara had not been informed of his release from detention and, indeed, Stonehouse's lawyers had deliberately withheld information of her husband's whereabouts for some days prior to this as it was clear that she was now seemingly in the pocket of the *Daily Express*. When advised of his release, the press pack was thrown off her tail with an elaborate police escort involving three vehicles, one of which was used to block the road to any would-be pursuers.

If Stonehouse had imagined his wife would greet him with a warm embrace, he was to be sorely disappointed, finding instead that the reunion was awkward and stilted. He was faced by an emotionally exhausted woman with a host of questions and a heart full of hurt.

She had tolerated his numerous infidelities as the worst-kept secret in the family, but Barbara now found herself confronted by a uniquely novel scenario with no map to help her chart her way. Initially overwhelmed with relief and elation at her husband's resurfacing, she would have had time to reflect, and undoubtedly there would have been a creeping resentment at his callous treatment of her and their family. Regardless, she remained loyal to her errant husband throughout this difficult period, appearing by his side at the various press conferences that ensued.

The publicity the case had attracted had swelled into a frenzy, with the two media giants of the time, Rupert Murdoch and Lord Beaverbrook, having engaged in a bidding war to buy Barbara's story. Beaverbrook's *Express* had won against Murdoch's *Sun* and *News of the World*, at a cost of 80–100,000 Australian dollars plus expenses, part of which had paid for Barbara's flight to Australia on Christmas Day. In retaliation, the Australian Murdoch enlisted his local contacts in his homeland to pursue Stonehouse and also sent journalists from the UK, who arrived as early as Boxing Day.

John Ballard, the assistant secretary at the Australian attorney general's office, became the conduit through which information about Stonehouse and his entourage's activities were communicated.

James Patterson, the highly experienced criminal lawyer Stonehouse had engaged, was a Liverpudlian who, following a brief stint in public relations, served in the maritime artillery during the war followed by the police force. He sensed greater opportunities in the New World and emigrated to Australia initially to take up a role with the police service there. He quit the police to study and qualify in law, and developed a busy and thriving practice. He had a reputation as a very effective lawyer.

Downing Street was becoming increasingly concerned about the whereabouts of Stonehouse's passport and the disagreeable likelihood that, if it were to be returned to him, he would take advantage of the liberty to vanish again, a scenario they were desperate to avoid given what was coming to light.

Initially, Stonehouse expressed his intention to resign his membership of parliament, writing to the Lord President of the Council and MP for Newcastle Central, Ted Short, to confirm this, which came as a considerable relief to the Wilson government. However, with his release from custody, Patterson advised his client that he should not resign as an MP, astutely recognising that to do so would remove his client's protected immigration status, which would likely result in his deportation back to the UK. For once, Stonehouse heeded the advice he was being given.

The MP was finding the intrusive attention of the press intolerable. He was trapped by the journalists camped outside his Melbourne address, brazenly rapping on the door at regular intervals to demand a comment, pursuing him and Barbara in hordes if they set foot outside, and chasing them on foot or in cars. Having gained his freedom from the law, Stonehouse found himself virtually a hostage of the media. He had previously referred to having been under enormous pressure and there were growing concerns as to his mental health as the intense scrutiny he received from the media took its toll. Whatever views may have been held of his questionable conduct there was no doubt that he was under immense stress, with the result that he sought the help of a psychiatrist. The more cynical may think that this was done in order not only to elicit sympathy, but also with an eye on his defence in potential criminal proceedings.

Somehow, on 5 January, he and Barbara managed to flee the claustrophobic coop in which they had felt confined. They had duly informed the police of their intention to leave the address but, to the alarm of the Australian authorities, vanished from the property before they had been given a chance to respond, leaving the surveillance team charged with observing him perplexed at how easily they had been sidestepped. All ports and airports were put on alert and furnished with the details for Stonehouse, Markham and Mildoon, His lawyer was contacted but, unsurprisingly, Patterson refused to divulge details of his clients whereabouts. It was rumoured that the Stonehouses had simply moved to another address in Melbourne, while some speculated that they had obtained a car and driven to Sydney. Patterson was warned that Stonehouse should be advised that he was likely to be arrested again.

The British authorities became acutely anxious as to the whereabouts of the Stonehouse passport, which had still not arrived from Miami. The Australian police gave assurances that they would hold it until discussions took place between the civil servants as to whether there were grounds for the passport to be withdrawn. Regardless, the ease with which the MP had slipped through their net threw the authorities' relative powerlessness to contain Stonehouse into sharp relief.

It transpired that the Stonehouses had hired a car and set off on the two-day drive from Melbourne to Sydney, phoning the police when they arrived to let them know of their whereabouts. The message was seemingly misinterpreted, with the police labouring under the impression that the couple had remained in Melbourne, holed up at another address. Realising very quickly that this was not the case, they put further pressure on Patterson to convey the warning of a possible further arrest and, with that, the contrite MP returned to the Victorian capital.

25

KNIVES ARE SHARPENED

January–February 1975

The Stonehouse affair was presenting the British government with not only legal and constitutional issues, but also more fundamental logistical problems. Trying to keep abreast of anything that the MP did was almost impossible; with satellite technology and instantaneous communication in their infancy, Downing Street was reliant on radio cyphers, teletext messages and long-distance telephone calls between the British consulate and their Australian counterparts. None of these were sufficient to maintain reliable surveillance of the MP's erratic movements or to know his vacillating mind.

The British government were keen to return Stonehouse to home turf, firstly to deal with the mounting constitutional crisis and secondly to ensure that he confront the consequences of his bizarre actions. There was a firm belief that he had been involved in criminal activities and that he ought to face prosecution. To achieve this, evidence would have to be gathered and, given the size of that task, it would take some time. Meanwhile, the Australians were proving reluctant to help with the politician's repatriation despite the mutual extradition treaty.

From the moment Stonehouse had been discovered, there were concerns he would attempt to disappear again and the British authorities were terrified of the further embarrassment of the MP vanishing and resurfacing in a country that did not share an extradition treaty with

Britain. They remained haunted by the scandal that had erupted over the case of Ronnie Biggs, the Great Train Robber, who had contrived to escape from Wandsworth prison, reappearing in Brazil with a young wife and child, only for the Brazilians to refuse to cooperate with the British authorities' request for his extradition and return to jail.

The Australians were themselves in a difficult position, hamstrung by the fact that, while the method by which Stonehouse had accessed the country had been unorthodox, his status as a British MP meant that he had technically done nothing illegal to merit deportation. There were, for the time being, no criminal proceedings in the UK that would support extradition and the Australians were loath to be perceived, either in their own country or abroad, to be at the beck and call of the British authorities.

Stonehouse exploited the clash of interests to remain in Australia and dance out of the clutches of his home country, astutely perceiving that though the two nations desired the same result, for different reasons, they would require a more coordinated approach to have any hope of achieving it.

On 7 January a meeting took place at the Australian attorney general's office in Melbourne between Detective Chief Superintendent Etheridge and Detective Inspector Townley, the two British officers; representatives of the Australian attorney general's office; the Department of Labor and Immigration; and the Victoria state police and the Commonwealth police. The universal view was that there needed to be huge improvements in communication and a coherent strategy pursued.

John Ballard, first assistant secretary in the attorney general's department, had already proved to be a significant character in recent events and would become even more so as matters developed. Opening the meeting by outlining the Australians' view, he clarified that they wanted Stonehouse to be extradited, but that proceedings would place the decision safely in the remit of the courts, a tactic that would allow ministers to avoid having to make a decision to deport, which would have proved politically highly embarrassing.

Ballard expanded on the extradition process. Firstly, an application needed to be made to the Australian police by their British counterparts for a provisional warrant, an ambiguous document that did not need to contain a full list of charges. The second stage would involve a formal requisition for extradition made by the UK home secretary to the Australian attorney general, which would have to specify the charges; followed finally by the extradition proceedings in court.

He added, 'The current situation is that Mr Stonehouse is technically free, however, should he attempt to leave Australia, Mr Cameron has authorised his arrest for offences under the Australian Migration Act. When Mr Stonehouse disappeared last Sunday, he was warned through his solicitor that he would be arrested. This prompted his return to Melbourne.'

Etheridge responded by explaining that the British authorities had established that they had clear evidence for one offence relating to the forged passport in addition to the DTI's ongoing investigation into Stonehouse's business affairs. He elaborated in detail the nature of Stonehouse's companies and the department's suspicions, having uncovered irregularities leading them to surmise that he had removed money from those businesses, which had in part been transferred to Australian banks, with some recent transfers from Swiss bank accounts to the Bank of New Zealand. He was frank in advising that the investigation had only just begun and would take six to twelve months to complete, going on to confirm that enquiries were also being conducted by the Metropolitan Police into other fraud offences but, again, these would take around six months to complete.

'So why are you here?' enquired Ballard warily.

'We're not here to interview Mr Stonehouse – of course, if he wants to speak to us we will listen to anything that he has to say, although he will be cautioned in accordance with the judges' rules.' Judges' rules, the precursor to the Police and Criminal Evidence Act (PACE), were the legal requirements for interviewing suspects.

Etheridge studied the group of men around the table before continuing. 'We're here to examine transactions that look to have taken place between Swiss and Australian bank accounts linked to him. We reckon there were "dummy runs" on those accounts undertaken by Mr Stonehouse shortly before his disappearance.' The room was silent, cigarette smoke coiling towards the ceiling. 'We're also very interested in listening to the taped interviews made by Mr Stonehouse to you when he was arrested on Christmas Eve. We remain convinced that Australia is not his final destination. He is getting desperate and looking for ways to avoid going back to the UK and facing the courts. We now hold his real passport but he's still got an account with the Bank of New Zealand with $A22,000; plenty for him to be able to pay to disappear again.'

There was a pause as the assembled group mulled over the implications, then Etheridge changed topic, describing the recent reunion between Stonehouse and his wife Barbara, referring to the occasion as not being 'particularly friendly'. Stonehouse had apparently made the accusation that Barbara had known all along what he was up to, also complaining that she was behaving 'more as a reporter than a wife', an astute observation given the recent contract that she had signed with the Beaverbrook newspaper group. The minutes held in the National Archives at Kew have been redacted on this topic; an unknown sentence has been removed on the basis that it is so sensitive.

Discussion returned to the thorny issue of the extradition process, concerns being raised that, while the British government could seek extradition on the relatively minor charge of fraudulently obtaining a passport, the proceedings could not be eked out for six months while they waited for the DTI and Scotland Yard investigations to be completed. Even if they were to prefer more serious charges, it was the view of the meeting that the magistrate in Australia would be unlikely to entertain the new matters. Furthermore, if Stonehouse was to be extradited on the passport charge alone, the UK prosecuting authorities would not be able to charge and try him in relation to the new charges.

With the problems highlighted, the meeting moved on to identifying possible solutions in the event that the UK government could not expedite their enquiries and complete them in two to three months, with two being identified. Both required the cooperation of Mr Cameron, the irascible minister of Labour and Immigration.

The first was to charge Stonehouse with offences in Australia under the Australian Migration Act, intended as a delaying tactic while their UK counterparts collated evidence for the more serious charges to come. The advantage of this approach would be that they could arrest Stonehouse if he tried to leave the country, but, as learned through bitter experience, the disadvantage was that they would find it difficult to keep the errant MP under constant surveillance.

The second option would be for Stonehouse to be deported. However, those assembled recognised that Clyde Cameron had been reluctant to follow this route while Stonehouse remained an MP and they felt it highly unlikely that the minister would agree now. Indeed, when Ballard reported the details of the meeting to Cameron, they took the same view that the case for deportation was very weak.

Etheridge suggested to the group that it would perhaps be better for the immigration officials to recommend to Mr Cameron that he simply request Stonehouse to leave Australia of his own volition; then, if he refused, it would give the minster greater opportunity to recommend to the Australian cabinet that the MP be deported. The Australian contingent agreed that this would be the best solution at present, acknowledging that, while the situation was politically highly sensitive and complex, if it was done soon, any further furore would have died down by the time parliament returned on 11 February.

While nothing decisive had been achieved, the meeting had helped to confirm that the British and Australian objectives were broadly similar. The various protagonists in the subsequent proceedings had now met and established a working relationship.

26

CAT AND MOUSE

January–February 1975

In the months following his arrest, Stonehouse and the authorities engaged in a game of cat and mouse, with Stonehouse's aim being to avoid returning to the UK while the establishment sought to prevent him escaping justice.

In what might be described as an act of impudence, the MP again exposed the tenuous grip the British authorities had on him when, on 9 January, he and Barbara arrived in Sydney by plane using an alias of Taylor. Claiming they were there to visit friends and that they had cleared this with the Commonwealth police, who now had Stonehouse under surveillance, they then planned to purchase a car in which to drive back to Melbourne.

To the great chagrin of Her Majesty's Government, on 10 January they were advised by the Australian Department of Immigration that the minister, Clyde Cameron, had decided not to deport Stonehouse, though there was a caveat that allowed a small ray of hope. 'Mr Cameron would be grateful for advance warning, if possible, should the House of Commons move to expel Mr Stonehouse,' read the cypher, indicating that with Stonehouse's expulsion the whole game changed for Cameron as the loss of MP status would sanction Stonehouse being deported.

If Stonehouse refused to resign by 'taking the Chiltern Hundreds', the government's preferred method, that would leave them only with the option for the House of Commons to pass a motion expelling him, on which point the attorney general gave clear written advice to the prime minister:

> Before any step is taken in the direction of a motion to expel Mr Stonehouse, he should first be given a clear opportunity to resign: if he refuses or fails to do so, he should at least be asked to give to the Lord President, or to his representative, his version of the events which have occurred and his motives, so far as relevant, for his actions. The Attorney General has in mind that Mr Stonehouse is reported to have referred to 'enormous pressures' being brought to bear upon him and even to 'blackmail'. Moreover, the state of Mr Stonehouse's mental health may be a relevant consideration. Such matters should, if possible, be clarified before the extreme step of a motion to expel is taken.

Having contrived to once again escape to Sydney from under the noses of the gathered press and British officials, enlisting the collusion of the Commonwealth police, even to the extent of arranging a police escort for thirty miles out of the city before allowing them the freedom to continue alone, the Stonehouses checked into a motel in Newcastle. There, Stonehouse took the opportunity to pen a three-page letter addressed to the lord president, Ted Short. He then telephoned the consulate's information counsellor, by the name of Tucker, at his home, making arrangements to meet urgently in a Canberra motel car park.

Drawing up at the car park, Tucker was met by Stonehouse and his wife. He described the MP as seeming calm and relaxed, although becoming animated when discussing the 'appalling treatment' he had suffered at the hands of the British press in Australia. Handing the civil servant the three-page letter, written on Noah's Newcastle Motor Inn notepaper, he explained that they had felt the need to meet in such a clandestine fashion so as to avoid the inevitable publicity. The letter made reference to the trauma he had suffered and how he had felt it necessary to consult a psychiatrist, going on to reaffirm his desire to remain in Australia and to that end stating his intention to resign as an MP.

Before he drove away from the meeting, Stonehouse commented to the bemused Tucker that he hoped this would be the last contact it would be necessary for him to make with any British official, an optimism that was to be shattered. Even as Stonehouse laid out his plans, the DTI had appointed two inspectors, Michael Sherrard, QC, and Ian Hay Davison, and a formal announcement was subsequently made to the press on 17 January.

Tucker immediately made arrangements to send a cypher to London with a transcript of Stonehouse's letter, which was received with some relief, with its promise of an early and painless resolution to the unfolding crisis. However, within twenty-four hours Stonehouse had qualified his desire to resign, fretfully seeking assurances that he could remain in Australia and would not be deported, information transmitted through a press report. Stubbornly, the British authorities pressed ahead, sending the necessary documents to organise his resignation to his solicitor in Melbourne.

There followed a flurry of correspondence between the parties seeking clarification, with the Australians requesting more information in order to prompt Cameron to review his decision to deport Stonehouse. Frustratingly, the British were unable to confirm Stonehouse's resignation immediately, ruefully confessing that his letter was not sufficient and that he would have to complete the necessary documents to take up the Crown office that would disqualify him from continuing as an MP.

On 15 January, Downing Street was dismayed to receive reports that Stonehouse was planning to fly to Bangladesh, where he had been granted honorary citizenship in recognition of his work in the

Bangladeshi war of independence. The British government contacted the Bangladeshi High Commission, who responded that they were unaware of any such request and concluded, following further enquiries by the British authorities, that they must regretfully decline to assist with Stonehouse's relocation to Bangladesh.

On the same day as the UK was negotiating with the Bangladeshis, the resignation documents were served on Stonehouse's lawyer. Patterson later confirmed that Stonehouse had read the paperwork, while making it clear to the consul general to Melbourne, Ivor Vincent, that he would advise his client not to sign.

That day had also seen the departure of Barbara, who returned to London, and the absence of her steadying, temperate influence perhaps partly explains why Stonehouse's behaviour deteriorated.

Late that evening, Vincent telephoned Stonehouse directly, finding the MP in an agitated state in the company of Patterson. Vincent reminded Stonehouse of his recent letter indicating his desire to resign, which had been received at a time when his Westminster colleagues were expecting to make a decision about his continued membership of parliament. It was Vincent's view that they had a right to a prompt response from Stonehouse and, if none was forthcoming, they would take the next steps to expel him.

If Vincent thought Patterson's presence would temper Stonehouse's response he was sadly mistaken as Stonehouse subjected him to what the consul general described as a 'tirade' against Britain, insisting that he would not be rushed into signing before passing the phone to Patterson.

'I'm not prepared to advise my client to decide whether to sign or not. It's not in his interests to make that decision now.' Barely allowing that fact to sink in, he elaborated, 'Once he signs that document, he loses his status as an MP and then he may be detained again. My client is in no psychological state to make such a decision. We are expecting a psychiatric report tomorrow, however; suffice to say my client is in a highly nervous and excited state of mind. He's been anxiously following developments as reported in the press.'

On that note he terminated the call, leaving a bemused Vincent to report back to Downing Street, from which he received further instructions that he was to speak with Stonehouse again as soon as possible. He was to advise that the MP should choose a dignified end to his career rather than letting a hostile House of Commons take the decision out of his hands, and Vincent was warned that the Australians were to be informed of developments only in the most general terms.

The following day Vincent tried without success to contact Patterson, leaving him with little option but to consult with the Commonwealth police and to approach Stonehouse's residence in Melbourne accompanied by his deputy. After some delay Stonehouse answered the door, treating them to a very frosty reception. When Vincent identified himself, the MP informed him curtly that he would not speak with him and instructed him to communicate through his lawyer, at which point Stonehouse jumped into his car and drove off, briefly returning a short while later to collect some luggage before leaving again without speaking with the two consular officials.

Undeterred, Vincent telephoned Patterson and, advising the lawyer of the urgency of the situation, requested a meeting that night or early the next day. Patterson coldly informed him he was unlikely to speak to his client until late that evening and that a night-time meeting was out of the question.

On the evening of 16 January, the persistent Vincent spoke with Stonehouse on the phone, patiently reminding him that, in the absence of a decision or a refusal to sign, ministers would have to put matters to the Commons. The politician lost his temper, insisting this was nonsense before dictating to the diplomat, whose patience was practically saintly, a response to be given to the lord president, Ted Short:

Dear Ted,

Thank you for your cable. Some newspapers are apparently reporting that I have announced that I will not resign. This is incorrect. The position is as follows. My solicitor has advised me very strongly not to resign because of the curious position with regard to the immigration laws in Australia. My solicitor has said that he would not take responsibility if I signed the document and that he would require an indemnity from me if I did so. My solicitor is seeking further legal advice . . .

Stonehouse paused, 'No, change that please.'

My solicitor is examining the legal position more closely and meanwhile I am awaiting further advice on the matter. I have noted in the press here a statement by Bob Mellish. I hope he has been misquoted. It certainly would be incredible for the House of Commons to follow what, apparently, he believes is the right course without giving my side of the story consideration. The press here have been quite hysterical and that, I suppose, is the root of the problem as far as you are concerned. I will let you know how this legal consideration proceeds and what my final decision is.

Yours ever,
John

Labour's chief whip, Bob Mellish had made some ill-advised comments to a pack of journalists who had doorstepped him at his home early one morning. The prime minister's private secretary immediately contacted him, admonishing him for the remarks he had made:

The prime minister hopes that the chief whip will from now on refrain from further tendentious observations in public

Front row (*left to right*): Stonehouse, his daughter, Jane, the author in bow tie and cowboy waistcoat. Centre: Elizabeth, the author's grandmother and Stonehouse's sister. Back row: centre with glasses is the author's grandfather, Tom, and on the right in the suede waistcoat, the author's mother, Patti. (*Author's collection*)

Stonehouse as Postmaster General on a ministerial visit with the prime minister, Harold Wilson.
© *Royal Mail Group Ltd, 18th October 1968, courtesy of the Postal Museum*

Prime minister Harold Wilson's wife, Mary, greets Stonehouse at the Labour Party conference, 1975. (© *Guardian News & Media Ltd 2021*)

A drawing by Osbert Lancaster of the Stonehouse trial taking place in Court 1 of the Central Criminal Court, otherwise known as the Old Bailey.

Josef Frolík, the StB agent who defected in summer 1969, revealed that Stonehouse had been a Czech agent. Frolík had been in London in the mid-sixties and had been sent home in disgrace after a drunken new year incident. Whilst he had never worked with Stonehouse, he had gleaned the information from files he had studied in the StB archives shortly before his defection. *(StB Archive)*

The last Postmaster General of the United Kingdom, John Stonehouse, before the role was abolished in 1969. *(David Cole/Alamy Stock Photo)*

Michael Hayes, a nephew of Stonehouse: he claims he was deceived into signing documents.

THE BULLETIN, MARCH 22, 1975

The author's father, Michael Hayes, in a photograph used in Australian publication *The Bulletin*. *(The Bulletin 1975)*

Stonehouse's mother, Rosina, at the age of eighty. *(Trinity Mirror/Mirrorpix/Alamy Stock Photo)*

Joshua Nkomo 44 M. 3 children President National Democratic Party Southern Rhodesia (elected Oct. 1960) formerly President SR African National Congress and in exile since 1959 (March). Will attend Federal / constitutional review conference London Dec. 5th as representative of Party. Formerly Trade Union organiser Bulawayo (railwaymen). During last 2 years much travelled Cairo, Accra, New York (for U.N.) at expense of Egypt and Ghana (considerable aid from this source). No political ideology – nationalist first but much influenced by Ghana line, pro-Lumumba and anti Tshombe. Popular among Africans in SR as first political leader and now NDP receives overwhelming African support. Nkomo will refuse to cooperate European politician (even Tredgold – former Federal Chief Minister – and Todd, former P.M.) unless they join NDP and renounce separate organisation. Sir Edgar Whitehead P.M. guaranteed not to arrest Nkomo on return to Salisbury from London although former

One of Stonehouse's handwritten notes on members of the African National Congress (in this case Joshua Nkomo) provided to the Czech State Security Agency and found by the author in their files. *(StB Archive)*

Karel Pravec, the Czech State Security agent who met Stonehouse in his room at the Hotel Kosodrevina on the slopes of Chopok Mountain in the Low Tatras in Czechoslovakia in 1967. Pravec took over as Stonehouse's handler from Robert Husak. He subsequently defected to the USA and confirmed that Stonehouse had been a Czech agent. *(StB Archive)*

THE POST OFFICE BILL

A Message from the Postmaster General

On 31st October I presented to Parliament the Bill on the reorganisation of the Post Office.

If the Bill is passed, it will enable us to make the changeover to the new Post Office some time in the second half of 1969.

The Bill provides the legal framework for the new Post Office. It does not, of course, say how the new Post Office is to be organised. These important matters will be worked out before the day of the changeover.

This leaflet gives some essential facts about the Bill. A fuller summary is also available. If you want one please ask for it.

John Stonehouse

The New Post Office

The Bill:— abolishes the office of Postmaster General;
sets up a new Post Office nationalised industry—to be called "the Post Office"—to run postal, telecommunications, Giro, remittance and data-processing services;
sets up a new Ministry of Posts and Telecommunications to take over the Postmaster General's radio and broadcasting functions, and to supervise the new Post Office;
sets up the Department for National Savings as a Government Department separate from the new Post Office.

What is the Bill for?

The Bill makes the new Post Office legally possible. It provides the legal framework in which the activities of the present Post Office will be carried on in future.

The Powers of the New Post Office

The Bill gives the new Post Office the powers it needs to run its services. The new Post Office will have the letter monopoly of the existing Post Office. It will also be given the Postmaster General's telegraph monopoly in a modernised form. It will also be able to do work for the Government and local authorities—for instance, post offices will still pay pensions and sell wireless licences.

The Post Office Bill, enacting the abolition of the position of Postmaster General, signed by John Stonehouse. *(© Royal Mail Group Ltd, August 1966–September 1969, courtesy of the Postal Museum)*

Queen Elizabeth with
the last Postmaster
General, John
Stonehouse (*far right*).
(© *Royal Mail Group Ltd,
8th February 1969, courtesy of
the Postal Museum*)

Stonehouse outside the Houses of Parliament. (*Ken Towner/Evening News/Shutterstock*)

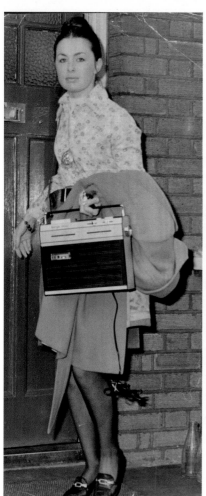

(*left*) Sheila Buckley, Stonehouse's parliamentary secretary. She and Stonehouse had an affair and later married. She faced trial at the same time as Stonehouse. (*ANL/Shutterstock*)

(*below*) Barbara Stonehouse in January 1975. (*Bill Howard/ANL/Shutterstock*)

The prison bus arriving at Bow Street Magistrates' Court delivering the incarcerated MP for what became known at the time as 'Stonehouse days'. (*ANL/Shutterstock*)

Stonehouse in his role as a minister with responsibility for aviation in October 1967. *(Fred Kaufmann/AP/Shutterstock)*

Stonehouse and Czech security agent Captain Robert Husak photographed by another State Security agent on a London street. *(StB archive)*

Stonehouse at his mother Rosina's funeral in Southampton in February 1981. Back row, from left to right: the author; Stonehouse; and his sister Elizabeth, the author's grandmother. The young boy immediately in front of Stonehouse is the author's brother, Vincent.

The passport photograph of Stonehouse's alter ego, Joseph Markham, from the court file held in the National Archives. (*National Archives*)

about Mr Stonehouse's conduct and mental condition. He does not dissent from the view that Mr Stonehouse should cease to be a Member of Parliament; but the fact remains that, if Mr Stonehouse does not resign and question of expelling him arises, the grounds for expulsion will be a delicate matter. He has not been charged – still less convicted – with any criminal offence. It will be important not to pre-judge possible legal proceedings; and it will be important that the Government in particular should seem to be holding the scales fairly. If the feeling becomes widespread that the balance of Mr Stonehouse's mind is disturbed or that the Government is acting other than fairly and judiciously, the feeling in parliament and more widely could swing round against the Government, in such a way as to cause a decision to expel Mr Stonehouse from the House of Commons to attract considerable criticism.

The whole pantomime came to a head in the following days. On 17 January, Stonehouse and his lawyer Patterson went to the consul's home. Vincent hoped that a more informal approach might lead to a positive outcome but, while it allowed all concerned to discuss matters more freely, the two-hour meeting ultimately failed to achieve the desired result of Stonehouse returning to the UK quietly.

Vincent made the point that, even if Stonehouse were to refuse to sign the documents, it would not significantly delay matters as a parliamentary select committee would rapidly be formed and proceed. He added that Stonehouse was losing popularity with the Australian public, citing editorials in the *Age* and the *Australian* that day urging him to return to the UK and apply to return under their new immigration laws, and suggested that they were losing patience with his petty shenanigans.

Stonehouse complained to the consul about the treatment he had suffered at the hands of the press over the preceding three years, in particular citing the *Sunday Times*'s 'Insight' report on the British Bangladesh Trust, while Patterson familiarised Vincent with Stonehouse's psychiatric issues. He suggested that there needed to be a delay as his client was 'too emotionally disturbed . . . to be able to present his case properly'. In his communiqué to Downing Street, Vincent commented that 'there may be something in this: he certainly displays the characteristics of a split personality.'

Stonehouse accepted Vincent's kind offer for him to stay overnight – or for as long as it suited the troubled MP – so they could extend their discussions without interruption but Stonehouse's stubborn streak came to the fore. If anything, his position hardened, leading Vincent to comment in his Downing Street cypher, 'Attempt to get him to relax and to adopt a helpful attitude was not successful. He was not open to reason. He remained tense and suspicious throughout and when under pressure withdrew himself both mentally and physically – in a psychological sense he went into a "fugue".' The message continued, 'Mr Stonehouse said that in no circumstances would he return to Britain of his own free will. If he went it would be in handcuffs. If extradited and brought to trial he would remain mute because he did not believe he would get a fair trial.'

Stonehouse obstinately reiterated his insistence that he would not resign unless he was granted leave to remain in Australia, adding that, even if he were expelled from the Commons, he would not resign from the Privy Council. Vincent believed that one of the reasons for his mulish attitude was that yet another adverse report had been published in the *Daily Mail* relating to the alleged comments made by the Labour Party chief whip.

Vincent's despondent belief was that persuading Stonehouse to return to Britain was a lost cause, an analysis with which Detective Chief Superintendent Etheridge concurred, reporting that Stonehouse had been observed withdrawing 8,000 Australian dollars from a Swiss bank account and was apparently brokering a deal with a national newspaper.

Stonehouse was determined to fight tooth and nail against the establishment. Twister was living up to his codename.

Within two days, Ted Short wrote to Stonehouse advising him that, as he had refused to resign, a parliamentary select committee would be appointed to investigate the matter and make a recommendation, though this was to prove easier said than done.

Stonehouse immediately went on the offensive. Considering his experience as a seasoned politician more valuable than his lawyer's advice, he gave an interview to the BBC on 21 January, in which he accused the British government of putting pressure on the Australian administration. He was highly critical of his colleague Ted Short. 'He was calling on me to resign right at the beginning before he had heard my explanation. To drum me out, a member of parliament, just like that without fully considering the issues is just ridiculous . . . lots of MPs go overseas on fact-finding tours. I have been on a fact-finding tour about myself.'

He continued, 'I am not here as a politician. I came here to escape all the hypocrisy of English politics and I have no wish to engage in public life in Australia. I will formally resign from the House of Commons just as soon as I know my position in Australia is secure.'

The interviewer asked Stonehouse whether his wife or Sheila Buckley had known of his plans, to which he replied, 'I could not possibly discuss it with anybody before I went. I could not involve anybody. It would have been a terrible thing to have done so.'

He steadfastly denied any fraud or wrongdoing.

Pressed further on whether he had contacted anyone in London, and in particular Sheila, after he disappeared, he protested, 'No, it's not true.' In fact, DCI Etheridge's travels across the globe, retracing the route that Stonehouse had taken, had exposed two telephone calls made to Sheila in London from Stonehouse's Honolulu hotel.

The sheer bravado of the interview left his colleagues outraged and aghast while the hungry public lapped up the drama playing out before their eyes, the first political scandal of gravity since the Profumo affair, highlighted in the new technicolour world of television with its almost 24/7 global coverage.

Certain quarters of the press were sympathetic to Stonehouse. In an opinion piece in *The Times*, Bernard Levin wrote of 'calling off the Labour pack', asserting that 'the indecency of Labour's behaviour should not pass without censure.'

On 22 January the *Australian* newspaper published an interview with Stonehouse, under the headline 'My Side of the Affair', in which he complained that the British government had, through Scotland Yard and the High Commission, deployed 'intense social and political pressures' on him and the Australian government to force his return to the UK. The overnight stay at the Consul General's home was referred to in both the *Australian* and the *Herald*, with the suggestion that Vincent's invitation for Stonehouse to stay longer, so he could await the arrival of his son in Australia, had been overruled by the foreign secretary, James Callaghan. It was alleged that the minister had ordered Vincent to 'eject' him from his home, an accusation that infuriated the British government as being not only potentially damaging but, in their view, factually incorrect. The press office was scrambled to attempt to redress the balance.

Downing Street had underestimated the rogue MP. The hope that he would step down without fuss had gone disastrously wrong as Stonehouse manipulated what appeared to be a straightforward criminal case into a political witch hunt, painting himself as the victim of a struggling government's ire in an attempt to deflect attention from their troubles at home.

Wilson and his cabinet rapidly learned the lesson that they would have to ensure that every action they took in the case was done with scrupulous fairness to avoid claims of a political conspiracy.

It was about this time that Stonehouse wrote to Cameron formally requesting permission to stay. Realising that some explanation was required as to the bizarre manner in which he had entered the country, not to mention the suggestion that he had done so in order to avoid the allegations of fraud and other financial irregularities, he had commissioned his psychiatrist to compose a report on his psychiatric state. While the Australians were already privy to the document, the British government were keen to find out what it had to say.

To this end a confidential call took place between Andy Watson, first assistant secretary in the Department of Labor and Immigration, and John Hay of the consulate general, during which Watson supplied the diplomat with an oral account of the contents of the psychiatric report. Both men were highly sceptical that Stonehouse was suffering from a genuine psychiatric condition.

On 28 January a motion was placed before parliament to 'consider the position of Mr John Stonehouse', as a result of which the government and opposition front benches supported the motion for a select committee to be appointed, citing his absence from the House and other factors. This reasoning caused some unease among backbenchers, with Enoch Powell counselling caution: 'If we are to cause a member to cease to be a member because of his absence, the House will have to inquire into the circumstances and background of any protracted absence of a member.' Though barely half the members voted the motion was nonetheless carried by a majority.

The select committee, once formed, considered the evidence, returning by March with the recommendation that Stonehouse should be expelled. The next step, to table a motion before parliament to debate the MP's expulsion, would prove more difficult to complete.

Stonehouse's penchant for dancing with the devil was again displayed during that January as he made moves to manipulate Ian Ward, a *Daily Telegraph* journalist, who had been instructed by his newspaper to fly from his base in Singapore to Australia specifically to report on the case. Initial attempts to contact the MP through Patterson had been fruitless until Stonehouse's ire was piqued by a purportedly exclusive article that appeared in the *Express*. This prompted him to telephone Ward, offering a genuine exclusive in retaliation. According to Ward there was a cost attached to the deal: Stonehouse was seeking financial assistance to help Sheila to 'escape' from London.

Both Ward and Patterson considered this a terrible idea, but their attempts to dissuade him fell on deaf ears. Faced with such stubborn insistence, discussions turned to how such an operation should be managed. Stonehouse proposed that Ward chaperone Sheila to Australia, though he also entertained the notion that a journalist already in London could escort her. Either way, he was firmly of the view that she should leave by a channel port and catch a flight from the continent so as to evade press attention. Despite his misgivings, Ward contacted his foreign editor in London, who declined the offer, much to Stonehouse's frustration, though he continued to court Ward's attention. The journalist responded eagerly and the two would regularly meet, inviting each other to their respective homes, Ward was at this time living at his mother's address, while Stonehouse had set up house at a place opposite Melbourne's Toorak drive-in cinema.

Stonehouse had become fixated on the proposal that Sheila should join him in Australia. He was increasingly concerned that the media would somehow trick her into incriminating herself, thereby inevitably implicating him. When the *Telegraph* refused to engage, Stonehouse asked Ward if he knew anyone in London who could help. Ward thought there might be and pulled out an old address book, flipping through to the relevant page, when, to his astonishment, Stonehouse snatched the book from his hands and copied the details. Ward was furious and an argument ensued, but Stonehouse remained unrepentant.

A couple of days later, while Ward was having dinner at Patterson's home, Stonehouse called to inform the lawyer that he planned to telephone the journalist's contact. Infuriated, Patterson repeated his opinion that his client's plan was ill advised, eventually handing the phone to Ward in exasperation. Another argument ensued and came to an abrupt end as Stonehouse hung up. Incensed, the journalist immediately dialled the operator, requesting to be put through to his contact in London. He was be informed that a caller giving the name of Thompson had already asked to be connected. Normally it would be a case of first come, first served, but Ward's professional standing as a journalist gave him priority and he was able to warn his contact of Stonehouse's intentions, thwarting the MP's plans. To Ward and Patterson's relief, Stonehouse then dropped the subject.

27

AN INSPECTOR CALLS

January–February 1975

By this time DCS Etheridge had returned to the UK where he needed to make further enquiries to build a case against Stonehouse and substantiate the charges that would be required in order to pursue any extradition proceedings. Working under considerable time pressure, the detective needed to focus his investigation and concentrate on the leading figures in the drama. It appeared that Sheila was pivotal and he was particularly keen to interview her over an assortment of letters, purportedly written by her, that had been found in Stonehouse's Flinders Street apartment. They strongly suggested she knew far more about the disappearance than she had admitted.

In the maelstrom that had followed Stonehouse's discovery, Sheila had retreated from the unwelcome press attention to her parents' home in Devon. Etheridge arranged to interview her at the Exeter Motel accompanied by Assistant Commissioner Crane with WPC Shields taking notes. Today a significant witness agreeing to such questioning would be afforded the protection of legal advice. Sheila was not offered this benefit despite it being evident to the extremely experienced officers that she was involved in the criminal conduct of her lover. Had she had that advice, what transpired would undoubtedly have been avoided. Responding to Etheridge's seemingly casual request to help with their enquiries, Sheila had thought nothing of agreeing to meet the officers.

The interviews were conducted over 29 and 30 January, when she was asked about Stonehouse, his business dealings and his disappearance from Miami. Producing copies of the letters, Etheridge began: 'These are copies of four letters which were taken possession of by police in Melbourne, Australia. Would you look at them and say whether or not you in fact wrote them?'

'Yes, they are in my handwriting,' she confirmed.

'I would like to discuss the contents of these letters with you. I am particularly interested in certain references which appear to us to have a bearing on matters we are investigating.'

'I am quite willing to help you on these matters, but I am not willing to discuss my personal affairs.'

Unabashed, the officer continued, 'Well, may we deal with these letters in date order, starting with the first? This is written at a time when, as far as the rest of the world knew, Mr Stonehouse was probably dead, and was in fact missing, after having apparently gone for a swim off the coast of Miami. Is it in fact a letter you wrote to Mr Stonehouse which was addressed to him in the name of D. C. Mildoon?'

'Yes.'

'When did you first become aware of the fact that Mr Stonehouse was not dead or missing?'

'I was living at 62 Fitzjohn's Avenue, which is the Highfield House Hotel, and had been living there for some few weeks, for want of somewhere better to live. A few days after the news report of Mr Stonehouse being missing, I received a telephone call at about midnight, to the best of my memory, and it was Mr Stonehouse. This was the first positive proof I had that he was alive, although I had a feeling that he was not dead. My intuition told me from a variety of examples of his behaviour that he might turn up somewhere. He did not tell me where he was. He sounded upset and his voice was high-pitched and distressed. I asked him whether I should tell his family that he was alive, and he said no and apologised for putting me in this predicament but insisted that his family were not told. This was the gist of the conversation. I cannot recall the details now, but it was left that he would contact me again by telephone. He did in fact telephone me again within a week, and to the best of my recollection he told me that he was in Hawaii, and I asked him whether he intended staying in America, or whether it was possible for him to get out of America. I was confused because I knew from press reports that his passport had been found among his effects in Miami, and he did not indicate to me that he had another passport. I believe it was at this stage that he told me that he was now using the name of Markham and that he had a passport. He was concerned that he was unable to know what news was being published about his disappearance, and asked me to let him know what was happening press-wise in the UK. At some later date when telephoning me – he telephoned on two or three occasions afterwards from places he did not disclose – he told me that he was worried about the use of the name Markham, and of the passport in that name being discovered, and he had therefore adopted the name of Mildoon in case he needed yet another identity. He asked me to write to him in the name of Mildoon, care of the Bank of New Zealand, Collins Street, Melbourne, and that is why I came to write the letters we are discussing.'

Probing a little deeper, Etheridge checked his notes, 'Referring to the letter . . . the letter is addressed to "My dear Dums". Was that your pet name for Mr Stonehouse?'

Sheila nodded, blushing. 'That is my nickname for Mr Stonehouse. The letters are written intending to convey a message to Mr Stonehouse personally, and when I refer to my friend, my boyfriend, my fella or George, I am in fact referring to Mr Stonehouse. Much of this letter and the others I am going to refer to contain purely personal things between Mr Stonehouse and myself, and in these I do refer occasionally to Mrs Stonehouse.'

'You wrote the following sentence: "At the moment, (saw her yesterday) she is questioned re self-service project. He lied about insurances to me. There's been a Mafia type murder in some place and they're tracing blood groups etc. They suspect B. of murder because of insurances S. has had to promise to retrieve if she's accused." What is the explanation for these words? What was the self-service project?'

Sheila took a deep breath. 'I was referring to the suggestion that he was involved in some secret service enquiries. This had just been in the press, and I assumed Mrs Stonehouse was being questioned about it.'

'"He lied to me about insurances." What did that mean?' the officer pressed her.

'I knew that he had at least one policy because I knew he went for a medical. I did not know that he had taken out other policies contemporaneously until Mrs Stonehouse told me and reports had appeared in the press. This seemed to me to be ridiculous in view of what had happened, and I was most concerned as to his intentions in relation to these policies. Indeed, as I go on later, I mention that Mrs Stonehouse was being suspected of murder because of the insurances, and this had all arisen because of the stupidity of taking out so many policies.'

Etheridge quoted further, '"S. has had to promise to retrieve if she's accused." What did you mean by this?'

Sheila sighed. 'I would like to say that that is a misleading sentence. What I meant to say is that I had to promise myself to do something about that; in other words, knowing that he was alive, I would have to disclose it if there was a possibility of Mrs Stonehouse becoming implicated.'

With these revelations Etheridge was duty bound to warn Sheila of the consequences of such admissions. 'From what you have told us, you knew that Mr Stonehouse was not dead and you were aware of a number of insurance policies in existence on his life. We suspect that in relation to these insurances a criminal offence has been committed and, in view of your close and personal involvement with

Mr Stonehouse, I feel that it is my duty to caution you before any more questions are put to you.'

This being done, he pushed on.

'"Industry is in 27 going through whole project. The lot. JCM probably arranged that." What does that mean?'

'I had been informed by my colleagues that the Department of Trade had visited 27 Dover Street, and that Mr McGrath might have requested this. I believe they may have been examining the books.'

Etheridge added, 'What did you mean when you said, "I do not recognise him as the same man at all. Two entirely different personalities, and I'm frightened to death. Like a schizophrenic (can't spell that)"?'

Sheila explained, 'In view of his behaviour, I did not recognise it as that of the conduct of John Stonehouse. The John Stonehouse I knew was a man of positive and brilliant thinking with a first-class brain, but the man I now heard about was a completely different man, totally unlike the man I know. I really believed at that time that something had happened to him mentally. He had turned from a totally rational politician and businessman into an irrational, illogical man.'

Eyebrows raised, Etheridge moved on. 'We will now deal with the letter dated 13 December 1974 . . . You have read the copy of this letter, and I believe you agree that it is written by you to Mr Stonehouse.'

'Yes,' Sheila responded.

'What did you mean by the following sentence? "I completely forgot to tell you of the end of that book you told me to tell you about. Well, the mystery was never solved, and a verdict was never reached, so it was all rather unsatisfactory." Did that refer to a book?'

Shaking her head, Sheila replied, 'No, it just referred to the whole Stonehouse situation which read like a book and the ending of which was totally unsatisfactory.'

'What did you mean by "My biggest problem, apart from industry – like flies – is insurance. The only one the female persisted about was the first, subsequents were forced by male who was never terribly intelligent, and this is front rag stuff now"?'

'The insurances were still the problem and really that is all I mean by that. My reference to "industry" does in fact refer to the Department of Trade and Industry, which was now becoming actively involved in the investigation.'

Etheridge went on, 'In this letter you refer to a Mr Howitt as "the only person to write where mail can be forwarded to me". Who was Mr Howitt?'

'It is my sister's address. And it was the name of the road. She lives at 11 Howitt Road, Hampstead.'

'"Nothing but Mr Royal to worry about at present." What did that mean?'

'I was referring to the insurance companies involved, and the heat of publicity.'

'In the last part of your letter you say, "I am the link so must be OK with concrete thing. May well be J and Mrs S is therefore terrorised by Royal etc. contract." What did that mean?'

'I believe I was saying that Barbara and Jane Stonehouse were frightened about the insurance policies. They believed he was dead, and it could have looked like murder.'

Having satisfied himself with the answers to the letter of 14 December, Etheridge moved on to his next topic.

'We will now deal with letter dated 17 December 1974: "There's a defect in that material I had. George has joined the Co-operation India Association, and has been named by another member as a good one. Uncle Bill originally started this, and now George spends all his time on the project, which is quite ludicrous, since that means that to see him a great deal is impossible. Because of this S. is a marked specimen." What does this mean?'

'All that referred to was the CIA and the alleged involvement with Czechoslovakia, as appeared from statements in the press.'

Etheridge pressed on, '"Uncle Harry is speaking about this to his big family this afternoon, and I am waiting for news nowish." What did this mean?'

'I was referring to statements being made by the prime minister to the House of Commons.'

The officer continued, '"The project on the ports thing is still OK – would you believe it." What did that mean?'

'I was referring to the fact that there had been no news on his Markham cover being exposed,' Sheila replied.

'"But the Scottish thing is still at it, barking up all the wrong trees"?'

'I was referring to Scotland Yard, and their missing person enquiries.'

Etheridge continued, '"I long to go to work in Africa, or anywhere else for that matter. Won't be able to leave because of eyes." Weren't you saying that you were longing to join him?'

'I just longed to get out of this situation, the press more than anything else. I could not move. I say Africa because there are lots of jobs for English secretaries.'

The officer pressed on. '"Oswald came through, but no news on all others yet"?'

'I cannot remember now exactly what I meant by that,' a flustered Sheila replied.

Scenting blood, Etheridge pursued it. '"Did you know that George was named by those other people I mentioned 5/6 years ago, and that is the reason the family dropped him?"'

'This refers to the Czechoslovakia business and I was being misled by the press myself.'

She explained that the family dropping him was reference to Stonehouse's fall from grace with Wilson and the Labour government in the aftermath of the spy allegations.

Unrelenting, the officer closed in on his prey. '"Have just heard from Uncle Harry marvellous news, is standing by George completely, a true friend, and has damned the ragsville. Says to leave the family and staff alone. Cheers from his large family and I am in tears of relief on that aspect. I would never have believed he would have stood by us like that. He told me and all of us everywhere that G's mother had had a heart attack and he blamed the R's entirely for that"?'

'That is an announcement made by the prime minister over the radio and it refers to Mr Stonehouse's mother,' responded a now weary Sheila.

'"I am so upset over his mother. She was getting on OK until Friday when all this broke re insurance project, so without wishing to be cruel, you can guess who is responsible. I cry all the time about her but cannot get in touch. George must not do anything as she is very elderly and it has to come anyway. She is in hospital and is being well taken care of. I pray for her every night so I will tell him (George) not to worry. Those bloody insurances." Was this the press concentration on the insurances?'

'I blamed the press comments on the insurances for his mother's earlier heart attack. It looked so bad. I am also telling him not to come back, because she is so old.'

Etheridge then moved on to the fourth and final letter. 'We will now deal with a letter dated 20 December 1974. "The ports project is still OK but quite frankly I cannot really see why, although it is really just Mr Rags who is blowing things up king-size." What does that mean?'

'I was still referring to the Markham passport. It was so bizarre I thought he would be found out almost straight away. The press are really blowing things up out of all proportion.'

Etheridge continued, '"I am labelled as the other woman by all rags, and I shall of course say no, but I hope he won't be clever and ask for my part of the port project and compare with his." What does that mean?'

'I was referring to an impending visit from the police, and believed I was to be questioned about my knowledge of the Markham passport.

I must, in my panic, have thought that the police had found out about the Markham passport, about which I knew nothing.'

The officer added, '"Disturbing news from MGH – that according to his edition of news but not mine – Linda Christine Sidney have ceased to carry on their good work. Trade is there but I thought they would carry on – this may be nothing because it came from unreliable newspaper, but could be bad news. I am expecting the I's at any time but will continue to contact George." What does his mean?'

Sheila explained, 'I heard from Mr Hayes that the LCS [London Capital Securities] had ceased to trade, and that the Department of Trade and Industry were investigating, but this within hours proved to be wrong.'

'Is there anything more you would like to tell us about the letters we have just been discussing?' Etheridge stared intently at Sheila.

'I would like to say that the "code" I adopted was really to confuse any person such as a bank clerk who might chance to open the letters I had written, and this was not a prearranged code, but I believed Mr Stonehouse might understand some of it.'

'We have referred previously to the Highfield House Hotel. Would you like to tell us the reasons why you moved into that hotel just a few weeks before these events took place. Was it prearranged between you and Mr Stonehouse that this would be a base for him to contact after he had disappeared?'

Sheila replied, 'This was not prearranged. I wanted to move from Vandon Court for some months for many reasons, and I thought it would be easy to get other accommodation. Notice was therefore given to the landlord and it was arranged that I would leave that accommodation on 31 October. However, it was not as easy as I thought it would be to get other accommodation and every effort I made fell through. I therefore moved into Highfield House Hotel on a temporary basis for the want of somewhere better to live. This was my suggestion entirely.'

Etheridge changed the tack of his questioning, 'Were you a director and secretary of Export Promotion and Consultancy Services Limited, also known as EPACS?'

'Yes.'

'Did you resign on 19 August 1974?'

'Yes.'

'Why was that?' the officer enquired.

'I don't really know why on that date.'

'Did he tell you to resign?'

'He did not tell me to resign, but he asked whether I would like to, and he suggested that I should. I believe this was brought about because Sir Charles Hardie, of the firm of Dixon Wilson & Co. [Hardie, former chairman of the British Overseas Airways Corporation, had been invited to become a director of the British Bangladesh Trust], appeared to be somewhat critical of the fact that the chairman's personal secretary was a director of one or more of the companies in which Mr Stonehouse was involved.'

'Were you authorised to draw cheques on the account of EPACS Ltd?'

'Yes,' admitted Sheila, 'my name has been on the mandate since 1970 and still is today, as far as I know.'

'You resigned as director and secretary on 19 August 1974, but after that date you continued to sign cheques on the company's accounts. Is that correct?'

'Yes, although I had resigned I was a member of the company. The mandate says "an official of the company".'

Etheridge continued, 'Did EPACS have banking accounts with London Capital Securities; Lloyds Bank, St James Street; Coutts, Strand; and the Midland bank, Victoria Street?'

'Yes,' she responded.

'You have been shown these cheques . . . Do they bear your signature?'

'Yes.'

'These are cheques drawn on London Capital Securities . . . '

Sheila was then shown a whole series of cheques on which her signature was found. Etheridge went to the crux of the issue.

'All of these represent money transactions of a company of which you were a director until 19 August 1974, and in respect of which you were authorised to draw cheques all the time. Can you help us at all as to the reason for these transactions?'

'The answer is no,' Sheila answered firmly.

'They represent large drawings in cash or to Mr Stonehouse personally. Have you any knowledge of any business matter in which EPACS was concerned that would require these payments to be made?'

'I have no specific knowledge of what this money was for. I suggest you ask Mr Stonehouse.'

Unperturbed, Etheridge continued, 'In fact, were you doing as you were told by Mr Stonehouse?'

'Yes.'

'Did you question any of these drawings?'

'No.'

'Have you personally received any benefit other than your proper wages?'

'No.'

'Was the position that Mr Stonehouse was your chairman and you saw him as your boss rather than a co-director?'

'Yes.'

'Are you, or were you, aware of your responsibilities as a director and officer of the company?'

'I think so. At all times I believed, and still do believe, that the chairman, Mr Stonehouse, is a man of the highest integrity, and I had no reason to doubt any action he asked me to take, which includes the cheques I have just examined. I have no specific knowledge as to the reasons for these cheques being drawn, and I did not ask Mr Stonehouse.'

Etheridge continued, 'Was there ever a meeting whereby you jointly authorised him to borrow money from the company, by way of a personal account?'

'I can't remember. There should be a minute if he was authorised.'

'What other companies were you a director of?'

'I think EPACS, Systems and Consultancy Services Limited, and Connoisseurs of Claret Limited, and I was the secretary of Global Imex.'

'Did you know anything about the accommodation address at 243 Regent Street, W1?'

'No, I read about it in the paper, but I have never been there.'

'How many bank accounts have you got?'

'Two, one of them is with LCS and the other is with National Westminster in Westminster.'

'Were all the cheques handed over to Mr Stonehouse?'

'Yes, but the cash cheques I would have handed over personally to Mr Stonehouse for security reasons.'

As the interview came to an end, Etheridge advised Sheila that he would certainly wish to speak with her again, adding that the director of public prosecutions would be informed and would consider prosecuting.

Panic rising in her voice with the realisation that she had been led to make such damning admissions, Sheila cried, 'I cannot see how I am involved. Do you really think I would be prosecuted?'

'You were a director of a company, and at all times authorised to draw on its bank accounts. You were a party to the removal of funds from this company, and it remains to be seen whether or not a criminal offence has been committed,' the officer replied flatly.

'Well, if he goes down on these cheques, I will go down with him.'

On that note, Detective Chief Superintendent Etheridge concluded the interview, not suspecting that this would be his only opportunity to speak with Sheila. She undoubtedly reported the events to Stonehouse. Just over a fortnight later Sheila had flown to Australia to join him, despite Barbara having returned to her husband.

* * *

Despite the somewhat fractious relationship between the journalist Ian Ward and Stonehouse, the MP seemed determined to persevere with the journalist quite simply to attempt to wring as much money as he could from his predicament. He had already attempted to broker an exclusive story with the letter he had written to Ted Short, an offer that fell through when the *Telegraph* got hold of the information through other sources. With Sheila's arrival in Australia imminent, Stonehouse sensed a second opportunity but made a simple error when he informed Ward that she had travelled to Brussels to catch a flight to Australia. It didn't take much investigation to determine that her journey would take her via Singapore and Perth, meaning the paper didn't need any exclusive from the MP: they just needed to lie in wait for their quarry at Perth airport.

Ward later recounted another episode with Stonehouse that occurred on the day before his wife's return to Australia, while the MP set up their new home near the Toorak drive-in cinema in Melbourne. Joining Stonehouse as he was unpacking, Ward's attention was drawn to a large metal trunk and, noticing the journalist's curiosity, Stonehouse boasted to Ward that he had picked the trunk up from customs where it had lain for some time. Confiding with a sly smile that the authorities were ignorant of its existence and significance, he commented in amusement that it would make a good chapter in his prospective book. As the trunk was unpacked Ward observed that the contents revealed a large quantity of women's clothing. These belonged, Stonehouse informed him, to Sheila. Among the dresses, blouses, handbags and shoes nestled a black slip which the

MP whipped from the trunk, whirling about the room clutching it 'as though he was dancing with the owner'.

Stonehouse was snapped rudely from his reverie when Ward coolly remarked that Barbara was soon to be joining him. He repacked the clothing and accessories into a red Samsonite suitcase, which he asked the journalist to store at his home. Ward agreed and deposited the case safely under his bed, along with a black attaché case. Stonehouse had discussed co-writing his book with Ward, and the case contained papers that related to his disappearance in Florida and odyssey to Australia, including the troubled fugitive's transit between the identities of Stonehouse, Mildoon and Markham. With Stonehouse's agreement, the full contents of the attaché case were photographed; prints were given to the MP and the originals were sent to the *Telegraph*'s office in London.

Ward left for Perth the day before Sheila's arrival on 16 February. The journalist's departure coincided with Stonehouse's arrival at his Melbourne home with flowers and a thank-you note for Ward's mother. Finding no one at home but the door open, he stepped inside and retrieved the two cases stored under the bed; the only sign of his presence were the flowers and note.

Arriving at Perth airport later that day, Stonehouse was surprised and not a little irritated to find Ward waiting with a photographer. He refused to be photographed with Sheila, obstinately ensuring that he remained behind the photographer at every step. With the journalist's use exhausted, the relationship between the men ended. But it would not be the last time that Stonehouse would see Ward.

28

THE LONG ARM OF THE LAW

February–April 1975

With any hope of Stonehouse agreeing to resign gone, Clyde Cameron made it clear that he was precluded from deporting him. With the reciprocal agreement that MPs from either country were able to enter without travel documents it would have set a dangerous precedent.

The only option that remained was extradition, as had been discussed at length at the meeting held at the Australian attorney general's office on 7 January. With the initial estimate that it would take six to twelve months to complete the investigation process, it was vital to expedite the procedure as all concerned were aware that the longer Stonehouse remained at large, the more time he had to calculate a scheme to extricate himself from his predicament. The MP continued to seek sanctuary abroad, although he also sought salvation through ongoing psychiatric and psychological evaluations, the initial results of which had established that he had suffered a mental breakdown.

Consideration was given to whether Stonehouse could be extradited on the passport fraud alone. A hurdle arose with the old established 'doctrine of specialty', which is a principle of international law that is included in most extradition treaties, whereby a person who is extradited to a country to stand trial for certain criminal offences can only be tried for those offences and not for any other pre-extradition offences. This was a considerable sticking point, with the authorities concerned that if they were to obtain the MP's extradition on the relatively minor passport offences, even if the ongoing fraud investigations were to lead to more significant charges after his extradition back to the UK, he could not be prosecuted for them.

The matter went to ministerial level on both sides. The Australians, ever pragmatic, were content to relax the rule, while the British felt that they could not, considering it a very dangerous precedent to set, concerned that in future the Australians and other countries would expect the same easing of the law. A decision had to be made whether to wait for the completion of the enquiries or proceed with the minor offence. The DTI and the police felt that, with a little more time, they would be able to substantiate the more serious charges.

As they strove to resolve their dilemma, both governments were aware that Stonehouse was still attempting to extricate himself from the mess he was in. Soon after Sheila arrived in Australia around 15 February, the authorities became aware that she had purchased tickets for a flight to New Zealand for both herself and Stonehouse, creating a new cause for concern in Downing Street, especially given a lack of reassurance from the New Zealand government that they would deal with the wayward MP by returning him home.

The Australian opposition questioned why Cameron was so slow to make a decision about Stonehouse's future in their country. While Stonehouse remained an MP, all concerned could understand the principle behind the decision not to deport but they expressed bafflement as to why the government refused to be drawn on whether Stonehouse could remain in the country. Cameron responded by seizing on reports on Stonehouse's mental health and the psychiatric diagnosis that, while the MP continued to have suicidal thoughts, he required therapeutic support.

The DTI inspectors contacted Patterson within days of their appointment, requesting to speak to Stonehouse and making tentative enquiries as to whether his client would be willing to return to the UK to be interviewed. The response was swift and negative, but Stonehouse conceded he would be willing to speak to them in Australia.

Arrangements were made for the inspectors to fly out to Australia, with 25 and 26 February fixed for the interviews to take place at the offices of the accountants Arthur Andersen in Melbourne. Unusually for the time, the interviews were to be recorded, a practice that did not become standard in police or other investigating agencies' interviews until the implementation of the Police and Criminal Evidence Act in 1984.

Press speculation continued to run amok, with the British media taking advantage of Stonehouse's absence to smear him with accusations of forgery, fraud, spying, adultery and more. No matter what one's personal view of Stonehouse, the savage media insinuations were clearly prejudicial to his right to a fair trial should the long arm of the law ever succeed in bringing him to heel.

Seeking new angles on the drama, some editors returned to another of the principal characters, Frolík, reporting that Scotland Yard had visited the offices of his publishers, leaving with a hefty statement from the ex-spy detailing his knowledge of Stonehouse's activities. Yet others followed up the tenuous tale regarding the MP's purported connection with the mafia and a Nigerian businessman, Sylvester Okereke, mysteriously found drowned in the Thames on 18 November 1974, some two days before Stonehouse's disappearance, attempting to create a link between Stonehouse and another body found encased in concrete in a warehouse twenty-one miles outside Miami shortly after his disappearance.

The cement-clad body was identified as that of David Shaver, whose name cropped up in a letter penned by Okereke, found at the MP's London flat, suggesting that Stonehouse was planning a business meeting with Shaver during his trip to Miami that November and referring to Shaver as a friend of the politician. It was implied that the meeting with Shaver was to discuss a £6 million cement deal, which the US police speculated had led the mafia to take steps to thwart Stonehouse's plans to gain a financial interest in the cement market and that Shaver's death had been a 'hit'.

The mafia, shady business deals and spying all blended to form a heady brew, infused by Stonehouse's reckless behaviour as he continued to court controversy and dissent wherever and whenever possible. His philosophy was to fight fire with fire, allowing himself to succumb to feelings of intense frustration and unfairness that the British press considered they had carte blanche to report whatever wild allegations they liked, regardless of whether they could be substantiated.

The DTI interviews took place as planned at the Arthur Andersen offices in Melbourne, though the estimated two-day time frame proved optimistic as the interviews dragged on for six, with Stonehouse naturally defensive and bullish. The point he was anxious to make the inspectors understand was that others had been involved and that he no longer had access to the documents, which it seemed were all located at his Dover Street office in London. It was during the course of these interviews that Stonehouse's mental health issues crystallised as he went on record maintaining that the person who was responsible for much of what happened was his other personality, Markham. Markham had usurped Stonehouse; Markham had arranged for the money to be moved; Markham had contrived to disappear. In time, transcripts of the recordings were to prove significant.

With each passing day the DTI inspectors discovered more evidence, piecing together the jigsaw of known facts as speculation and rumours about apparent business irregularities gained substance and fell into place.

Running in tandem with the DTI investigation was the Scotland Yard enquiry into the life insurance policies and credit card frauds, which were perhaps a little easier to investigate, though the alleged insurance fraud was not without its problems, there being no established principle in English law acknowledging that a crime in the UK could be perpetrated from abroad. It was unclear whether any fraud had in fact been committed as Barbara had never actually made any claim against those policies. The prosecution could not use Barbara as a witness as a wife could not give evidence against her husband in a criminal trial, a principle since abolished. It was to their great discredit that the newspapers implied that Barbara may have been responsible for her husband's murder, a disservice perpetuated even in the Home Office file on the affair in which a passing suggestion was noted that she had prior knowledge of her husband's antics. There remains to this day no evidence to suggest that Barbara was ever knowingly involved in her husband's plans. Why would she have been? Stonehouse's plan was to disappear with his mistress and a large sum of money.

With pressure mounting on both the Australian and British governments to resolve the whole sorry saga, on 24 February the opposition in the Australian House of Representatives forced a debate on the affair, impelling Cameron to give the assurance in his address to the House that if Stonehouse was expelled from the House of Commons they would deport him within seventy-two hours. In response, the Australian prime minister asserted that his government would not permit Stonehouse to remain in the country, citing Stonehouse's recent breakdown and psychiatric problems as valid reasons precluding them from giving him leave to remain under Australian immigration legislation.

While Downing Street was relieved to hear this, the Australians were growing increasingly frustrated at the slow progress of Scotland Yard's investigations. Simultaneously, Cameron's declaration contributed to Stonehouse's increasing desperation. Frantically, he applied for a Swedish passport, but the Swedes politely declined.

By mid-March 1975 the police considered that they had gathered sufficient evidence to charge Stonehouse with offences of fraud and forgery. A meeting took place between the DPP and attorney general to discuss a strategy at which it was decided that, once before the court, steps could be taken to retrieve the miscreant MP. The DTI investigation was taking considerably longer, though it had unearthed sufficient evidence for some charges to be preferred. Years later, one of the DTI lawyers, Ian Mayes, QC, suggested that if they had been given more time others would have appeared in the dock alongside Stonehouse, including his accountant. Nonetheless, with the evidence that they had, charges were placed before the metropolitan magistrate at Bow Street, London, on 20 March and a warrant for the MP's arrest was finally issued.

Shortly afterwards, in Canberra, a relieved Cameron received the news and a requisition seeking the MP's extradition was lodged with the Australian authorities. The acute political embarrassment caused by this saga was at long last to be alleviated and placed in the hands of the courts.

On the morning of 21 March, armed with a warrant issued by the local magistrate, police arrested Stonehouse at his Melbourne home, though this was only a temporary holding mechanism while the formal documentation and requests were drafted and lodged by the British government. The MP was taken to Melbourne police station, where he was processed and put before the local magistrate. Patterson was immediately pressed into action, ensuring the case was adjourned to allow time for a formal requisition and supporting documentation to be filed, and securing that in the interim Stonehouse was granted bail.

Stonehouse's return to his apartment revealed that the police had also seized the draft manuscript of his book along with other documents and cash. Immediately going on the offensive, he complained to the press that he considered that this was politically motivated, suggesting that the British authorities wanted to discover what revelations and accusations he was to make, a charge upon which the British government chose to make no comment.

Days later, Sheila was also arrested. The formal documents for requisition now lodged with the Australian courts had allowed the long arm of English law finally to collar the two fugitives.

29

END OF THE AFFAIR?

March–May 1975

Now that proceedings had commenced, the screw was tightening and, under the mounting pressure, Stonehouse's fragile state of mind was fracturing. In early January 1975 he had already been seen by a psychiatrist who had identified concerns about his mental health, since when the debilitating effect of the police and DTI investigations, the incessant and invasive press attention, the daily struggle with the British and Australian authorities and the uncertainty regarding his future had continued to take their toll.

Another significant factor was the complicated state of his marriage and his relationship with Sheila. Barbara had briefly returned to the UK and had only agreed to re-join her husband in Australia on the proviso that Sheila remained in England. Stonehouse failed to live up to his promise. In February, Sheila had flown to Australia to join her lover. Stonehouse had seemingly assumed that, having gathered Sheila, Barbara and their children safely around him in Australia, his previous living arrangements could continue uninterrupted. Barbara had other ideas subsequently revealing the death throes of their marriage to the newspapers at the conclusion of her ex-husband's trial. A misplaced phone call on a stopover in Singapore had alerted her to the mistress's imminent arrival. The resulting argument with her husband became physical, with Barbara suffering facial injuries.

Stonehouse stormed out, threatening to end it all, only for his son to intervene. It proved to be the end for Barbara. While the couple remained married, Barbara, in her mind, had moved on.

With Sheila's arrival, arrangements were made for her to share a nearby apartment with a male friend, a TV cameraman, who later described to a newspaper how Stonehouse would surreptitiously come over, hiding his car behind bushes to evade the press so that the lovers could spend days together. There were even occasions when Stonehouse's children would join them for dinner at the apartment, having seemingly accepted Sheila's presence in their father's life. Stonehouse aspired to accommodate both women in his life, as if it wasn't complicated enough already. While Sheila seemed ready to accept anything that he wanted, Barbara had put up with enough. Despite having endured years of her husband's infidelities, compounded by the humiliation of his abandonment and betrayal, loyalty and love had led her to drag the family halfway across the world to be by her husband's side. But it was now too much to bear. She was inescapably confronted with the truth that this man had been prepared to remove himself from her and his children in the most callous way.

Matters came to a head a week after the MP had been arrested when, over the Easter weekend, Stonehouse had taken the two women in his life for a picnic at a lakeside beauty spot near the Maroondah Dam. Stonehouse seemed almost oblivious to the excruciating discomfort to which he was subjecting them. Having normalised the situation in his own mind, he assumed it would be perfectly natural for the others to accept it. When the conversation moved on to plans for the three of them to return to Melbourne, Barbara's patience snapped.

'I won't have that girl there,' she hissed to her husband's bewilderment.

Despite his protestations, Barbara stood her ground, maintaining that if Sheila joined them in Melbourne she would immediately return to the UK. Stonehouse lost his temper.

'I can't let you leave, Barbara, you've got to come back with me,' he insisted.

Realising that his wife was serious, Stonehouse leapt to his feet, shouting, 'If you leave me, Barbara, I will kill myself.'

With that he ran towards the lake's shore as if to throw himself over the edge of the dam, both Barbara and Sheila racing after him. Coming to a standstill, he turned to face them, collapsing in tears into Sheila's arms. He had made his choice. Within days, Barbara was back in England.

* * *

While this personal drama was unfolding, the parliamentary select committee report recommending his expulsion had been published, advice which was to be usurped by Stonehouse's arrest on the extradition warrant. Patterson visited the home of the consul general with his daughter, where a candid conversation about his client suggested that he was tired of the MP's antics and his impromptu press conferences, despite advice to the contrary. He also reiterated his concerns about Stonehouse's mental health.

Amid the complications of their private lives, the two fugitives were also required to appear in court for preliminary hearings on the extradition proceedings, where they were faced each time with the dogged Etheridge, watching, listening, waiting and planning, determined to bring his man to justice.

Stonehouse was becoming ever more desperate to evade the clutches of British justice; his failure to persuade the Australians, Bangladeshis and Swedes to provide refuge had been testament to that. On 12 April, news filtered through that his daughter had appeared in Mauritius bearing a formal request for citizenship and a passport for her father. In a flurry of behind-the-scenes diplomatic activity, the Mauritians initially advised that they had not considered the application, and subsequently declined the request. When challenged, Stonehouse retorted that he had been compelled to act, having been informed that, with his expulsion from parliament, he would have seventy-two hours to leave Australia and would be in need of a new country in which to live.

In the meantime, a second select committee had been convened to deal with the question of Stonehouse's continued membership of parliament, returning on 29 April with a recommendation that he should 'come before the House and show why his continued absence should not result in his expulsion' before 6 June, laying down the gauntlet with a stern warning to Stonehouse.

Having been the subject of a parliamentary select committee investigation and report, the time had come for a definitive decision as to how to deal with the Stonehouse affair. Harold Wilson was uncomfortably conscious of the extensive international interest and the immense strength of feeling that it had generated with the public, in his own party and in parliament. His government had struggled to maintain their narrow majority and Stonehouse was partly responsible for narrowing it even further. Wilson was painfully aware that his premiership was hanging in the balance.

Ted Short, a highly experienced and respected MP and minister, had been charged with the task of reviewing matters and reporting to the cabinet. What has remained obscured was that he too had been conducting a secret life, engaged as an StB agent with the codename Skot, making him undoubtedly highly sensitive to the spy allegations against Stonehouse. Perhaps his motivations for seeking his colleague's removal were not based solely on the party's interests.

The political and legal ramifications of seeking the runaway MP's expulsion were discussed at a cabinet meeting on 22 May. In typical Wilson fashion, the decision was fudged, delaying any decision to later in June. They were to discover that the Stonehouse saga would take a further twist that would absolve them of the need to conclude the exercise. Matters on the other side of the world were about to render the entire process redundant.

30

EXTRADITION

May–July 1975

May saw the two sides assiduously preparing for the extradition hearing: attending conferences with lawyers and remand hearings, collating evidence and putting in hours of legal research as the date loomed for the case to go before the magistrate. The date of 26 May had been set and a smaller courtroom had been selected in order to manage the media presence and make proceedings easier for the magistrate and advocates.

The fugitives' lawyers used the hearing to argue that there were procedural irregularities, contending firstly that the warrants were bad due to duplicity: two warrants had been issued, one on 21 March and the second on 29 April, and it was submitted that the magistrate had no power to act upon the second warrant and that the original warrant failed to comply with the Justices Act, which required that a separate warrant should be issued for each of the charges laid before the court. On that basis, they maintained, the case should be dismissed. The second legal argument employed was that the action was contrary to natural justice in that the defence was prevented from challenging the affidavit evidence presented on behalf of the Crown to establish that it satisfied the requisite burden of proof. The technical and complex arguments meant very little to many of the gathered throng, most of whom had flocked to witness the personal drama as opposed to the legal niceties. The submissions failed to persuade the magistrate, who found in favour of the Crown. With these preliminary legal arguments determined, the substantive hearing could now continue.

Realising the game was up, Stonehouse changed tack. With the inevitable staring him in the face he was now anxious to return for the parliamentary debate to preserve his status as MP. He had another plan. He instructed Patterson to make an offer to return to London voluntarily without the need for the extradition proceedings and, if required, in the custody of the police; the magistrate was duly advised that Stonehouse had provisionally booked a flight for 1 June, with Patterson hastily adding that this had been contrary to his advice. The magistrate expressed his displeasure at the prospect of Stonehouse skipping bail.

This strategy had blatantly been adopted to create problems for the Crown's case, both in Australia and the UK. Had it been successful, Stonehouse would return to present his case to parliament and defend the criminal prosecution, while Sheila would be left to fight the extradition, which could potentially go on for many more months, making the prosecution of the conspiracy charge in London virtually impossible. Correctly judging this to be the case, the Australian magistrate implacably ruled against the defendants.

John Hay of the British High Commission attended the court to witness the events first hand in order to provide a report to Downing Street:

> although remarkably attractive and seemingly composed, [Sheila Buckley] is really rather a silly person who has been brought to her present situation by infatuation with Mr Stonehouse. He, however, seems fully in control of the situation. He looked the healthiest person in the court last Monday morning, taking a lively interest in all that was going on. Writing all the while on a thick quarto pad (presumably for his book) and consulting from

time to time with his lawyer. He is also making as much as possible out of the request by the Select Committee of the House of Commons that he return voluntarily to Britain, pointing out that, though willing to do so, because of the extradition proceedings, of which the Select Committee were aware, he cannot within the time envisaged.

The offer to return immediately raised concerns from DCS Etheridge, who suspected Stonehouse of looking for another means to escape while in transit back to the UK, though he conceded it might be just another political stunt. The Australians, meanwhile, were relieved and rather smug that the political embarrassment had moved from Canberra to London.

Stonehouse frantically sought alternative ways to evade facing his accusers, following up his 'offer' with a letter to the consulate general on the very same day seeking assurances that he would be granted bail pending the outcome of his criminal case and an opportunity to give a personal statement to the House of Commons in order to put his side of the case. Under the protection of parliamentary privilege, he intended to raise the stakes for the government by suggesting that the case against him was politically motivated. When the British consul general conveyed the news to James Callaghan, his initial response was that consideration would be given to the request but that he would need to consult the DPP and attorney general, during which time the extradition proceedings would continue.

Aside from his anxiety to sidestep his current legal quandary, Stonehouse continued to follow parliamentary events and was highly aware of the debate gripping the UK concerning the nation's continued membership of the EEC, an association to which he was very much opposed, considering it excluded the country's ability to maintain trade and relations with the former British colonies and the Eastern Bloc states, with whom he had personally gone to great lengths to nurture connections. He was therefore extremely keen to be present when a referendum to decide the issue would take place on 6 June.

At this point the proceedings were adjourned. The court reconvened on 30 May and Sheila's lawyers immediately applied for an adjournment and legal aid so that they could appeal the magistrate's decision to the High Court, an application supported by Patterson and opposed by the British government, to which the magistrate responded by adjourning to 13 June to consider the submissions. The adjournment had thwarted any plan Stonehouse had to return for the 6 June, which he believed was also the deadline by which he should appear before the House of Commons to explain why he should not be expelled for his self-imposed absence and conduct.

In London, the DPP and attorney general met to discuss the recent developments, giving their view that the extradition proceedings should not be withdrawn. They issued a letter advising the MP that they intended to proceed and he would have to abide by the Australian court's extradition order. Even once the order was made, Stonehouse would have to wait fifteen days before it was activated, a statutory requirement that he could not waiver. A commotion followed, with Stonehouse's frenzied attempts to derail the process turning the matter into a political stand-off with the British government. Letters flew back and forth between Stonehouse and London in which he demanded assurances that while he was using his best endeavours to return to London in time for the June deadline, any parliamentary debate should be delayed to allow him to be present. Downing Street refused to budge on the 12 June debate, with the chair of the second select committee, George Strauss, writing an exasperated response to Stonehouse's repeated requests, 'The Select Committee has not made a deadline for your return by June 6th, or any other date. Its sole recommendation in regard to time is that at least a month should elapse between the publication of its second report on April 29th and consideration of the expulsion motion by the House, in order to give you the opportunity of either attending the House or resigning.'

The contents of Strauss's letter were conveyed to Stonehouse in a telephone call. The MP asked for a message to be passed to the prime minister, advising that he was now considering his position but that, in the circumstances, he would now contemplate petitioning the Queen, judging that the government's decision preventing his return gave rise to grave constitutional questions.

While they attempted to deal with this, Downing Street was alarmed to receive reports from Ballard that the Australian police believed Stonehouse was in possession of a passport, possibly with a green cover, suggesting it could be Irish, and that a BA flight had been booked for 5 June, adding that they feared that he may have plans to escape by sea. A port alert was issued.

On 5 June, there was a definitive response from Downing Street to Stonehouse's request delivered by the British consulate, reiterating their view that the proceedings would not be withdrawn nor could they give assurances at the prospects of bail for the MP should he return, stating that this would be a matter for the court. Stonehouse phoned the British consulate asking to speak with the governor of Victoria, Sir Henry Winneke, and, when it transpired the governor was indisposed, left an indignant message requesting a meeting the following day at which he demanded to be issued with a passport immediately as he wished to travel back to the UK. When challenged as to what the position of the Australian court was, Stonehouse retorted, 'The position of the court, though important, is insignificant compared with the constitutional issue,' and that if he was not granted a passport he would consider this an 'unjustifiable impediment'.

Stonehouse missed the EEC referendum, in which 68 per cent of those who voted opted to remain in the EEC. Infuriated by the bureaucracy, Stonehouse decided to take matters into his own hands and tried to deliver to the governor a hastily handwritten document petitioning the Queen to allow him to be present for the debate to defend himself. When told that the governor did not have authority to accept the petition, the MP threw a copy of the document into the doorway and left, later sending his daughter, Jane, to the British Consul General's office, where she dropped off further copies of the petition.

Considerable debate arose within cabinet as to how to manage the developing situation, with members determined not to allow it to appear that Stonehouse's actions had changed the government's position. Outwardly, they were clear that their stance remained as per the recommendation of the select committee, but privately they acknowledged that it was inevitable that the government would need to delay matters now that Stonehouse had expressed his intention to return. They had no intention of letting him know that, though, as they were determined to keep up the pressure.

On 8 June, Stonehouse announced to the press that he planned to fly back to London the following day, having arranged a constituency meeting for 11 June. On the morning of 9 June he attended Melbourne Magistrates' Court to seek the resumption of the hearing that had originally been adjourned to 13 June. He wanted the court to proceed immediately to order his extradition. Having become tired with his lawyer's advice contradicting his own wishes, the MP had dispensed with Patterson's services. Stonehouse addressed the magistrate himself, describing how the British government had wilfully refused his request to defend himself in the House and rather grandly stated that he considered he had a 'greater duty to the UK constitution than to the court'. The magistrate was unimpressed and refused to resume the hearing, at which a petulant Stonehouse reiterated his intention to leave as planned.

Four tickets for the BA flight had been booked. It was suggested that two of those tickets had been purchased by the *Daily Express*. The world's press were waiting at the airport, as were the Australian police, when the Stonehouse entourage swept in. Sheila was not present; she intended to remain to continue her fight against extradition. In a blaze of publicity, amidst a melee of press, airport officials, bemused passengers and police, the MP was arrested as he attempted to leave the airport lounge to board the plane. As two of his children embarked and returned to the UK, Stonehouse was charged with a further offence of obstructing justice and taken before the magistrate, who had no hesitation in remanding him in custody for breaching his bail. To add to the unfolding drama, the otherwise verbose politician refused to speak at the police station and remained mute throughout the hearing.

Though largely staged by Stonehouse himself, the turmoil of events had an adverse impact on his fragile mental health and being remanded in custody was the final straw. Some asserted that this was yet another ploy to manipulate events and public sympathy; nonetheless Stonehouse's mental state created enough concern for him to be transferred to the hospital wing of Pentridge Prison, where he was seen by a consultant psychiatrist, Mr Allen A. Bartholomew, on 10 and 11 June. Bartholomew reported, 'When I saw him he was clearly aware of my presence and shook my proffered hand in greeting and then turned his back on me. I asked him how he was and whether there was anything that I could do for him. He put his finger over his mouth, sat on the bed and wrote on a piece of paper.'

The MP proceeded to answer all questions put to him by the psychiatrist by writing on a pad of paper and, despite a suspicion from some quarters that he was malingering, after the second day of examination the psychiatrist concluded that Stonehouse was mentally ill, even though he 'may be consciously protesting' and that this may cause problems for the hearing scheduled for 13 June. There was even the suggestion of 'underlying schizophrenic illness' and a question as to whether he would be 'fit to plead'. The prosecutors were advised and the news filtered back to London, where the authorities remained suitably reassured that, while his mental health may affect his ability to attend court, it did not prevent the magistrate from giving his final judgment.

There had been a further cabinet meeting at which the Stonehouse affair was discussed and an agreement reached that, with his imminent return and the questions that had arisen regarding his mental health, the expulsion debate would be postponed, resulting in Ted Short announcing the decision to parliament on 11 June. Stonehouse had finally got his way.

With the emergence of Stonehouse's mental health issues, the hearing on 13 June was adjourned to 17 June, during which time he was granted bail subject to conditions. The same day, a report appeared in *The Times* citing Stonehouse's psychiatric issues, the information having been leaked, leading inevitably to repercussions at the hearing on 17 June, when the case was adjourned to 30 June to allow the magistrate to consider transcripts and make his final decision. While the Crown was convinced Stonehouse would be extradited, there were concerns that they would not be successful with Sheila. As the court retired, Stonehouse asked the prosecutor, within earshot of the press, who had disclosed the information about his psychiatric condition, maintaining that this development was very damaging, to which the prosecutor chose to make no comment.

The court reconvened on 30 June, when the magistrate gave judgment, finding that the charges had been substantiated in respect of both defendants and granting warrants for extradition. With this, the bail for both defendants was withdrawn and they endured fifteen days in custody as they awaited the statutory period permitted before the execution of the warrants. In the meantime, Etheridge, who had been present throughout the process, made arrangements for a temporary passport to be issued to Stonehouse and for escorting officers to accompany the two fugitives on the flight back from Australia. He and Townley were to escort the MP, while WPCs Shields and Jackson would chaperone Sheila.

As his final days in Australia ebbed away, Stonehouse began to turn his mind towards his return. On 9 July, he wrote to the speaker of the House of Commons requesting the opportunity to make a personal statement. While the likelihood of Stonehouse being expelled from parliament had receded, there was still the prospect of the MP losing his position through bankruptcy. He was aware that the first steps had been taken to recoup monies that he appeared to have appropriated through his business dealings, although this was a process that would take a considerable time to run its course.

On 17 July 1975, Stonehouse and Sheila were transferred to Melbourne airport and boarded flight BA979 for the long haul back to London. The adventures in Australia were over and the couple were now on their way home to face the music.

31

BOW STREET

The Protest, 18 July 1975

It seemed a terrifically exciting and daring plan, having the children throw eggs at the passing police vehicles as they sped towards court. The reality, however, so often fails to live up to the fantasy.

Patti Hayes had been transfixed by the events unfolding since Stonehouse's discovery in Australia, observing the pantomime of court hearings and press conferences that he had given with a growing sense of fury.

Outraged by Stonehouse's behaviour, she became increasingly resentful as she contemplated the trouble his recklessness had brought to her husband and family. With Stonehouse's return to the UK, she felt compelled to express her anger, calculating that some sort of public protest was most likely to catch his attention. One of her main grievances was his seeming utter ignorance of the massive ructions he had created within the family and the way he expected them to rally around him as if he were the innocent victim of the entire, bizarre spectacle. Instead he was a man who had misused his position as a high flyer in the political and business world to bring a tidal wave of distress, anguish and ruin crashing down on his extended family, not only poor Barbara and their children, but also dragging his nephew Michael and his young family under with them.

Before these events, Michael's legal career seemed to be taking off, with the family enjoying an idyllic life on one of the many new housing estates that were springing up across the country at that time. Life had been sweet, but Stonehouse's exploits had soured everything, causing tensions between husband and wife and arguments and recriminations.

With the news that the MP was returning to the UK from Australia, Patti was resolved to mark the moment by registering her indignation, considering the court where he was due to appear to be the perfect platform.

As Michael was getting ready for work that July morning, Patti mentioned that she was planning a day trip with the children, though she may have omitted to specify that it would involve a journey to London, knowing that Michael would disapprove and an argument would inevitably ensue. To avoid adding to Michael's miseries, she had turned to her brother, David Taylor, to talk about their troubles and her profound sense of betrayal at the intolerable worry and uncertainty the situation had brought upon her husband and children. She had given birth to their fifth child the year before and the family were now facing losing the security of the life they had built with her husband's livelihood in jeopardy as a result of his uncle's indiscretions. So the siblings hatched a plan, putting to use David's early career in journalism. Though he was now pursuing a successful career as a producer with Yorkshire TV, he still had many contacts in Fleet Street.

After breakfast, Patti kissed her husband goodbye and, as soon as he left, packed the children into the Ford Escort estate and made the long drive to London, where she planned to meet up with her brother in Covent Garden, close to Bow Street Magistrates' Court. It had been reported that Stonehouse was due to land at London Heathrow that morning and be produced at the magistrates' court.

Patti and her brother had made only the loosest of arrangements, having decided where to meet but not yet having formulated a plan beyond that. The journey to London was uneventful. Patti sang songs and chatted with her children to pass the time, becoming quieter as they entered London and she concentrated on finding her way through the city streets, eventually finding a lucky parking spot close to the rendezvous.

She met with her brother at an Italian restaurant in the web of roads sandwiched between Covent Garden and Bow Street and, as the children devoured their ravioli, Patti and David discussed their plans. The news had filtered through that Stonehouse's flight had been delayed and it was touch and go whether he would make it to court that day. In an effort to keep on top of the latest developments, David kept disappearing from the restaurant to consult with a number of his old Fleet Street colleagues for updates on Stonehouse's progress.

Over the course of their long lunch Patti and David formulated a plan, bearing in mind that it was vital that they themselves did not fall foul of the police.

Sitting opposite our tomato-sauce-streaked faces, the pair struck upon the idea to persuade the two eldest children, myself, now aged nine, and my sister, seven, to hurl eggs at the passing convoy of vehicles as they entered the precincts of the court in the hope that this would attract plentiful press attention and sufficiently convey the disdain with which Patti looked upon Stonehouse's behaviour. She figured that she wouldn't get into trouble with the police if it could be depicted as an escapade undertaken by her wild and wayward son and daughter while she had been distracted with the care of her other children. She was a little unclear as to how they would explain how the children had got the eggs, but dismissed this as a mere detail. She and David then carefully explained their plan to us, as we enthusiastically spooned Italian ice cream into our sticky mouths, finding in me a more than willing accomplice. I was animated with the idea of causing some mischief, particularly adult-sanctioned pitching of eggy missiles at the police. With that, David disappeared again, this time to the nearest convenience store where he bought half-a-dozen eggs.

A solemn stillness had settled over Bow Street that stifling summer afternoon and there was a sense of calm before a storm. Eventually David was able to give Patti the news that the plane with Stonehouse had landed and that he was expected at any moment. As we waited impatiently, the clock on the restaurant wall ticking, in a tableau reminiscent of the scene in *High Noon* in which Gary Cooper sits, alone in his sheriff's office, awaiting his fate.

My sister and I marched resolutely alongside Patti and David the short distance to the court and took up our posts on the pavement, behind a line of temporary metal barriers that had been set up at the driveway into the court building yard, where the prison vans would unload their cargo of unfortunate detainees. An egg was surreptitiously deposited in each of our small, sweaty palms along with final whispered instructions that we should watch out for the line of police cars and vans and, as the vehicles passed, fling the eggs and run. Showing us the best vantage point to stand, on the curb of the driveway a few feet from the large wooden doors of the courtyard, Patti and David retired to a discreet distance to watch over us. The road was deserted save for the odd passer-by and, in my memory, eerily quiet.

Anticipation rose as we waited expectantly, if not a little diffidently, at the allotted spot. The occasional journalist and photographer loitered by the entrance to the court, but the scene was calm, all things considered.

Suddenly there was a shout. 'They're coming!'

The clang of the Black Maria and the siren of the dark-blue Rover police escort heralded their arrival in Bow Street.

With those words and the rising clamour of the approaching vehicles pandemonium descended on the street as people flooded from pubs, cafés, shops and side streets while, like locusts descending voraciously on a field of wheat, a swarm of journalists and photographers suddenly swooped, encircling my sister and me. Our view of the road became blocked by the jostling journalists and our bravado and resolve swiftly melted away as we were swamped in the melee. I contemplated for a moment the fragile missiles I clutched but feared to throw them, afraid that the eggs would strike the crowd of people in front of me, and the repercussions that would follow.

The vehicles carrying Stonehouse and Buckley swept left into the courtyard of Bow Street Magistrates' Court. The heavy, metal-studded, wooden doors had swung open, almost unnoticed, immediately slamming shut with the passage of the last vehicle, depriving the prurient throng of a view of the alleged miscreants being ignominiously led to the cells.

Patti and David watched the crowd dissipate, leaving us standing staring at the eggs in our hands, as the moment for protest passed and, thankfully for us all, without incident.

My sister and I skipped back across Bow Street to join our mother and uncle and we retired to a nearby café to await the outcome of the court hearing. News soon came that the pair had arrived too late to be brought before the court that day and would now have to wait until the next morning before facing their accusers.

With this news, Patti disappeared with the two toddlers to tend to the baby and David took up conversation with a colleague, leaving my sister and me bored with our perceived incarceration in the café. Unnoticed, we slipped out without the boring adults knowing where we had gone, it being perfectly usual in those days for children to wander widely without adult supervision. At liberty, we found that there wasn't an awful lot for children to do – despite the odd photographer perched outside the court, the crowds had well and truly disappeared – but then our attention was drawn to a TV camera set up outside the main entrance to the court. A reporter stood armed with a microphone, nervously checking his notes before addressing the lens. We took up a strategic position behind the reporter, dangling chimp-like, we were later informed, from the old blackened railings that encircled the court building.

Imagine the scene some hundred or so miles away: Michael, settling in his armchair after a taxing day, with a glass of beer and a TV dinner, to watch the national early evening news, no doubt wondering where his wife and children were as the opening credits spilled from the family's newly acquired colour television.

The programme opened with the story of his uncle's case and relayed the afternoon's events at court, covering the drama of the delayed flight, the rush to get to court and the missed deadline.

'We will now go to our reporter at Bow Street Magistrates' Court.'

As Michael watched the reporter, his attention was caught by two children in the background playing on the court railing. Food spilled on to his creased shirt front as he recognised that the urchins were in fact his eldest son and daughter.

Patti would have had some explaining to do.

32

HER MAJESTY'S PLEASURE

The first court hearing, 19 July 1975

Bow Street Magistrates' Court was one of several courts that fell within the petty sessional division of the City of Westminster, ranging from the old Victorian wood-panelled courts, like Bow Street and Marlborough Street, to the brand-new, purpose-built courts of Horseferry Road and Wells Street resembling bland 1970s office blocks more than formal, stately courtrooms. Even those later courts were designed to make a statement to anyone who had fallen on the wrong side of the law, a show of state power over the individual. Whether by design or oversight, there were no conference rooms to speak of, meaning interviews with clients detained in the court cells had to be conducted through the wicket of the cell door amid the noise and distraction of fellow detainees, jailers and other lawyers.

Court 1 in Bow Street Magistrates' Court was, even in those days, peculiar and rather archaic, its oak-panelled walls, brass and glass fittings and library of books ornamenting the area behind the magistrates' seats, lending it the air of a Victorian study rather than a courtroom.

Here it was that John Stonehouse and Sheila Buckley, after a desperately uncomfortable night in Bow Street police station, appeared to face justice for the first time on British soil to answer to charges of conspiracy, fraud and theft amounting to around £175,000 (£1.3 million today). It was to be the start of a long, drawn-out process, partly through Stonehouse's interference and in part because the Crown needed time to collate the evidence. The police investigation was still ongoing and the police and prosecution had to be wary of the singularly sensitive political nature of the case.

It was not only Stonehouse and Sheila who had landed in London that late July afternoon but the Australian lawyers, the reappointed Patterson and counsel George Hempel, who had flown in at their own expense to assist him.

The courtroom was packed with lawyers, the press, curious members of the public, court officials and jailers, but the excited buzz instantly fell into a reverential hush with the harsh rap at the magistrate's door. As it swung open, the justice strode to his seat, nodding to the clerk. The defendants were asked to stand; they were formally identified and had the charges read to them.

The initial hearing dealt with procedural matters primarily to determine the court the case should be heard in and a timetable. The trial would ultimately take place at the Central Criminal Court. At that time, before a case could proceed to the Crown Court the prosecution had to serve the evidence it relied upon to the defence. The defence could either accept or dispute the evidence provided. If the evidence was to be disputed, the magistrates were required to consider the prosecution case and any representations the defence made to dismiss the charges on the basis that there was insufficient evidence. Stonehouse would of course be contesting matters, which would require a lengthy hearing given the complexities of the case and number of witnesses to be called. With the preliminaries resolved, there remained the question of bail.

Stonehouse felt that, because he had voluntarily returned to the UK and had publicly announced that he intended to resume his life as a politician, the issue of bail would be a formality. He was about to be abruptly disabused of this assumption.

From the perspective of a criminal defence lawyer, it is unsurprising that the prosecution opposed bail. The representative for the director of public prosecutions, described by Stonehouse as a 'large, florid man', raised objections to the MP being freed, submitting that there was a substantial risk that he would abscond for a second time, which if he did so abroad, would result in protracted and expensive extradition proceedings.

The prosecutor described the elaborate methods used by Stonehouse to acquire new and false identities, and his approach to the Swedish prime minister for a passport, mentioning also that it had come to their attention that he had been looking to flee to Mauritius and Bangladesh, concluding that this clearly demonstrated a desire to evade justice in the UK.

Stonehouse's Australian barrister, Mr Hempel, who had, through an expedited process, been granted rights of audience in the UK, applied for bail. The magistrate was not particularly receptive and gave him short shrift when it was suggested that Stonehouse's duties and responsibilities as an MP were a 'special reason' for bail to be granted.

Stonehouse recorded the magistrate's response in his book *My Trial*, published in 1976: 'Are you telling me that he is entitled to special consideration over and above that of a normal citizen because he is an MP?' he demanded, the disapproval in his voice rippling just below the surface of his words.

'Certainly not, sir,' the barrister retorted.

'I certainly hope not. I misunderstood you. He is in the same position as any other ordinary member of the public,' he said reproachfully, glancing from the lawyer to defendant then back to the lawyer.

The barrister was barking at a closed door and without further consideration the magistrate refused bail, stating that he was of the view that the MP would fail to surrender to bail because of the nature, seriousness and number of charges he faced. That abruptly ended the hearing as the justice quickly retired from court.

Stonehouse sat frozen in horror at the prospect of being held in prison with all the ritual humiliation and discomfort that would entail. There had been no objection to bail for Sheila and, subject to conditions, she was to be released.

After the magistrate rose, there was pandemonium in the courtroom as the defendants were led back to the court cells. The lawyers earnestly conferred among themselves and the press filed into the waiting area and spilled on to the street.

Stonehouse had instructed an English solicitor, Michael O'Dell, who appeared to have limited experience in criminal law and admitted that this was to be his first big criminal case. He immediately lodged a bail application before a judge in chambers for the following Monday, which was summarily refused, paving the way for repeated applications in the ensuing weeks.

July to August 1975

Geoffrey Robertson had only been plying his trade as a budding barrister in the magistrates' courts of London and the Home Counties for eighteen months. The dashing young lawyer had been called to the bar in 1973, not long after arriving from his homeland of Australia at the start of the decade.

While only recently qualified, he already had a number of notable cases under his belt, having been involved in the successful defence of the underground *Oz* magazine on obscenity charges, where he was led by John Mortimer, QC, the creator of every lawyer's favourite character *Rumpole of the Bailey*. He had also been on the defence team representing Peter Hain, a future Labour minister in the Blair and Brown cabinets, who had been charged with conspiracy involving the organisation of anti-apartheid demonstrations against South African rugby and cricket tours. Robertson had quickly developed a reputation as a clever, eloquent and pugnacious lawyer.

These cases had brought him to the attention of Stonehouse, who reckoned the charismatic anti-establishment counsellor was just the sort of person he wanted in his corner to fight against the institution he had long been part of.

Geoffrey had become aware of the case when he had returned home to Sydney for Christmas 1974, continuing to follow the spectacle as it played out in his homeland when he returned to London to take up arms for the downtrodden and forgotten.

Stonehouse and Robertson were introduced at a conference in the legal visits room at HMP Wandsworth one fine July day at a meeting in which Stonehouse was naturally concerned with obtaining bail, while young Geoffrey was keen to make his mark, making him easy prey to the challenge.

Within the week, the barrister had taken his place in Court 1 at Bow Street Magistrates' Court. With Stonehouse remanded in custody, he had to be produced each week for the court to reconsider the issue of bail. During this period, what became known as 'Stonehouse days' were weekly occasions when the courtroom would be packed to the rafters with members of the press reporting on the unfolding drama. In the midst of all this, Stonehouse's daughters stoically sat, providing reassurance and support that their father desperately needed.

Despite all Robertson's preparation and eloquent advocacy, the chief magistrate was having none of it and refused bail, citing yet again that Stonehouse was a flight risk.

'But this is the face that has launched a thousand headlines!' blurted out the incensed counsel.

Robertson faced a monumental task, but if ever there was a man for the job, he was the one to achieve it, despite the awkward fact that, for the time being, Stonehouse continued to languish in jail.

* * *

As an astute judge once said, when portraying the effects of the first-time experience of custody or prison, 'Do not underestimate the effect of that first clang of the cell door.' While Stonehouse had spent a little time in custody in Australia, incarceration in the hot, crowded, stinking, Victorian prisons of London was a different experience altogether. Stripped of even the most basic facilities such as adequate plumbing – with no toilets in cells as there are now – prisoners had to make do with buckets and submit to the daily chore of slopping out when their doors were opened.

Stonehouse had been transported to Wandsworth, a daunting experience, but he adapted to prison life while on remand at both Wandsworth and Brixton with impressive resilience and resourcefulness, even drawing on his experiences, after his release, to challenge the home secretary with some authority, having encountered the conditions first hand.

He was provided with his own cell, though there was some suggestion of placing him in the hospital wing amid fears that he might harm himself, a story which appeared in the newspapers in the days after his remand, which he found very irksome. This, in addition to the submissions made by the lawyer for the DPP at the first hearing, the press coverage, the parliamentary commission, as well as being denied an opportunity to make a parliamentary statement, led him to believe that he was the victim of some political conspiracy.

He was desperate to have a voice, to be heard above the tabloid and political clamour that was drowning him out. He struck on the idea to write to the newspapers to make a statement about the latest 'fake news' story, but he suspected that his post, even legal correspondence that should have been privileged, was being intercepted and censored by the prison authorities, who would never permit a letter to the press to reach its destination. With that in mind, and flying in the face of prison regulations, Stonehouse penned a letter and arranged for it to be smuggled out and made available to the national newspapers, who gleefully published it in its entirety.

Dear Sir,

I would like to make it clear that I have no quarrel with the prison authorities, in fact your officers have treated me with courtesy and consideration. As far as I can see the food is excellent and make no protest about the food.

My accommodation is quite satisfactory, and I am content with it.

According to a report in the *News of the World* and other newspapers, I requested to be transferred to the hospital upon my arrival here. That report is not correct. I made no such request whatsoever. I have been advised that it has now been reported that I will nevertheless be transferred to the hospital. I would object most strongly to this as I am perfectly fit.

My objections relate solely to the conduct of the British Government in not making it possible for me to make a statement to the House of Commons. I should make it clear that such a statement would not be on my own case. My own case will be conducted in the courts of law. The statement will consist solely of such facts of which the House is not yet aware.

The denial of bail was on instruction of counsel acting for the Director of Public Prosecutions. Those instructions came from the Attorney General and it was therefore a political act designed to frustrate any bail appeal.

Conversely if the Attorney General had given instructions that bail was not to be opposed, bail would presumably have been granted. Since my arrest on 21 March I have consistently been granted bail by the Australian courts. It would be extraordinary of the English courts to grant me less. The opposition to bail is clearly politically inspired.

Yours faithfully,
John Stonehouse

The publication of the letter meant that Stonehouse had embarrassed the authorities yet again. The extraordinary episode served to highlight one of the unusual features of this case: the way in which it was being played out – and to some extent tried – through the lens of the media in a manner that had not previously occurred in the UK. Following more closely US-style litigation in which both parties try to sway public opinion through manipulation of the press, normal *sub judice* rules were being pushed to their very limit, not only by the press themselves, fighting to be first to break ever more scandalous stories, but, perhaps for the first time, by the defendant at the centre of the furore.

Each week, Stonehouse was produced at Bow Street Magistrates' Court and his barrister would again dutifully apply for bail, only for this to be refused by the magistrate. At the hearing on 28 July, in a sign of things to come, Stonehouse adopted different tactics, choosing to dispense with his lawyer and hoping that his appearance alone in the dock would draw some sympathy from the bench. The MP made his submissions only to be disappointed to find that his solitary presence had proved insufficient to move the magistrate to grant bail.

Stonehouse's continued incarceration increased his belief that pernicious forces were at work. After several failed attempts to obtain bail, at the early August hearing Geoffrey Robertson had, with Stonehouse's agreement, decided not to apply for bail as they considered it a pointless exercise. Whether it was the letter's publication or other factors to which Stonehouse had alluded in that letter; or the miscreant MP being unable to misuse his parliamentary privilege now that parliament had gone into summer recess, no one can say. Unprompted, however, the magistrate suggested that he was minded to grant bail. The Stonehouse legal team swiftly put into place a bail package to include hefty sureties from friends amounting to £40,000 (£325,000 today), as well as his having to report daily to Holborn police station.

With his reclaimed freedom on 4 August 1975, he felt that finally he could launch his defence.

33

BUSINESS AS USUAL

August 1975

After the trauma of Stonehouse's incarceration and the intrusion of the press into every aspect of his life, one might have thought that he would have wanted a time of quiet contemplation, an opportunity to prepare with his legal team for the trial to come. On the contrary.

When his lawyer, Michael O'Dell, picked him up from prison the route was blocked by an excited crowd of reporters outside the gates. The newspapers later described how, with the car unable to move, Stonehouse stepped from its shell to face the melee, agreeing to demands for a statement, but, rather than discuss his own case, he used the occasion to highlight the plight of the many remand prisoners unfairly detained at Her Majesty's pleasure, insisting that something must be done to assist them. 'What I say is, "Wake up, England!"' exclaimed the politician, before leaping back into the vehicle, which immediately sped off, hotly pursued by a posse of journalists.

If Stonehouse thought his speech would earn him some respite, he was sadly mistaken and the car was pursued through the streets of London by some of the more determined journalists. Eventually pulling up outside his flat in Sancroft Street, Kennington, Stonehouse was observed experiencing considerable difficulty in gaining access. In an attempt to avoid the journalists waiting outside his home, he attempted to enter at the rear of the premises, where, frustratingly, he found he could not open the gate to his back garden. Undeterred, Stonehouse was observed clambering over the gate, only to be further frustrated by the locked back door, leaving him no choice but to hammer on the window, shouting, 'Barbara, Barbara, let me in, it's me, John,' until the back door swung open to allow him to step into the haven of his bemused family.

Tenacious reporters set up camp outside the apartment. Whether this was an attempt to get rid of them or because he just could not resist the lure of rebuking the establishment publicly, Stonehouse was drawn back out again fifteen minutes later but announced to the waiting pack that he would not be answering any questions. The newspapers, ever eager for drama, duly reported his comments:

'The bail system is full of humbug,' he proclaimed.

'Mr Stonehouse, are you above the humbug?'

'I'm not above humbug. I said, "No questions",' he reiterated sternly, as if reminding himself that he was not to be drawn into any further dialogue, before retreating back into the flat.

* * *

Stonehouse threw himself back into the maelstrom of political life, resuming his position on the backbenches, stubbornly ignoring the monumental issues needing to be resolved in his life as if the events of the previous year had never happened and all was back to normal. The period between his release on 4 August 1975 and his 'resignation' on 27 August 1976 became one of Stonehouse's most prolifically active spells in parliamentary affairs and saw him regularly contributing on topics as diverse as NATO, UK fisheries policies, matters concerning his own constituency, and crime and punishment, the latter issues having become particularly close to his heart. It seems that in parliament he found some solace and sanctuary from the madness that continued to surround him, finding himself dogged in the 'real world' by journalists doorstepping him, harangued by disgruntled constituents and members of the public, pursued by creditors and haunted by the criminal case, all while attempting to salvage what he could from the wreckage of his personal life. The business of politics was perhaps the one area of his life in which he felt some semblance of familiarity and control.

His experiences of the justice system and its apparent unfairness, specifically when trying to obtain bail, gave Stonehouse a keen interest in reforming the criminal justice system. He spoke often in parliament, whether to table amendments or otherwise, on the introduction of the Bail Act 1976, which to this day forms a cornerstone in the criminal legal process, as well as showing particular concern about the conditions that prisoners faced.

In one exchange on 13 February 1976, a long debate ensued on the issue of unconvicted prisoners in which Stonehouse used his personal ordeal to great effect:

> I suppose that I must declare an interest, in view of the fact that, in the middle of last year, I spent six and a half weeks in Brixton Prison on remand, when bail was refused me on instructions to the Director of Public Prosecutions by the Attorney-General. At any time now my bail may be revoked and I could find myself back in a solitary cell in C wing in Brixton. It is not fanciful to suggest that I might even this very day be sent back. It is well known that the police, when they have problems in making a case stick, harass the defendant, find reasons to suggest that he is breaking bail conditions and get him back inside. Under my bail conditions I have to report to the local police station between 8 a.m. and 10 a.m. Some time ago I was delayed at my home by an incoming telephone call and I reported at seven minutes past 10 a.m. The police in charge of my case rang my solicitor and told him that if I was late again I would be arrested and put back in Brixton.

Later in the exchange with the spokesperson on behalf of the government, Dr Edith Summerskill, Stonehouse asked, 'If people on remand are presumed to be innocent and are not there for punishment, why are they locked up without any communication outside their cells from 4 p.m. to 7 a.m. next day?'

Dr Summerskill responded, 'I was coming to the conditions under which they are kept. Incidentally, the period concerned is 5 p.m. until the following morning. The right honourable gentleman was wrong when he said that they had nothing to eat from 5 p.m. I am informed that they have a hot drink and a bun or something similar to eat during the evening.'

'I must correct the minister. I know what goes on because I was there. Tea is served at four o'clock and then the cell doors are banged shut. Prisoners are then left on their own until six o'clock, when hot tea – evil stuff – is brought in. That is all they get,' retorted Stonehouse, asserting an authority that was hard for his peers to counter.

34

COMMITTAL PROCEEDINGS

13 October to 6 November 1975

Barbara had stood stoically and steadfastly by her husband, playing down the trauma of loss and betrayal she had suffered at his hands, the epitome of unquestioning loyalty, certainly in public. From other quarters, the story was very different as Stonehouse obtained scant support from the parliamentary Labour Party, many of his colleagues considering his behaviour abhorrent and extremely damaging, though a few who felt some sympathy chose to sit by silently. He cut a forlorn and isolated figure at that autumn's conference in Blackpool where the press indulged their spiteful pleasure in publishing photographs of the MP sitting alone in the banks of empty chairs put aside for delegates. To her great credit, Mary Wilson, the prime minister's wife, approached Stonehouse to speak with him and enquire how he was in a moment of rare compassion in that brutal world.

Stonehouse's mental state had continued to be a concern as the MP maintained the view that he was not acting as himself and that psychologically his personality had been usurped by an alter ego, Markham. This analysis had been upheld by his Australian psychiatrist, who considered that the Markham personality was a genuine symptom of his mental health as opposed to a ruse to escape justice. This aspect was to be pursued by his lawyers, who cited the fact that, from the moment he was discovered in Melbourne, the MP had claimed to have suffered a mental breakdown, asserting to the psychiatrists in Australia that Markham and Mildoon were personalities who had from time to time taken over his own, a pronouncement on which he had elaborated in his interviews with the DTI inspectors over those six long days in Melbourne.

In October 1975, Stonehouse received a visit from the eminent psychologist, Lionel Haward, at his Andover home. Haward, generally credited as the 'father' of forensic criminal psychology to which field of research Stonehouse no doubt added, pursued a particular area of expertise in examining the artwork produced by those accused of criminal activities. Having been engaged to assess and provide a psychological report he was not to be disappointed, being immediately struck by an array of abstract artwork scattered around the Stonehouse home and, on enquiring as to the identity of the artist, Stonehouse confirmed it was his own work. Further probing as to the period in which certain pieces were painted and what events had been taking place in the politician's life at those times added context to the shapes and patterns that he observed beyond the surface of the canvases.

The renowned, if controversial, psychiatrist R. D. Laing was approached to assess and prepare a report on the MP's mental state, specifically to address the area of concern suggesting that Stonehouse was malingering and feigning his alleged mental conditions. Laing had developed a technique to elicit whether indeed a patient was adopting such a strategy. It was his opinion that Stonehouse's condition was genuine.

The committal hearing had been listed to take place in early October. Stonehouse's barrister, Geoffrey Robertson, had advised that, in his view, there was no case in respect of at least some of the charges that the MP faced. Firstly, the assertion was that the alleged fraud was in fact perpetrated outside of the jurisdiction, in Australia, while the law at that time suggested that any fraud needed to be committed within the jurisdiction of England and Wales; and, secondly, no steps had ever actually been taken to attempt to claim on the insurance policies.

Compounding the fraud allegations, the prosecution had also preferred charges relating to fraudulent applications for legal aid. Stonehouse had benefited from the assistance of legal aid, but, as he was still drawing an MP's salary, it was means tested, requiring the completion of a form for the court to consider whether his disposable income exceeded the threshold that would allow him to be granted legal aid, leading the prosecution to claim that he had provided misleading information.

The young barrister had spent the summer and early autumn scrutinising the Crown's case, considering the witness statements and exhibits, and holding numerous conferences with Stonehouse to consider them all and discuss the best ways to challenge the charges.

* * *

The first day of the long-awaited committal proceedings had arrived. They were to take place at Horseferry Road Magistrates' Court, a brand-new building designed for the needs of criminal justice of the 1970s, in stark contrast to the archaic Victorian courts at Bow Street.

Again the journalists and TV crews descended en masse, as they did throughout this saga. Stonehouse arrived with his lawyer, looking calm, relaxed and in control, passing with dignity through the crowd while, no doubt warned by his legal team, declining to make any comment to the press.

The proceedings lasted six weeks, following the longstanding procedure which placed the onus on the Crown to establish that there was a case for Stonehouse and Buckley to answer, a responsibility shouldered by the prosecution's representative, Henry Tudor Price. Sheila was represented by another up-and-coming barrister, Gerald Gordon, who would later become a QC and highly respected High Court judge sitting at the Old Bailey.

The procedure involved the prosecution calling their witnesses to give evidence before the court where they would, in turn, be questioned by the Crown and defence advocates. The witnesses' statements would then replace the original statements they had made to the police. Any non-contentious witnesses would simply have their police statements read to the court without having to give evidence themselves.

One of those who had been warned to attend court to give evidence was Stonehouse's nephew Michael, who had spent a miserable year clearing up the shambles left by his uncle, leaving him tense and resentful. This would be the first time since his grandmother's birthday party in November 1974 that the two would come face to face.

Michael had been under a great deal of stress, both personally and professionally, at that time, being in the process of completing on the purchase of a new home just outside Southampton, dealing with the logistical issues of moving his family from Wiltshire to Hampshire, while also conducting his career as an associate solicitor at the Winchester practice, where his workload was varied and heavy.

He attended court on 15 October 1975 and spent the best part of the day giving his evidence to the magistrate, a distressingly uncomfortable experience but at least he did not have to speak with his uncle directly.

The hearing developed its own rhythm, with the magistrate being most accommodating to the MP. The court sitting times would normally be between 10.30 a.m. and 4.30 p.m. with an hour for lunch; however, at Stonehouse's request, the magistrate permitted the court to sit until 3 p.m. to allow the politician to attend to his duties at parliament, which was only a short walk from the court.

Personal statement, 20 October 1975

Stonehouse had long been agitating to make a statement to the House of Commons in an attempt to provide some explanation for his bizarre behaviour, not only to the chamber but, perhaps more crucially, to reach out to the public who would ultimately form the jury that would try him, having long since formed the belief that the authorities and press were conspiring against him.

The MP had been frustrated that, during the period of his remand in custody, he had been prevented from making a statement to the House but now that he was free, he pursued this objective with renewed vigour. He approached the speaker of the House, Selwyn Lloyd, to canvass the idea, who in turn suggested Stonehouse draft something for him to consider. Lloyd, a reserved and prickly man, had many years of experience on the frontbench of government in the Anthony Eden administration and had been a significant figure in the Suez crisis of the mid-1950s as well as having some involvement in the Profumo scandal of the early 1960s. Lloyd was therefore no stranger to political intrigue and scandal, and was also very conscious of his responsibilities with the sub judice rules and anxious to avoid any criticism for having turned a deaf ear to any issues that Stonehouse might bring up which might jeopardise the subsequent trial.

Stonehouse quickly produced a draft of his proposed speech. Perusing it thoroughly, Lloyd found much within the document that caused him concern, and the censor's pencil came out, removing vast tracts. Lloyd made it very clear that he would not tolerate anything being said that might jeopardise the criminal court process and the speech was to be read strictly as he, the speaker, approved it, without variation or deviation, otherwise Stonehouse would not be allowed to address the House. Reluctantly Stonehouse capitulated and the date of 20 October 1975 was fixed for his address.

Stonehouse's lawyers were firmly of the view that he needed to step out of public office and that having him so prominently in the public eye not only increased his unpopularity as a serving MP in the ruling Labour Party, but also meant that he could use the protection of parliamentary privilege to press his case if he so wished, a ploy the lawyers were keen to avoid. It seemed that Stonehouse had just about been persuaded to relinquish membership but, before doing so, he was adamant that he be given the opportunity to set the record straight and explain himself to the House of Commons. It was with some trepidation that Geoffrey Robertson took a seat in the public gallery to witness his client's next move.

Stonehouse faced opposition from a large number of his colleagues in the Labour Party who were set against him making such a speech. It had been the subject of some debate in the press, fed by leaks from various quarters suggesting that there would be a mass walkout at the point when he stood to address the House.

The Commons was busy as Stonehouse took his seat, running the gauntlet of disapproving frowns in an atmosphere of palpable tension, while the prime minister was on his feet concluding another aspect of parliamentary business. Having completed his tasks, Wilson departed, but the majority of MPs remained to witness the spectacle.

Clutching a copy of the speech in his hand, the speaker addressed the expectant House.

'Before I call upon the right honourable member for Walsall, North, Mr Stonehouse, to make a personal statement I want to make one or two matters clear. Responsibility for the decision to allow the right honourable member to make a statement is mine. If the House wishes to introduce a new standing order dealing with personal statements, I am sure that any occupant of the chair would be grateful. I certainly have not found this an easy matter to decide. The right honourable gentleman's affairs and absence have frequently been referred to in the House. A select committee was set up and has reported. I am of the opinion that, in those circumstances, I should allow the right honourable member to make a statement about his absence. As to the precise contents of the statement, the task of the chair in this case has been to ensure that nothing should be said in it concerning matters which are sub judice and that it does not involve attacks upon other members. The convention of this House is that a personal statement should be listened to in silence.'

Having made his statement Lloyd ceded the floor to a rather nervous Stonehouse, who stood and addressed the House. After a preamble, he said, 'I am grateful to you, Mr Speaker, for your agreement to my request to make a statement. It is not easy for me, nor is it easy for the House. The events surrounding my disappearance last November, and since, have created tremendous press publicity, and everyone's consideration of my experience has been coloured and influenced by that media treatment. There have been incredible allegations made against me.'

'Order. The honourable gentleman must be very careful. He is not now reading from the text which has been agreed with me,' scolded the speaker.

'I have made a few textual changes,' baited Stonehouse.

'Let there be no misunderstanding about this. The right honourable member is entitled to say only what I have passed.'

'In particular,' Stonehouse persevered, 'you will see this in the text, Mr Speaker, I deny the allegation that I was an agent for the CIA. I deny the allegations that I was a spy for the Czechs. I can only regret that the original stories were printed. The purpose of this statement is to explain, as best I can within the traditions of the House, why I was absent from the House for such a lengthy period.

'The explanation for the extraordinary and bizarre conduct in the second half of last year is found in the progressions towards the complete mental breakdown which I suffered. This breakdown was analysed by an eminent psychiatrist in Australia and was described by him as psychiatric suicide. It took the form of the repudiation of the life of Stonehouse because that life had become absolutely intolerable to him. A new, parallel personality took over – separate and apart from the original man, who was resented and despised by the parallel personality for the ugly humbug and sham of the recent years of his public life. The parallel personality was uncluttered by the awesome tensions and stresses suffered by the original man and he felt, as an ordinary person, a tremendous relief in not carrying the load of anguish which had burdened the public figure.

'The collapse and destruction of the original man came about because his idealism in his political life had been utterly frustrated and finally destroyed by the pattern of events, beyond his control, which had finally overwhelmed him. Those events which caused the death of an idealist are too complex to describe in detail here, but in the interests of clarity as well as brevity I refer to them as follows.

'Uganda was a country in which I worked for two years in the development of the Co-operative movement. I was active also in developing political progress and became, for instance, a character witness for one of the accused in the Jomo Kenyatta Mau Mau trial in Kenya.

'Later, as a backbench member of parliament, I campaigned vigorously for African independence and became vice-chairman of the Movement for Colonial Freedom. Much of my backbench activities at that time – conducted, incidentally, from this bench – were concerned with advancing this cause. I believed in it sincerely and passionately. But those ideals were shattered in the late 1960s and the 1970s as Uganda and some other countries I had helped towards independence moved from democracy to military dictatorship and despair.

'The Co-operative movement in Britain had been a great ideal for me from an early age. Co-operation was almost a religion for me. It was not only a way to run a business; it was a way of life from which selfishness, greed and exploitation were completely excluded. I became a director, and later president, of the London Co-operative Society, the largest retail Co-operative society in the world, in active pursuit of those ideals. I did not do it for money. The honorarium was £20 per year. But I was pursued by the communists in that position during that period. I was bitterly attacked, and at that time . . .'

'Order. The right honourable gentleman must say only what I have passed.' The exasperation in the speaker's voice was evident.

Unperturbed, Stonehouse continued, 'That time was a most traumatic one for me and wounded my soul deeply. It had become cruelly clear that my Co-operative ideals were too ambitious, for, in truth, they could not be achieved, given human motivations. I felt as though my religion had been exposed as a pagan rite.

'Bangladesh is a country which I helped to create, and, with my honourable friend the member for Mitcham and Morden, Mr Douglas-Mann, I was one of the first in the House to take up the cause of self-determination for East Pakistan following the terrible events of the military crackdown in March 1971, when 10 million people had to flee for their lives to the safety of India. I became deeply involved as a result of first-hand experience in Bengal during the struggle for freedom. I sponsored several early-day motions concerned with Bangladesh, including one which attracted over 100 signatories, calling for the recognition of an independent and sovereign Bangladesh. That motion, in July 1971, was most significant in the progression of events towards the independence which finally came in December of that year.

'Bangladesh made me a citizen in recognition of my identification with the cause. I was enthused at that time with hope, but the hopes turned to tears as the conditions in that country deteriorated. Another of my ideals had collapsed.

'After the Labour defeat of 1970, I became active in export businesses, a field in which I had been successful as a minister and one in which I felt I could make a contribution in assisting British exports. I had hoped to establish personal financial security after a few years and then to return to full-time political activity. My enterprises were successful.

'However, early in 1972, I was approached by Bengalis residing in this country who wanted me to assist the establishment of a bank to cement relationships between Britain and Bangladesh. This involved me in very great problems, which could have ruined my career and public standing, and I was left a broken man as a result of the nervous tension I suffered throughout that period. That experience contributed heavily to my breakdown.

'In 1974, with the collapse of many secondary banks and the problems of the British economy, the strains became even worse. There seemed no escape from the awesome pressures which were squeezing the will to live from the original man. Everything he had lived for and worked for seemed to be damned.

'In this House itself, I felt a big weight bearing down on me. It was physically painful for me to be in the chamber because it was such a reminder of my lost ideals. I was suffocated with the anguish of it all. The original man had become a burden to himself, to his family and to his friends. He could no longer take the strain and had to go. Hence, the emergence of the parallel personality, the disappearance and the long absence during the period of recovery.

'That recovery took time, and in the early stages the psychiatrist in Australia advised that I should not return to England until I had recovered, as a premature return would inevitably do further harm to my health. At the time of the disappearance, no criminal charges were laid or anticipated; they did not come till four months later.

'In view of the facts, I hope that the House will agree that the right honourable member for Walsall, North had no intention of removing himself from the processes of justice as established by parliament.

'I am not allowed by your ruling, Mr Speaker, to refer to what you consider to be controversial subjects, and of course I accept your judgement; but I remind you, Mr Speaker, that one man's meat . . .'

'Order. The right honourable gentleman is again departing from the text.'

'Yes, Mr Speaker. I am simply explaining that I accept your judgement entirely, but a personal statement is a personal statement, and I must advise the House that half of my original statement was deleted by you. However, I fully appreciate your position, and I am deeply indebted to you for your sympathy, understanding and forbearance in the difficult circumstances which I have involuntarily created for you and the House during these past eleven months. I am very grateful to those honourable members who have extended understanding in my turmoil – especially to my honourable friends the members for Mitcham and Morden and for East Kilbride, Dr Miller, the right honourable member for Down, South, Mr Powell, and the honourable members for Chippenham, Mr Awdry, and for Horncastle, Mr Tapsell. I express thanks also to the right honourable member for Worcester, Mr Walker, and the then foreign secretary, who both helped me through a terrible crisis in 1973. I thank the clerks at the table and their assistants, who have been exceptionally helpful in recent months.'

At that, Stonehouse slumped back into his seat among the clamour as his colleagues rose to their feet to attract the attention of the speaker to pursue their own objectives.

It is clear that Stonehouse was continuing to advance a psychological defence for his actions whenever and wherever possible, determined to bring it into the public domain, no doubt conscious that the magistrate conducting his committal proceedings would read about it and ever cognisant that the general public would now be fully aware of it. He had achieved his goal to communicate with the public at large who would be his ultimate judges.

Unfortunately for Stonehouse, the media were less than sympathetic and in some quarters openly ridiculed him: in particular, *Private Eye*. He appeared on no less than three of the magazine's front covers in 1975, the first of which showed a picture of a man between two police officers standing at a urinal with the headline 'Missing Member Held'.

* * *

After the drama of his personal statement, the MP returned to the relative mundanity of the magistrate's committal proceedings. Days stretched into weeks as Stonehouse slipped into a routine of arriving early at court, partly in an attempt to evade the attention of the press but most importantly to review with his legal team the evidence that was due to be called by the prosecution that day.

His barrister recalled Stonehouse's attending each day carrying a case containing reams of questions scribbled out on parliamentary notepaper in distinctive green ink which, during long conferences required all of Robertson's powers of persuasion and diplomacy, to pare down to those that were pertinent to the case. His counsel also recalled fondly how most days they would be joined for lunch by Barbara, who would bring their meal in a small hamper, complete with cutlery.

At the end of the prosecution evidence, Robertson made submissions as to whether there was a case for Stonehouse to answer in respect of each of the charges. The arguments had made their mark and after due consideration the magistrate adjudged that there was insufficient evidence on the most serious of the charges relating to the insurance frauds, and promptly dismissed them. However, he found that there were cases for Stonehouse to answer to in respect of the remaining matters and committed them to the Central Criminal Court for trial.

That is normally the end of proceedings in a magistrates' court, but discussions had taken place between Stonehouse and his barrister on making a statement to the court. Given the press restrictions on what can be reported before a trial takes place, permission must be given by the court in order for any more detail to be reported. Stonehouse, against his lawyers' advice, asked for restrictions to be lifted.

Keen to put his side of the story, being constrained by the sub judice rules and, frustrated that the address he had given to parliament had been heavily censored by the speaker, Stonehouse was eager to have another opportunity to state his defence in some detail.

At the close of the case, Robertson advised the magistrate that his client wished to make a statement, an unusual step, but not entirely unheard of. Stonehouse, ever-conscious of the presence of the press, was determined to end the proceedings with the last word on matters and, rising to his feet, he read a prepared statement. It gave a flavour of things to come and expanded on issues he could not raise in his personal statement. It attacked the press and the government, and suggested that his prosecution was malicious and politically motivated.

His book *Death of an Idealist* had just been published in an attempt to explain what was widely regarded as inexplicable, reiterating with considerable emphasis the assertion that his actions were of a man not in his right mind, a message he was keen to broadcast more widely in the public domain.

'The problem with the prosecution is that they operate with such limited objectives and with such limited vision that they cannot see the wood for the twigs, let alone the trees. The prosecution have ignored the fact that the offences with which I am charged are completely out of character. My book *Death of an Idealist* shows my background. I present it as an exhibit.'

At this point, a hardback copy of his book was produced to the magistrate and given the exhibit number 663. Stonehouse was anxious to set out in detail his argument and the 240-page tome was to be his defence statement.

Finishing with a flourish, he asserted, 'I will not present my defence now to be squandered on those who have sought to make public entertainment out of my problems.

'I have nothing to hide, and that is why I asked, against legal advice, for reporting restrictions to be lifted. I am not a forger. I am not a thief. I am not a "con" man. I am not – most petty and ridiculous of all charges – a fiddler of legal aid. I have done my muddled, unhappy, but nonetheless honest best. I ask no privilege, except the right of every Englishman to a fair trial.'

The magistrate thanked him for his statement and asked for the copy that he held in his hand to be signed and initialled where there had been amendments.

Whatever one's view of Stonehouse, and while acknowledging he heaped so much of the trouble he experienced on himself, his views about the British press still resonate through the years, with many of his complaints concerning the behaviour of newspaper and police complicity borne out by the Leveson inquiry. The use of the media by the 'establishment', as he put it, to peddle their own message and manipulate public opinion continues to this day.

35

THE BEAUTY PARADE

November 1975–April 1976

Stonehouse's case was considered of such public importance that the Crown elected to engage both a senior treasury counsel, as well as juniors, with the team being embellished with Michael Corkery, QC. In the numerous obituaries written in the aftermath of Corkery's death, the picture painted was of a tall, imposing figure, with clear blue eyes, always dressed immaculately and possessed of a charming manner. He had served as an officer in the Guards during the second world war so carried that military air. He was described as 'affable' in the robing room, likened to a P. G. Wodehouse character, referring to friends and colleagues as 'good egg' or 'good cheese', and was never shy of cracking the odd joke. This almost casual exterior camouflaged an extremely hard-working and eloquent advocate who had gained a formidable pedigree, with a long list of notable cases under his belt, not least having been junior counsel on the Stephen Ward trial, a case that had been central to the Profumo affair and the demise of the Conservative government in 1964. This deadly combination would inevitably win over many a jury.

With this in mind, Geoffrey Robertson, for all his youthful exuberance and talent, would need a QC to lead the defence. Stonehouse had very clear views indeed, considering that the candidate needed to possess the necessary gravitas so that they would not fear taking on the establishment and, further, if they were part of the establishment then even better. With this in mind he initially approached Lord Hailsham, who had been Lord Chancellor under the Heath Conservative government of 1970 to 1974, who politely declined.

Robertson drew up a list of other candidates for Stonehouse to consider and there then followed a series of interviews with some of the finest legal minds in England.

Stonehouse took up residence at his barrister's chambers, conveniently located just off Fleet Street in what had been the home of Dr Johnson opposite the Inner Temple Church, where the contenders would meet with Stonehouse and Robertson to discuss what had been billed by the press as 'the case of the century'. John Mortimer, QC, was a contender but, after due consideration, aided by copious quantities of tea and biscuits, Stonehouse settled for Richard Du Cann, QC.

The *Independent*'s obituary in 1994 described Du Cann in glowing terms: 'as an advocate he was formidable. He demanded of himself, his pupils and others only the highest standards. Lean and spare in appearance, he commanded the attention of the court. He presented his cases, whether for the prosecution or the defence, fearlessly and with penetrating logic and persuasion.'

Robertson would describe him as being old-school, in that he preferred to remain aloof from his clients, always choosing to refer to 'Mr Stonehouse', resisting the temptation to be on first-name terms.

Stonehouse appeared less impressed with his prowess as an advocate than the fact that his brother was Sir Edward Du Cann, who had been a prominent Conservative politician and at that time was the chairman of Lonrho. He considered that Richard would possess a similar nous for business, which, in his view, would greatly assist in his defence. With the team assembled it seemed that Stonehouse was all set for the trial ahead.

On 22 January 1976 Stonehouse made his first appearance at the

Old Bailey where, to his dismay, he discovered that a number of the charges that had been dismissed by the magistrate had been reinstated on the court indictment. The trial was fixed for April 1976.

Stonehouse was outraged that the prosecution could revive the charges and was unable to let this betrayal rest. The Hansard reports disclosed, in the wake of the January hearing, his focus on questions regarding the reinstatement of charges by the prosecution and how many resulted in acquittals at the Crown Court.

By this time Stonehouse had ceased to hold the Labour whip. He joined the newly formed centre-right English National Party, advocating, among other things, the abolition of income tax and a devolved English parliament. His impending date with justice opened him to merciless humour from some of his parliamentary colleagues. Shortly after the preliminary hearing in January 1975 the following exchange occurred:

> *Mr Stonehouse:* On a point of order, Mr Speaker. You will be aware that this afternoon the Secretary of State for Social Services was unable to answer supplementary questions regarding the provision of National Health Service pay beds for those who come from abroad to take advantage of them.
>
> *Mr Hamilton:* From Australia.
>
> *Mr Stonehouse:* From Australia and elsewhere.
>
> *Mr Hamilton:* And from Miami Beach.
>
> *Mr Stonehouse:* The Secretary of State was unable to answer the supplementary questions because of Question No. 38 which appeared later on the Order Paper. I attempted to forgo that Question so that she could reply, but apparently that was not in

order. In view of the interest being expressed in this matter, can the Secretary of State be given an opportunity to reply to that Question now?

Mr Skinner: Further to that point of order, Mr Speaker. In considering this matter perhaps you could take into account the fact that it is quite possible that the right honourable member for Walsall, North, Mr Stonehouse, will get his pay bed soon enough.

Mr Speaker: I have had no such request. I am very dissatisfied with the progress made at Question Time today. The Chair has many responsibilities, but unfortunately they do not extend to long-windedness. I wish they did. We have had some very long questions and answers today.

* * *

Stonehouse continued to prepare his case with his team, a situation that was soon to change when, on the eve of the trial, he announced that he was dispensing with the services of his advocates, Du Cann and Robertson. A number of explanations have been presented, with Stonehouse claiming that he wished to save the legal aid fund money, while two of the junior barristers present at the time offered different views as to why this happened. Michael Grieve, QC, who was to be noting junior for Stonehouse, suggested that a conflict arose between Stonehouse and his senior counsel, which meant that they could not continue to act, as they were professionally embarrassed, an event likely to have arisen with regards to the medical defence that Stonehouse intended to pursue, whereas Ian Mayes, QC, the junior instructed by the DTI to attend the trial in order to take note of the proceedings, believed that Stonehouse had taken this step for tactical reasons, taking his cue from the Peter Hain conspiracy trial, where

Hain had successfully defended himself without a barrister. Hain's case was substantially less complicated and had elicited considerably more public sympathy as it was believed that he was the subject of a South African security services plot to frame him.

No matter the reason, the decision was to prove crucial in the course of events and his nephew, Michael, maintained that it was a fundamental mistake on Stonehouse's part: he would probably have been acquitted of many of the charges had he retained his representation.

36

THE TRIAL

The First Day, 27 April 1976

The Central Criminal Court, otherwise known as the Old Bailey, was animated on the fine spring day that would see the start of the Stonehouse trial, with banks of press photographers, television crews and journalists stationed outside the court to capture the protagonists as they entered.

Stonehouse's arrival on foot, from the direction of the Holborn Viaduct, was greeted with a shout from one of the awaiting throng, which scurried towards him, desperate to get that candid photo or telling remark below the three carved figures, the Recording Angel, Fortitude and Truth, who silently gazed down on the melee from the pediment of the portico of the main entrance. Stonehouse was engrossed in conversation with his solicitor, Michael O'Dell, and ignored the intrusive shouts as they entered.

Court 1 of the Central Criminal Court is an awe-inspiring courtroom and, to the uninitiated, and particularly a defendant, it is an intimidating and austere arena, its dark, wood-panelled walls testifying to many moments of drama; from Crippen to Christie, it has borne witness to the basest depravities to which humanity can sink.

It is not a court built for comfort, whether for judge, jury, advocate, witness or defendant. I have heard the pleas of visiting judges begging for cases to be transferred to one of the more modern and comfortable courts in the new part of the Bailey. However, as a backdrop to any courtroom drama, it is second to none.

The dock is an island of wood and brass, rising in the centre of the room, providing the defendant with a unique vantage point while giving no doubt to all as to who is the focus of proceedings. To the left of the dock is the bank of hardbacked wooden benches where the twelve members of the jury sit, and situated to the jury's left is the witness box, which is level with the judge. To the defendant's right is a bank of wooden and leather benches where the advocates, solicitors and their clerks sit, while around the dock are seats reserved for the press. In the eaves of the courtroom is the public gallery where family, friends and members of the public peer down to provide support and solace or simply to seek entertainment. Last, but certainly not least, the court clerk, stenographer – with the advent of digital recording, no longer required – and ushers seated in the well of the court squint up at the unfolding drama.

The advocates' dining room on the fifth floor would have been a fascinating place to eavesdrop that day, with the Crown's senior treasury counsel and counsel for both defendants discussing recent developments, and in particular Stonehouse's decision to sack his defence counsel.

Sheila Buckley's defence team could have only despaired as it is always the case that, as an advocate where there are co-defendants, you are not only concerned with the Crown's case against your own client but also the impact of any controversy concerning the co-defendants on your client's case. This may be damaging enough when the co-defendant is legally represented, but the prospect of dealing with any of the accused litigating in person, with all the inherent pitfalls and embarrassments, eliminated the possibility of conducting those quiet conversations with fellow counsel intended to avoid problems arising.

The waiting area outside Court 1 was filled with press, counsel, solicitors, clerks and court staff. The magnificent Edwardian dome with its painted murals lent an air of splendour to the events unfolding beneath it.

Stonehouse took his place in the dock next to Sheila Buckley, the pair dressed impeccably, as ever, Stonehouse in a dark suit with a lilac shirt and matching handkerchief, affecting tanned relaxation, masking the gut-wrenching nerves roiling beneath. Sheila, not to be outdone, was also stylishly dressed. Her style and beauty had been the cause of considerable press comment throughout the process, and she was determined not to disappoint during the trial, to play to perfection the role of the classic femme fatale in this saga. Stonehouse was stubbornly determined to undertake his own advocacy, though he was still accompanied in court by his long-suffering solicitor, Michael O'Dell, to help prepare his defence.

Prosecuting for the Crown was Michael Corkery, QC. His junior was David Tudor Price, who would later become a judge and the common sergeant of London in the 1980s.

Defending Sheila Buckley was Lord Wigoder, QC, who had, only the year before, entered the House of Lords as a Liberal peer and brought the weight of experience of having prosecuted and defended throughout his career at the bar, making him very much in demand.

His resumé was impressive and he was not averse to being in the public eye, an attribute that suited him to this case. He had represented clients including Lord Wigg, the former paymaster general, who was acquitted of kerb crawling; the artist Francis Bacon on a charge of possessing cannabis; and, in 1966, he had conducted the successful defence of Alfred Berman, one of the defendants in the Richardson gang trial.

In the immediate lead-up to this trial, he had also appeared in a number of IRA trials, including acting for a defendant in the notorious Guildford Four case. His junior was Gerald Gordon, who had conducted Sheila's defence at the committal proceedings.

Mr Justice Edward Eveleigh had been appointed as the judge. His gaunt countenance, like a bird of prey, conveyed a warning to all that he was not to be trifled with; he had built a reputation for being tough on sentencing and intolerant of tardy counsel. He also seemed to relish press attention and took particular pleasure in seeing his comments reported. In 1973, while sitting at the Inner London Crown Court, he described the late arrival of lawyers to courts where they were representing defendants on legal aid as a 'public scandal'. 'It is a scathing indictment of the profession that this should happen,' he announced. 'I wish the press would publish it in the biggest possible letters.'

These attributes no doubt led to his selection to preside over the trial. He would not be cowed or fazed by the huge press interest, nor impressed in any way by the defendant's background. Eveleigh was coincidentally an old boy of Stonehouse's school, Peter Symonds College in Winchester. He clearly had no intention of allowing Stonehouse a platform to turn the case into a political trial and, to his chagrin, Stonehouse was soon to discover that he would be given little quarter.

37

APPLICATION TO ADJOURN

27 April 1976

Most Crown Court criminal trials of any length will start at quite a sedate pace as, for the first day or so, preliminary issues, legal arguments, judge, advocate, defendant and witness availability and jury selection are resolved.

The Stonehouse case was no exception and much of that first day was spent with the judge hearing legal argument as to whether the prosecution should be allowed to reinstate five of the charges that had been dismissed by the magistrate at the committal proceedings. To his eternal credit, Richard Du Cann had remained to oppose the Crown's application on the MP's behalf. The contest lasted four hours as the two heavyweight counsel sparred in the wood-panelled arena.

After due consideration, the judge acceded to the prosecution request to have those charges added to the indictment, a decision that rather made a mockery of the six long weeks spent by the magistrate considering whether there was a case against Stonehouse in respect of each of those charges. Alarmingly, the legal exchange served to highlight the fact that Stonehouse would be hopelessly out of his depth arguing such matters on his own, but, after Eveleigh's ruling, Richard Du Cann had no option but to step back and leave his client to his own devices, wishing him well.

In all, Stonehouse faced twenty-one counts; Sheila faced six.

Once the legal argument had been completed, the judge moved to the next stage, the arraignment. Now that there were further charges on the indictment, Stonehouse and Sheila would be asked formally whether they pleaded guilty or not guilty to those counts.

Just as the judge announced that the arraignment should take place, a voice piped up from the dock. Gazing up from the papers on the bench the judge saw that Stonehouse was now standing in the dock. As the judge attempted to continue, Stonehouse interrupted him again. It was to prove an ill-advised move. The newspapers reported on the exchange that followed.

'Your Lordship, I would wish to make an application . . .'

'Before hearing any application, Mr Stonehouse, you need to be arraigned,' his lordship reiterated.

Stonehouse continued, 'Certain information came into my possession on Thursday last confirming that the prosecution in pursuing this case were in fact pursuing a largely political case.' He was referring to the transcript of the police interview he had given in Australia, which he had only received late the previous week.

The judge, momentarily stunned by this apparent impudence, stared down from his eyrie as a bird of prey might before swooping in for the kill, his countenance abruptly transforming from cordiality to open hostility as the 'P' word was mentioned.

'As a result of this information,' Stonehouse continued, 'I knew that I would have to ask my counsel to withdraw and decided to do this last Friday . . .'

'Mr Stonehouse, please sit down. This is not the time for making such an application. It can be dealt with later . . .'

Ignoring the judge, Stonehouse continued to speak over him, 'This information means that I have to ask for an adjournment, my lord.'

The judge swooped. 'You will sit down or be taken down and there you will stay until you decide to obey the direction of this court. If I am wrong, there is another court that will decide.'

'There is information that requires an adjournment . . .' Stonehouse faltered.

Anger rising, the judge struck again. 'YOU WILL SIT DOWN OR BE TAKEN DOWN. MAKE UP YOUR MIND NOW.' The force of the judge's irritation seemed to cause the wood-panelled walls to vibrate. Lowering his voice, he continued. 'You are not going to delay these proceedings,' he hissed.

Stonehouse stared back, aghast.

Collecting himself, and no doubt reminding himself that the defendant was unrepresented and required some latitude, the judge continued, 'You will be able to make your application when I have finished what I have to say. You should wait and then at that point you can speak. It will not do, you interrupting me as I am speaking.'

Suitably chastened, Stonehouse thanked the judge for his guidance.

The charges were then formally read to the defendants, both of whom confirmed that they were pleading not guilty to all counts.

'Now you can make your application, Mr Stonehouse.'

Standing up, Stonehouse began to advance his arguments. 'There are three applications I wish to make, my lord.' Half expecting an interruption, he paused before continuing. 'The first is that I seek an adjournment of two to three weeks in order for me to complete the work I need to do in light of my decision to defend myself. Giving me this time will assist in shortening the proceedings once they have started.'

As he listened, the judge made a note.

'My second application is for me to be able to tape record the trial and my third application is for me to be able to conduct my defence from the well of the court alongside the other advocates.'

There was a pause as the judge considered Stonehouse's words and his own notes. 'I must refuse your applications to adjourn and to tape the proceedings. I have ordered, and indeed you have been provided with, a table in the dock on which to place your papers and make a note and prepare your case. I will not allow any further delay in the proceedings.'

The judge then stated that he would reserve his decision on whether Stonehouse could conduct his defence from the well of the court or from the dock, later coming to the conclusion that Stonehouse should remain in the dock.

The lines were drawn, with Eveleigh determined to give Stonehouse no scope to turn proceedings into a political trial.

With these preliminary matters out of the way, the judge moved on to the job of selecting a jury. At that time, both prosecution and each defendant were entitled to object to a particular person sitting on a jury. Each defendant was entitled to up to seven peremptory challenges, meaning that if they took exception to a prospective juror they could object to them sitting on the trial. This right to peremptory challenge was reduced to three challenges per defendant in 1977 and then completely abolished in 1988.

In the days before jury nobbling and intimidation became an issue of significant concern to the authorities, the defence and prosecution would be provided with the names and addresses of the fifty or so people selected for jury service, from which a panel of twelve would be selected, in order to enable the defence and police, if they so wished, to undertake their own checks as to suitability. Stonehouse had concerned himself with where members of the jury were living in the hope of ensuring that a predominantly working-class group was appointed, which he considered would be more sympathetic to his plight. Armed with this information, he and the other parties set about selecting a jury panel from the fifty people assembled in Court 1 of the Old Bailey.

Seven men and five women were selected; Stonehouse objected to four women, the Crown objected to one person and Lord Wigoder, on behalf of Sheila, objected to five women. Stonehouse seemed happy with the choices that he had made, although he was concerned that there might not be anyone on the panel with any experience of running a business.

The jury was sworn in, each member being asked to stand and affirm that they would 'faithfully try the defendant and give a true verdict according to the evidence.'

The judge warned them that the case would last between two and three months and, with that advice and no doubt filled with excitement mixed with trepidation at the prospect of being players in the drama to come, they were stood down for the day to return for a 10.30 a.m. start the next morning.

Michael O'Dell had submitted a written request of the court to have a 'noting brief' granted on the legal aid order. This would allow for a junior barrister, normally within their first year of being called to the bar, to be instructed to take a longhand note of the proceedings. A young man, Michael Grieve, was designated, having met and become friends with Geoffrey Robertson, who had no hesitation in recommending his friend to undertake the job. Fully robed and wigged, he would sit in the well of the court, later describing how he would fill a counsel's notepad every day and hand the completed document to Stonehouse in the dock so that, as the trial progressed and the stacks of notepads grew around him, Stonehouse became almost completely hidden from view.

The scene was now set for the next part of the show.

38

THE CROWN'S CASE

28 April 1976

The phoney war was now at end and the protagonists were all assembled for the trial proper to start.

A sharp rap at the judge's door signalled his entry and the court rose in anticipation as he strode the ten or so feet from the door to his seat, all parties bowing as he sat, before following suit.

Before the jury were called into the court, Stonehouse stood up and addressed the judge. 'My lord, can I please take this opportunity to apologise for yesterday? It was entirely due to my misunderstanding and no disrespect was intended.'

The judge smiled weakly. 'Think no more about it. Things are bound to happen, particularly when you don't know all the rules. As long as you bear in mind that you will be heard and that you have to take it from me about procedure.'

Meekly, Stonehouse took his seat in the dock.

The jury entered, shuffling solemnly along their benches and, once settled, the judge addressed them gravely, warning them to ignore all that they had read and heard in newspapers, to cast out anyone else's views and not to speak of the proceedings they were engaged in with anyone.

Mr Justice Eveleigh nodded to Mr Corkery, QC, who, surrounded by a mountain of papers, rose purposefully to his feet.

A hush fell over the grand wood-panelled chamber as he gathered himself, all eyes in the packed court settling upon him, ears straining to catch his first words. Journalists' pens were at the ready to note every word that was to be uttered.

'Ladies and gentlemen of the jury,' he began conversationally, 'the judge rules on the law and the jury must listen to the evidence and arguments and apply common sense when considering that evidence. Only consider the evidence of witnesses, cast out of your minds any matters you may hear about outside of this court. What I am about to tell you will take at least two days, so please bear with me.'

A skilled advocate, he leaned languidly on some of the piles of paper in front of him, adopting an almost conspiratorial tone with the jury, delivering his speech slowly and deliberately so that they – and the press – would appreciate the significance of each carefully crafted word.

'Ignore comments in the press, in magazines, on TV, ignore reported interviews with family and friends . . .' This was a reference to the plethora of interviews that Stonehouse, his wife Barbara and others had given. 'Cast out of your minds any prejudice and do not be influenced by political beliefs. This is a crucial trial involving grave dishonesty; politics do not come into it whatsoever. Ladies and gentlemen, another aspect you must bear in mind is that you are, in fact, conducting trials in respect of both defendants. Do not lump them together. They are separate and distinct; each is entitled to a separate trial and separate consideration.'

He moved on to outline the cases against Stonehouse and Buckley in a summary that was actually to take three full days, the participants and audience hanging on every word, the only movement the scratch of pens from the bank of scribbling journalists.

'What I am about to tell you is rather like a jigsaw puzzle – most of the pieces are there, although there are some that are missing. However, ladies and gentlemen, the Crown say there are more than enough pieces to show overwhelming dishonesty.'

With a craftsman's skill, the prosecutor proceeded to construct the case against Stonehouse.

He started by setting the scene to give clues to the motivations behind Stonehouse's actions, beginning with the summer of 1969 when the cabinet minister had seen the writing on the wall for the Labour government and, in anticipation of losing the next general election, plans were put in place to set up businesses to allow him to step seamlessly into the life of a high-flying entrepreneur. Three companies were set up in 1969, with the assistance of his nephew, Michael Hayes, who was a director in some of those companies along with Stonehouse, Buckley and John McGrath, the accountant.

He described the aftermath of the general election defeat at the hands of Edward Heath's Conservatives when Stonehouse had failed to retain a place in the shadow cabinet. Relegated to the backbenches, the MP was able to slip into his role as an international businessman and entrepreneur.

Unfortunately for Stonehouse, the businesses on which he had pinned all his hopes for the future did not thrive as he had foreseen and it became clear by July 1974 that they were on the verge of collapse, bringing shame and bankruptcy down on the businessman's head. With ruin staring him in the face, he resorted, Mr Corkery suggested, to desperate measures to avoid his downfall, scheming to fake his own death and set up a new life for himself and his mistress, the second defendant, Sheila Buckley.

Having painted a picture of the turmoil Stonehouse had created, Mr Corkery set out to illustrate the steps that he took to alleviate the problems he faced.

'He made an escape plan. It was a very clever plan, very elaborate, and very ambitious. It was an utterly dishonest plan.'

The use of the word 'dishonest' was deliberately emphasised repeatedly during this address, so that it was indelibly etched on the minds of the jurors right from the outset.

Corkery paused to allow his words to hang in the air for a few moments before continuing. 'The defendant brought his substantial talents and great capacity for detail upon it.'

He set out what the prosecution asserted were the systematic and deliberate steps taken by Stonehouse to fake his death in Miami on 20 November 1974 and to set up his new life with his mistress, while also ensuring that his wife and children were not left destitute.

The prosecution, as is the custom in all criminal trials, had provided the jury with a dossier of relevant and admissible documents to help signpost the way through the trial. Referred to as the 'jury bundle', this portfolio is often contained in lever-arch files with clearly marked dividers. Before the trial, the defence is supplied with a schedule of the documents that the prosecution propose to rely upon and during the course of the trial further documents may be added to the bundle.

He described how the Crown would show that Stonehouse had taken deliberate and elaborate steps to perpetrate the fraud by creating the two false identities of Markham and Mildoon with the intention of faking his own death so that his wife could claim on large insurance policies that he had taken out in the summer of 1974.

He recounted how Stonehouse had procured loans through his various businesses, acquiring almost £300,000 by unscrupulously doctoring and creating documents, citing in particular the minutes of a purported EPACS directors' meetings in which it was erroneously stated that McGrath and Hayes were present to authorise the borrowing. 'People are put down as being present at meetings when they never were and, like so many documents in this case concerned with Mr Stonehouse, they are bogus, false, spurious, dishonest.'

The jury were directed to a schedule in their lever-arch file. That schedule referred to the twenty or so company bank and credit card accounts along with a list of Stonehouse's personal bank guarantees. 'You will note that the third column shows the state of Mr Stonehouse's accounts on 20 November 1974.'

The jurors huddled over their files, their eyes scanning the long, closely typed list until they settled on that fateful date.

Reading the long list of overdrawn accounts, Mr Corkery explained. 'You will see that the total at the bottom is £375,000. In other words, Mr Stonehouse, on the day he pretended to die, owed these particular banks and credit card companies £375,000 [roughly £3.7 million today].'

Corkery went on to outline how Stonehouse had then laundered the money through various channels, funnelling it into the numerous accounts held in the names of Markham and Mildoon. 'This attention to detail shows the devious ingenuity of Mr Stonehouse in his determination to make sure his tracks were well and truly covered so nothing could lead along that winding track to show Mr Stonehouse still existed.'

Next, he guided the jury's attention to the accused's disappearance, recounting how Stonehouse had undertaken a dummy run in the United States at the beginning of November 1974, using an American Express card in the name of Markham. He then chronicled the fateful days of 19 and 20 November 1974, when Stonehouse had staged his drowning, by detailing the business meeting in Miami that he and a co-director, James Charlton, from London Capital Securities, had attended with officials from the Miami bank; the crucial arrangement to meet Mr Charlton in the hotel bar at seven in the evening of 20 November, only for him not to show; and the ominous discovery of his discarded clothes at the beach kiosk.

Of the police search of Stonehouse's hotel room, Corkery remarked, 'Once more he showed his great attention to detail. He had left behind everything a man going swimming would leave behind.' His passport, watch, money and clothes were found in the room.

From there, he described Stonehouse's journey to Melbourne, via San Francisco and Hawaii, specifying that he had stayed in Honolulu for four days from where he had telephoned Sheila on two occasions. He clearly implied that Sheila must have been complicit, given that the story of her lover's disappearance was very much in the news.

Relentlessly, Corkery moved on to events as they unfolded in Melbourne after Stonehouse touched down there on 27 November 1974, cataloguing the numerous bank accounts, no fewer than twenty-seven, that were opened in the names of Mildoon and Markham, and describing the life that he set up before coordinating the furtive rendezvous with Sheila in Copenhagen. This was presented as a litany of calculated manoeuvres that the prosecution maintained were the deeds of a man in full control of his faculties, intent upon creating for himself a new and comfortable life on the other side of the world, while abandoning all his responsibilities at home.

With dispassion, Corkery depicted how the house of cards constructed by Stonehouse had collapsed, thanks to the eagle-eyed bank employee whose suspicion had alerted the Melbourne police, the drama of the surveillance and the arrest adding a final twist to the tale.

Almost as an afterthought, Corkery moved on to the charges on the indictment related to Stonehouse's use of the credit cards that he held in his own name, contrasting how they had ordinarily been little used, except in the weeks immediately before his disappearance when he had indulged in a spending spree. 'He made up his mind to go and he decided quite dishonestly to have a good time at the expense of the credit card companies,' was Corkery's conclusion.

He reported how Stonehouse had applied for American Express and Diners Club cards in the name of Markham, as a requirement for which American Express wrote to the business address for Markham asking for a reference, receiving in reply a recommendation signed S. R. Alexander which, Mr Corkery alleged, was another of Stonehouse's many forgeries. 'So far there is Mr Stonehouse sending off his own reference recommending credit; as a result of that false information, they granted him an American Express Card.'

Having completed his summary of the case against Stonehouse he turned his attention to co-defendant Sheila Buckley who faced six charges, setting out that the aim of the prosecution was to show that she had knowledge of the frauds they claimed had been perpetrated by Stonehouse, and that she had passively and actively engaged in assisting him in his enterprise.

'Mrs Buckley is a very astute lady who clearly knew a great deal and was clearly a participant,' he declared to the court, emphasising each word with a staccato stab of a finger. He stated that there was substantial evidence to demonstrate her knowledge and willingness to be a partner in this operation, 'intending clearly to benefit as his new wife, either as Mrs Markham or Mildoon.'

To this end, he referred to her role in the companies to which she had been signed up as a director, asserting that she had tacitly been involved in Stonehouse's manipulation of those firms' finances to their mutual benefit.

Part of the evidence suggesting her participation was contained in the series of 'Dear Dums' partially coded letters she had written to Stonehouse. One of these was certainly sent on the apparently carefree shopping trip to Swindon that Sheila had taken with Patti.

Copies of the letters had been supplied to the jury in the lever-arched files and they were able to follow as the prosecutor read aloud several excerpts to demonstrate how Sheila must have known of the fraud and assisted Stonehouse in its execution.

The letters had been deeply personal and extracts had previously been salaciously published by the newspapers, but the conscientious Corkery kept on point and quoted only those sections that were relevant to his case, although he did ask the jury to consider their general contents in order to gain a flavour of the nature of the relationship between Stonehouse and Buckley and how much of a willing accomplice she was. In them she referred to him as 'my boyfriend' and described the anguish that his 'drowning' had caused, in particular

275

lamenting the scrutiny she had been subjected to by 'Mr Fuzz', her codename for the police, and the press.

Quoting from Sheila's fourth letter to Stonehouse, Corkery recited, 'I'm afraid to say that yours truly was on the front page of two thingies yesterday – I am labelled as the other w.'

In another fragment, Sheila's words were delivered by Corkery describing how 'B' – Barbara Stonehouse – had been suspected of committing murder because of the five insurance policies Stonehouse had taken out to benefit her in the event of his death, and that 'S' – Sheila – promised 'to retrieve if she is accused'.

Her letter reproached Stonehouse for having taken out the four additional policies to the original, fretting that he had 'overdone it' and mentioned 'the male who was very terribly intelligent and this was front rank stuff now'. This, the prosecutor attested, was a poorly veiled reference to Stonehouse and the fact that the story had hit the front pages of the newspapers.

Another extract he chose to present was a passage in which Sheila wrote about 'Mr Royal', a reference to the Royal Insurance Company with whom he had taken out one of the insurance policies. 'Oh why did he have to do it, what a twerp. I am much wiser than him,' she scolded. 'I could almost hate him for perhaps ruining our lives.'

Each of these selections supported the Crown's contention that Sheila was a knowing and willing participant in the duplicity.

At the end of three riveting yet arduous days, the prosecution opening was concluded, bringing to an end the first week of the trial. The next task for them was to produce the evidence and prove the defendants' guilt.

39

THE OPENING SALVOS

4 May 1976

Week two of the trial would be another short week, punctuated by a bank holiday. The protagonists reassembled in court on Tuesday 4 May, when the prosecution were due to call their first witnesses. Albert Stokes was a chartered accountant who had been involved in auditing the accounts of the British Bangladesh Trust and his evidence described how the bank had operated in the first year, confirming that all loans that had been extended had been repaid in that year and that the accounts, as he put it, were 'tidy'. However, there were further loans made in the second year about which the bookkeeper had some doubts and which had caused the auditors to put a qualifying note on the year-end accounts.

Stokes told the court that this had clearly irked Stonehouse, leading to an agitated conversation between the two men. 'I think the phrase he used was a "baby bank" and he accused me, as auditor, of strangulation of a bank which would remain on my conscience for the rest of my life.'

The accountant had expressed his doubts to the directors of the trustworthiness of the borrowers to which their reply, to his disquiet, was that they were satisfied that they were financially stable.

Stokes described how one of the loans was made to Finsec Holdings Limited, a subsidiary of the bank, the recipient of which was a person by the name of Ms S. Black which, as Stokes informed the jury, was the maiden name of Mrs Buckley. He had telephoned Finsec and he told the court that Mrs Buckley had answered the phone. He said that when he asked for Ms Black, Mrs Buckley had paused and then said that there was no one there by that name.

Once the Crown had completed their examination in chief it was the turn of the defence to cross-examine the witness. As Stonehouse was the first named on the indictment, he was to begin, asking his questions from his place in the dock.

'Mr Stokes, in asking you questions I shall refer to myself as Mr Stonehouse in order to avoid using the first person in any of my questions. This should allow you to answer the questions objectively and without confusion as to whom I may mean.' Stokes nodded his understanding. 'There is a community of feeling between accountants who join the association. It is like belonging to the same club, they understand the way that one another think – is that not correct?'

'Yes,' replied Stokes.

'Is it correct that, over the years, there have been changing opinions among accountants on such matters as discount, cash flow and inflated values?'

'Yes.'

'And that acceptable accountancy practice in 1972 would have been considered inappropriate in 1952?'

'Yes,' nodded Stokes.

Suitably encouraged, Stonehouse went on, 'It is also the case that accountants change their views on the way they undertake their audits according to changes in the economic environment?'

'Audits generally follow the same principles but changing economic climates have to be taken into account when audits are done,' agreed Stokes.

Stonehouse was growing more assured with every question he was asking and seemed to be enjoying the experience, tipping over into overconfidence, which resulted in a further clash with the judge. When the judge followed up one of Stonehouse's questions with one of his own, the MP interrupted him, provoking another spark of irritation.

'When I begin to speak it is better for you to stop for a second, because it will help you,' the judge reprimanded him.

Unperturbed, Stonehouse moved on to another topic. 'I am going to ask you about the collapse of a secondary bank, London and Counties Securities. Do you recall this?'

'Yes, I do.'

'Can you recall that the collapse of this bank was a symptom of what was going on in the market?'

'I don't recall that,' answered Stokes.

Stonehouse was manoeuvring his cross examination to focus on political issues that had led to the collapse of a number of secondary banks, one of which was his own bank, the British Bangladesh Trust. In attempting to establish that these banks had in fact collapsed because of the government's poor handling of the economy, perpetuating the secondary-bank crisis, he hoped to show that it was not fraud on his or anyone else's part that had caused the collapse of his bank but the incompetence of Edward Heath's Conservative government, and that his prosecution on this and the other charges was a conspiracy by the authorities to discredit him and lay the blame at his door.

'The financial correspondents have been suggesting that, while the performance of London and Counties Capital would soon be forgotten, it would be seen that the trouble lay deeply embedded in the political and monetary climate of that time?'

'Yes, I agree.'

Stonehouse saw his chance and pursued the line of questioning further, citing the financial difficulties of many companies during 1973 and 1974 and the near-collapse of the Crown Agents as a result of the secondary banks' collapse, troubles which had embroiled other MPs, such as Jeremy Thorpe, who were involved in the City at that time.

Stokes agreed that it was necessary for the government to step in to restore the confidence of overseas investors in the Crown Agents.

'Is it not true that, unless the government had been prepared to come in with an £85 million loan, the Crown Agents and all that it entailed would have gone bust?'

'I think that was possible,' replied Stokes.

'Are you aware of the government's so called "lifeboat committee"?'

'I am.'

'Is it true that several banking organisations, including the Bank of England, had been trying to step in to shore up the secondary banks, to shore them up with £200 million fund to save depositors?'

'Yes, it was,' responded Stokes.

'Are you aware that a large number of secondary banks received support loans?' Stonehouse pressed.

'Yes, I am aware of that but even they eventually collapsed.'

'Do you know how much support my company had received from the lifeboat committee?'

'To my knowledge . . . none,' replied Stokes.

Stokes had been in the witness box most of the day and it was at this point that the judge took pity upon him and the jury and adjourned proceedings. With the usual warnings not to discuss the case with anyone, the witness and jurors wearily withdrew.

Stonehouse conceded in his book *My Trial* that he nervously scanned the newspapers for their reactions and was encouraged and flattered by the press's view of his performance. 'Stonehouse grills Crown witness,' trumpeted one headline.

Day two of the Stokes cross examination took on a far more aggressive tone as Stonehouse challenged the accountant about his crude investigative work.

'Why should you set yourself up and play amateur detective when the simple thing would have been to ask a director or official, "Is it not true that Miss S Black and Mrs Buckley are one and the same?"'

'I chose to make my own investigations in my own way,' Stokes responded defensively.

'That's humbug,' retorted Stonehouse.

The cross-examination continued for the rest of the day, with Lord Wigoder asking more limited questions on Sheila Buckley's behalf, before a rather relieved witness left the court.

Stonehouse had, in his own way, been quite effective, even managing to play the political trial card, but it has to be conceded that he had so far dealt with just one witness and would face a considerable number before the matter could be laid to rest.

It was now the eighth day of the trial. Sheila had not been able to attend as a result of a very painful cricked neck. However, after the excuses had been made on her behalf by her counsel, the trial continued. Stonehouse had tried the patience of the judge so there was some relief that the next few witnesses were not questioned so laboriously.

Gerald Hastings, Stonehouse's old RAF chum, described the events leading to his purchase of £12,000 worth of shares in Stonehouse's bank, London Capital Securities and the Bangladesh 'Shangri-La Project'. He was followed by a freelance publicity consultant, Edward Bedford, who dealt with further issues regarding shares in Stonehouse's companies. The court also heard from Susan Hill, the friend of one of Stonehouse's daughters, who described how he had persuaded her to become involved in the purchase of £20,000 worth of shares.

There inevitably comes a time in any trial when, in order to save time, expense and everyone's patience, the prosecution and defence agree certain facts without the necessity of calling a witness or reading a statement. This is normally drafted into a formal document and reduced to a paragraph or two of facts that are then read to the judge and jury, forming a collection of evidence that is treated with equal weight as all the other testimony that the court hears.

The prosecution's case asserted that Stonehouse required birth certificates and passports to pursue his plan to adopt a new identity in Australia after his faked death in Miami, thereby demonstrating forethought and long-term planning. It was an unarguable fact that Stonehouse had obtained these documents. Was it necessary to call witnesses, including the widows of the deceased Markham and Mildoon? Even Stonehouse realised that having the wronged widows put through the trauma of giving evidence before the court would not help his case.

Having dispensed with his advocates, Stonehouse had rashly taken the view that he would fight all the charges levelled at him, including two charges relating of 'uttering forged applications for birth certificates of Mildoon and Markham' and 'uttering a forged application for a passport in the name of Markham'. It was a tactical error. His counsel would have advised him simply to admit his guilt and focus on the charges he could defend.

Whether it was Corkery's persuasive skills or otherwise, an agreement was reached with Stonehouse for some admissions to be made and so on 13 May a short document was read to the jury confirming facts about the birth certificates and false passport application. The three death certificates of Mildoon, Markham and McBride, and the evidence to show that Stonehouse had falsely used the name of Neil McBride to certify the photograph accompanying his application for a passport in the name of Markham, were then shown to the jury.

Despite this, Stonehouse obstinately retorted, 'The facts in these admissions are quite correct, but they are irrelevant to the charges.'

40

RELATIVE VALUES

11 May 1976

Michael had travelled up from his home in Hampshire, passing the tense train journey to Waterloo by trying alternately to distract himself by studying the countryside as the train rushed by or with the newspaper spread on his lap – no doubt attempting to anticipate how the day would unfold, what his uncle might have in store for him. The family had noted that Michael had been withdrawn and distracted and while he had busied himself with work and settling into the family's new home, his loss of appetite, lack of sleep and poor concentration were all tell-tale signs. He had lost weight and had suffered Patti's wrath when he had absentmindedly left his infant son out in the early spring sun while gardening. Even the sight of his beloved Southampton winning the FA Cup final was but momentary respite from worry.

His anger with his uncle had not yet subsided in the wake of his own world having been turned upside down. His career been put in doubt while he was doing his best to provide for his wife and five children and to keep up with the mortgage payments. Part of his resentment towards his uncle was that he felt sure that Stonehouse was perfectly oblivious to the trauma he had unleashed.

Arriving at Waterloo, Michael took a cab across Waterloo Bridge and along the Strand to the Old Bailey, asking the taxi driver to drop him at the end of the road, having caught sight of the crowd of photographers. As he stalked towards the court he was surrounded, the click and whirring of the cameras punctuating the questions fired at him about his thoughts about the coming day. Michael remained silent but, remembering his wife's advice, gave them a cheery wave and smile.

Having run the gauntlet of the press, he should have been relieved to slip into the relative quiet of the court building, but would have felt the knot of tension in his shoulders tighten as he awaited his turn in its precincts. A smoker, he would have sought the solace of an Embassy Regal as he paced the bare floor, drawing hard on the cigarette, seeking comfort it could not provide.

A court usher regularly popped his head round the door to check on him, his raised eyebrows giving the appearance each time of someone surprised to find that Michael was still there as the tension in the air grew as thick as the cloud of cigarette smoke.

Meanwhile in Court 1, Corkery had completed the admissions and exhibits relating to the passports and proceeded to call John Harris, a cousin of Stonehouse, whose evidence proved to be relatively minor and uncontroversial, doing no more than simply confirm that he, his wife and two daughters had been furnished with a hundred £10 shares each in the British Bangladesh Trust and telling the court that, in early 1973, Stonehouse had asked him if he would become a share nominee and hold shares worth £15,000. He had agreed after assurances had been received that he would not be financially liable, declaring that Stonehouse told him the shares would be guaranteed by EPACS. This, the prosecution pronounced, was yet another family member or friend used by Stonehouse to achieve his dishonest aims.

Michael's apprehension would have reached its crescendo when the usher finally asked him to come to court. Having waited all morning, he was about to come face to face with his uncle.

Resolutely, he followed the usher into Court 1, trying not to be intimidated by the austere magnificence of the chamber nor the dozens of eyes that followed his progress as he took his place as directed, perching in the witness box overlooking the court.

He could not have helped but glance around the courtroom before taking the oath, his attention momentarily resting on the two figures in the dock, no doubt reflecting uneasily that this was the first time he had seen them in the flesh since October the previous year at Horseferry Road Magistrates' Court, and it would be the first time that he had spoken to his uncle directly in just under two years.

Corkery led Michael through much of the evidence in chief. Michael confirmed that he was a solicitor practising in Winchester, having qualified in 1973, and that, while he was still an articled clerk – a trainee solicitor – with a firm of solicitors in Sunderland, he had visited Stonehouse at his country residence near Andover in Hampshire in December 1969 where Stonehouse had told him that it was unlikely that Labour would win the next general election and that he needed to prepare for a life outside government. Stonehouse had ambitions to start his own business empire and explained that Michael could assist him in achieving this aspiration.

Michael described Stonehouse's instructions to form three companies: Export Services and Consultancy Services, Connoisseurs of Claret, and Systems and Consultancy Services; all three were incorporated in March 1970 for £100 each. He confirmed that Stonehouse had instructed that he, Sheila and a third individual named Rainbird should be the named directors, although it remained 'on the shelf' until June 1970 when Labour lost the general election, at which point his uncle had been appointed director and taken control of the three companies.

Corkery then asked Michael to consider some documents he had placed before him in the witness box, which transpired to be the minutes of company meetings showing that Michael had been present. Without hesitation, Michael stated that he had not been at those meetings. Asked whether he had been present at an EPACS meeting where a resolution had been passed by the board for a payment of £2,000 to be made to Stonehouse or a similar meeting a year later where another was passed for a further payment of £10,000 to be made to Stonehouse, he firmly declared that he had not. Michael also confirmed that he had not seen the minutes until after Stonehouse's disappearance in November 1974, when he had started to look into his affairs.

The prosecutor moved on to Stonehouse's disappearance and Michael recounted how he had received instructions from Barbara to act as the family's solicitor to resolve Stonehouse's affairs, attending the offices in Dover Street in this capacity. To his alarm, he had discovered the manufactured directors' minutes, the unauthorised bank loans and that large sums of money had been paid into various private accounts, reluctantly but inexorably forming the view that the companies were insolvent, compelling him to bring in the liquidators to wind up the businesses. He was also tasked with dealing with the four life insurance policies taken out for the benefit of Barbara and his children, confirming that he had written letters on behalf of the family to the companies concerned advising of Stonehouse's death.

Finishing his line of questioning, Corkery thanked Michael and took a seat, opening the floor for Stonehouse to cross-examine his nephew. The courtroom fell deathly silent as he rose in the dock, gathering himself. Michael looked across the court, outwardly displaying an impassive demeanour to mask his inward agitation.

His uncle fixed him with a piercing stare, intently scrutinising the witness for any chink in the armour he had donned during the examination in chief.

Stonehouse no doubt fondly imagined that the witness before him was the same malleable young man to whom he had peddled his heady dreams and aspirations in those exhilarating days of the 1960s and early 1970s: an unwise assumption, given what had followed. Reinforced by his inflated ego, Stonehouse was convinced that he could intimidate his nephew into accepting the points he wished to impress upon the jury.

But Michael was not that same young, impressionable man. In the years since, Michael had been abandoned by the person who stood before him now, forced to clear up the shambles created by his uncle's disappearance, betrayed by a man he had once admired.

Each advocate adopts their own style and approach to questioning a witness, some opening with soft questions that they are sure they will agree with, gently conditioning them to eventually concur with them on more contentious issues. Others will immediately go for the jugular and challenge, often aggressively, the witness with their client's case. Whatever the individual approach, the golden rule for all advocates is rarely, if ever, to ask a question to which they do not already know the answer.

Stonehouse immediately launched into his cross-examination in machine-gun-like fashion. The rat-tat-tat of questions shot across the courtroom, intending to wound, barely waiting for the witness to finish answering the preceding question. Again the newspapers reported the exchange verbatim.

'Did you try to consult with Mr Stonehouse before deciding to wind up the companies?' he barked.

'As far as we could see, the major reason the company was insolvent was that Stonehouse had withdrawn more money from the company than was available in the company for anyone to take out,' Michael retorted.

'Did you ask Mr Stonehouse for an explanation?' Stonehouse's voice rose in mock anger.

'Mr Stonehouse wasn't there to ask,' Michael snapped back. 'We recommended to the shareholders that the companies should be voluntarily wound up. Matters were put in the hands of liquidators . . . What happened after that was a matter entirely for them.'

'In other words, you passed the buck to a firm of liquidators who are specialists in the job of liquidation?' Stonehouse shot back testily.

'I cannot agree with your suggestion of passing the buck.' Michael seethed, annoyed to have allowed his temper to be provoked and hearing his voice rise in anger. Attempting in vain to get his temper under control, he spat his fury towards the figure in the dock. 'Clearly there was no possibility of the companies' ever being able to trade properly or profitably. There was no business. There were considerable debts including one of £40,000 to a clearing bank. It was your financial manipulation which resulted in the disappearance of considerable funds from the company.'

Oblivious to the assembled throng, the men's eyes locked in rage, a reflection of a deeper desire to inflict some physical retribution on each other. Shaking himself from the momentary paralysis brought on by the verbal altercation, the judge took advantage of the lull in hostilities. With quiet diplomacy he suggested that that was a convenient point to conclude the day's proceedings. He instructed the jury to retire and to return the following morning, with the admonition not to discuss the case with anyone. After the last juror had left, the judge turned to Michael and asked him to step out of court, directing him to return the next day with the same instructions.

12 May 1976

Court 1 simmered with eager anticipation at the prospect of uncle and nephew crossing swords again, the dramatic conclusion of the previous day's proceedings having whetted the newspapers' appetites. The press gallery was crammed full of rapt journalists. With the judge, jury and protagonists ensconced, Michael took his place in the witness box.

The focus of Stonehouse's cross-examination would be on the life insurance policies he had taken out to support his wife, Barbara, and their teenage son, their two daughters already being financially independent, pursuing their own careers in London.

Michael had been instructed, as the family's solicitor, to resolve his uncle's affairs after his disappearance and it was his conduct in this matter that formed the course of Stonehouse's cross-examination. As Michael explained, no claims had been envisaged by Barbara in the immediate aftermath of Stonehouse's disappearance in November 1974 because there was no proof of his death.

It was in pursuing this line of questioning that Stonehouse was again to bring about conflict, not with Michael, as everyone had anticipated, but with the judge. Stonehouse wanted to establish that there had been no fraud perpetuated as no steps had been taken to lodge claims against the insurance policies.

Initially, Stonehouse's cross-examination concerned letters Michael had written. 'You wrote to the Yorkshire Life Insurance Company on behalf of Mrs Stonehouse, advising them that her husband had taken out a life-insurance policy and that you were the instructed solicitors. You did this because a newspaper article had reported this?'

'Yes, I did so,' responded Michael.

Stonehouse continued, 'The letter said that the family could not claim.' He quoted aloud from the letter, '"The position was that until we had some form of proof of Mr Stonehouse's death we would not be able to submit a claim." This was written only some two weeks after Mr Stonehouse's disappearance?'

'Yes, that is the case.'

'And the only reason you had written to the insurance companies was to advise that you were acting on behalf of Mrs Stonehouse and that the only reason you had done this was because the newspapers had reported that Mr Stonehouse had insured his life for £119,000 shortly before his disappearance?'

'Yes, that is correct.'

Stonehouse produced a hefty sheaf of newspaper articles and began to read a number of extracts referring to the insurance policies, the

Czech spy allegations, that he was the victim of the mafia hit and the disappearance of £1 million from a Bangladesh charity.

Cutting Stonehouse short, Justice Eveleigh turned abruptly to Michael in an attempt to short-circuit the line of questioning. 'Did you become aware of a large number of newspaper items detrimental to the reputation of Mr Stonehouse, both in financial affairs and insofar as his loyalty to the country were concerned?'

'I was aware, my lord.'

Failing to recognise the judicial hint, Stonehouse recommenced his questioning. He began to read yet another newspaper report to Michael.

The judge's patience snapped. He raised his voice as he wagged a talon-like finger at Stonehouse. 'I hope you're not seeking to try me. Let me make that quite clear to you.'

A dangerous glint in his eye, the exasperated judge asked the jury to retire, watching grimly as they filed out, intrigued by what was about to happen in their absence. Once they had left, he told Michael to leave the court and wait to be recalled.

Turning to Stonehouse, the judge admonished him, 'I am not going to allow you to read these reports in order to get before the jury evidence that is not being proved in this case.' He waited a beat to ensure Stonehouse was following. 'I have allowed you a good deal of latitude and I am not going to allow you to prove facts other than in the proper way. It is not my personal inclination, it is just that it is not allowed. If you wish to put evidence before the jury as to what was in Mrs Stonehouse's mind, you should call her as a witness.'

Having satisfied himself that he had made his point understood, he summoned Michael, who resumed his place in the witness box, the jury following shortly afterwards.

Stonehouse moved on to another line of questioning, but the opportunity to highlight the significant issues he had sought to elicit from Michael had been lost and, almost before the witness realised it, Stonehouse had finished and taken his seat. To Michael's relief the questioning from Sheila's legal team was short and to the point. Before long his ordeal was over and he was homeward bound.

Up until Michael's cross-examination, Stonehouse had, according to the newspapers, performed beyond expectation, with some reports referring to him as 'Stonehouse, QC'. However, his handling of Michael's evidence had been horribly damaging. He conceded in his own book that this had been the turning point in the case against him.

41

LONG, HOT SUMMER

May–June 1976

Following Michael, the court heard the evidence of Alan Le Fort, the accountant who had been employed by Stonehouse in 1972 and had been responsible for managing the accounts of Global Index, Connoisseurs of Claret and EPACS.

Le Fort told the court of his concerns regarding the money drawn out of EPACS by Mr Stonehouse and the transfer of funds between the companies. He described how unhappy he was that loans received by the companies were used to pay Stonehouse's consultancy fees. This, he told the court, had resulted in his resignation.

However, under cross-examination he had to concede that various companies had consulted Stonehouse personally and paid him between £3,000 and £13,000, also confirming that Stonehouse could choose to receive the money personally or, as he had done, have his fees paid into EPACS.

Le Fort further admitted that Stonehouse had used his own money to keep the British Bangladesh Trust afloat when the secondary-banking crisis had hit the United Kingdom in the early 1970s: 'There were occasions when people would come into the bank saying they wanted to withdraw their deposits. There was a crisis because the bank did not have the money to pay and Mr Stonehouse was contacted. He would withdraw his own personal money to enable the bank to meet those commitments.'

He also recalled other occasions when Stonehouse helped the bank with funds. The British Bangladesh Trust wanted to avoid showing the loss on its share portfolio in the end-of-year accounts.

The prosecution's junior counsel, David Tudor Price, re-examined Le Fort, and this was when the accountant recalled that, in regular morning meetings, Stonehouse would direct him where money should be moved between thirty-five to forty accounts, going on to say that by 1973, four of Stonehouse's companies were suffering solvency problems.

The end of that third week saw two further significant events. A female juror had fallen ill and had to be discharged so the jury was now down to eleven. The second was that Stonehouse had decided, after reviewing all the evidence, that out of the hundred witnesses tendered by the prosecution, he required fifty of them to be called so he could cross-examine them with the net effect that the time estimate for the trial would be extended from three to five months. The trial was already predicted to cost £250,000 (£1.7 million today), a figure that would increase considerably as a result – another casualty of having a litigant in person.

The summer of 1976 was a long, hot one. The lack of air-conditioning in the old wood-panelled court was taking its toll on the participants, causing tempers and nerves to wear thin and creating increasing conflict between Stonehouse and the judge. Michael Grieve, Stonehouse's noting junior, recalled how he would get off the morning tube at St Paul's, perspiration rolling down his back, shirt clinging to his skin with no prospect of respite from the heat in that baking courtroom.

Stonehouse's cross-examination of Michael had revealed very blatantly that he was hopelessly out of his depth, his continual attempts to raise correspondence or newspaper articles to attack the prosecution case increasing Eveleigh's ire and rendering Stonehouse irritated and frustrated with the judge's interference.

On 18 May the newspapers reported a Stonehouse meltdown as he cross-examined his former personal assistant, Philip Bingham, about correspondence that had arrived at his office in Dover Street.

In the midst of questioning Bingham, Stonehouse suddenly disappeared from view as he bent down in the dock. He reappeared hoisting two carboard boxes and a bulging plastic bag, balancing them precariously on the brass rails of the dock.

'This is what I am up against,' he wailed to the judge. 'These people threw them out on the street without any regard to my interest. This is the sort of thing going on and will be revealed in your court, my lord.' He hurried to continue before he could be interrupted. 'This correspondence was thrown out any old how. No one had any regard for my interest. They were so influenced by all the adverse press publicity they did not bother with me at all.'

The piteous figure in the dock slumped, seemingly overcome by the insurmountable nature of his task. 'I'm too upset to go on, my lord.'

The judge informed him that he was not going to permit an adjournment. 'No one can blame you for being emotional, but you won't listen to advice. I will now show you the way to do it.'

'I do feel very emotional,' blurted Stonehouse.

'I must make things clear to the jury,' continued the judge. 'Their heads must split if you go through things in minute detail like those letters for they will say, like me, "Where does this all fit in?"'

'I don't know if the stuff on the dock is similar to the material put outside Mr Stonehouse's office,' interjected the witness. 'Any letters received were put inside the office. I had lost faith in Mr Stonehouse after he disappeared, but this in no way made me fail in my duties.'

The next day, Stonehouse continued to cross-examine Bingham with the purpose of casting his own activities with the bank in a purely altruistic light, and rebutting the prosecution's case that he had acted fraudulently.

'Is it true that Mr Stonehouse was personally idealistically involved in the cause of Bangladesh?'

'I believe he was, when it gained its independence,' responded Bingham.

'Did you believe that he genuinely thought that the bank would form a bridge between British financial interests and Bangladesh?'

'That was the prospectus.'

'The position was that Mr Stonehouse responded to the invitation of Bengalis to assist them in establishing a new institution which would assist the Bangladeshi community?'

'I believe that bank was formed to do that.'

'Did Mr Stonehouse insist that he should be unpaid as the bank's chairman because he wanted the work he was doing for the bank to be idealistically interpreted?'

'No, I would not put it like that. I know that he was unpaid. But I don't know why.'

'Are you aware of allegations made in the *Sunday Times* by a reporter called Anthony Mascheravas?'

Sensing that Stonehouse was yet again about to read newspaper articles to the witness and digress into irrelevant areas, the judge interrupted. 'What is the purpose of this questioning, Mr Stonehouse?'

On this occasion, Stonehouse was ready for him. 'Mr Mascheravas is a Pakistani agent trying to undermine my position, as I had become a citizen of Bangladesh, to which Pakistan is violently opposed.' He continued confidently, 'This was part of the campaign by Pakistan to undermine Mr Stonehouse and the *Sunday Times* fell for it at that time by printing the inaccurate allegations that had been fostered by Mr Mascheravas.'

'I remember Mr Stonehouse telling me something of this nature back in 1972,' nodded Bingham.

'It was the case that these unfounded allegations in the *Sunday*

Times had led to a Department of Trade investigation which had sent shivers down the spines of the British Bangladesh Trust?'

'Yes, there had been an investigation by the Department of Trade.'

'And it was the case that Mr Stonehouse had been subjected to harassment, tension and persecution by Scotland Yard over these allegations? Did it not become clear that Scotland Yard was conducting a campaign of intimidation to various Bengali shareholders, trying to get them to make statements?'

'Yes, prospective customers had been frightened off because of approaches by a Fraud Squad detective,' Bingham agreed. 'The bank did not develop in 1973 as fast as officials had hoped.'

After a night's rest, Bingham returned to the court to complete his testimony at a session during which Stonehouse again suffered the judge's ire when asking another inadmissible question.

Interrupting the MP in full flow had elicited a look from him that only added fuel to the flames.

'The licence you have been given in this trial exceeds what I have ever in my experience known in any court of law. I simply tell you that because of the look on your face. Be careful, because I shall insist on you being 100 per cent within the rules of procedure.'

Unabashed, Stonehouse continued his questioning of the witness. 'It's correct that financial inducements have been paid by Britons to promote trade in Bangladesh?'

'I do not know that, sir. I have read in the newspapers that that is common practice in some countries.'

No doubt Bingham was delighted to get out of the witness box, soon to be replaced by another personal assistant of Stonehouse, Philip Gay, who confirmed that he had joined Stonehouse after leaving the army and that he had later become a director of some of his companies.

The prosecutor quizzed him about an entry that had been made in the minute book for EPACS. 'Can I refer you to one of the minutes dated October 3rd? You will see that there is a minute of a resolution that there should be overdraft facilities for £10,000 with the company's bankers, Lloyds Bank?'

'Yes, I see.'

'The minute shows that you were present.'

'I was not present,' he said firmly.

'There is another entry in the book dated November 4th. Do you see that?'

'Yes.'

'It states that there was a meeting of directors and that you were authorised to sign the companies' bank accounts.'

'There was never any such meeting.'

Like Bingham before him, Gay found himself having to return the next day.

'How did Mr Stonehouse's disappearance make you feel?'

'I was very upset and distressed by the press reports.'

'How did you feel when he reappeared?'

'I was shocked when I realised that he had made a conscious decision to disappear.'

Stonehouse stood to cross-examine him. 'Have you had the opportunity to obtain an explanation from Mr Stonehouse?'

'No. I've never had any explanation of these bizarre occurrences and I have never sought one.'

'Can you explain why the mail from my offices in Dover Street was not sent on to me after my reappearance?'

'I didn't send the mail on as I felt some antagonism towards Mr Stonehouse, who had brought matters upon his own head.'

Taken aback, Stonehouse responded defensively, 'Do you think that was a fair way of dealing with Mr Stonehouse?'

'Yes. I felt Mr Stonehouse had walked out or opted out.'

Stonehouse felt it best to turn to another topic. 'Had you been responsible to convey the news of Mr Stonehouse's disappearance to Mrs Stonehouse?'

'I had been. I told her that I had spoken to Mr Charlton on the telephone in Miami and that he told me that Mr Stonehouse had disappeared, presumably while swimming. Mrs Stonehouse broke down at this point, assuming that her husband was dead. I subsequently went to Miami and spoke to the police about the disappearance and their investigations,' he added.

Stonehouse was keen to expose the prejudice whipped up by the press and politicians while he was still in Australia with no opportunity to resolve the problems that had been publicly broadcast with his disappearance. Whether this impressed the jury was a moot point.

42

LIQUIDATION AND INSURANCE

24 May 1976

James Charlton was a former secretary of the British Aircraft Corporation and had been a non-executive director of London Capital Securities. He was called by the prosecution to describe the events that led up to his former business partner's disappearance from Miami Beach on 20 November 1974.

He was soon followed by Michael Francis, confirming that he was instructed to administer the liquidation of EPACS in February 1975. He added further nails in Stonehouse's coffin with the revelation that he had discovered unrealised assets in the company, firstly £34,300 due from Stonehouse on a loan account and secondly $12,500 that Stonehouse had received from the Garrett Corporation, which had not been recorded in the company books.

Stonehouse commenced his cross-examination of Francis by taking him through various company documents and who had been responsible for them, a line of questioning clearly of importance to the defendant. However, the judge, who was by this stage barely able to hide his irritation and frustration, intervened. It had reached the point that the press were more interested in the judicial clashes than the evidence when recording the exchanges with the defendant.

'This is a typical example of the gross waste of the court's time,' Eveleigh huffed, slamming his pen down and throwing a darkly disapproving stare at Stonehouse. 'What is the object of this? I cannot see how this witness can be expected to help us on this.'

'I am simply trying to identify where the responsibility lies,' replied Stonehouse, glibly.

Staring down his nose, the judge exclaimed, 'What does it matter? Ask your next question please.'

'I have an important issue to raise, my lord.'

The judge sighed and requested the eleven jurors to leave the court. After they had retired, the matter was discussed, the judge taking pains to make it quite clear that he was not going to entertain what he perceived as irrelevant and peripheral questions.

Given the judicial disapproval, Stonehouse decided there was nothing of further use to elicit from the witness.

The court heard further accounts of financial mismanagements and cover-ups, painting a comprehensive picture of the politician's manipulation of the various companies and the bank that he had set up, although it had to be noted that Stonehouse did not face charges connected with the British Bangladesh Bank. Most of the charges, and in particular the conspiracy charges, related to his group of companies, principal among them EPACS.

26 May 1976

On the twenty-third day of the trial, evidence was called relating to the life-insurance policies Stonehouse had taken out for his wife, totalling £125,000, with the Crown asserting that Stonehouse had faked his death in order to allow his wife to claim on insurance policies, thereby attempting to defraud the insurance companies of that sum. As wives could not be compelled to give evidence against their husband, the prosecution could not call Barbara to quiz her on the circumstances leading to the insurance policies, which meant other ways had to be found to prove the fraud.

John Martin Jones, a sales consultant with Canada Life Assurance Company, confirmed that a policy had been taken out with them insuring Stonehouse's life for £25,000, and Stonehouse cross-examined him at length, firstly seeking to confirm the legitimate need for such policies to be taken out. Jones was reported to have told the court, 'There were two reasons Mrs Stonehouse needed the extra cover. One was that Mr Stonehouse was committed in various business matters and had signed over his existing insurance policies as security for those activities. The second was that an explosive device had been attached to Mr Stonehouse's car near Heathrow.' It was a fitting setting in which to allude to 'the Troubles': the IRA had attacked the Old Bailey in 1973.

'When I heard the news of Mr Stonehouse's disappearance I wrote to Mrs Stonehouse to express my condolences.'

Mr Jones confirmed that he had received a reply from Mrs Stonehouse dated 3 December. As extracts from the letter were read aloud, the court heard that the news had been a 'nightmare', however Barbara still hoped that her husband was alive. Jones read on, '"I am about to see the police this afternoon to look into another area of search as a result of a very similar case we have just heard of, but it is pretty depressing and nerve-wracking. The press have been unbelievable, but at least we have been surrounded by good friends and family. I will be in touch if we have any news."'

The insurance man was released from Stonehouse's cross-examination after agreeing that Mrs Stonehouse had not made any claim against that insurance policy.

The jury then heard evidence from Marbans Roopral from the Norwich Union Insurance Company about another life policy taken out for a period of five years for £25,000, followed by William Terry, a life supervisor with the Phoenix Insurance Company, who also confirmed a policy for £25,000 had been taken out with them.

It was during Stonehouse's cross examination of Terry that the court glimpsed the nature of his defence as he was asked about the report prepared by the doctors at the time they examined Stonehouse when the policy was taken out, highlighting a potential issue with the brief remark, 'Special attention emotion stability'.

43

THE MYSTERIOUS MR MARKHAM

28 May 1976

The early summer heat simmered as characters, major and minor, shuffled across the stifling stage.

The prosecution had successfully painted a picture of the complex and confused affairs created in the Stonehouse business empire, the Crown demonstrating indisputably that Stonehouse had robbed Peter to pay Paul, using funds from one business to bolster another business with loans and fees as well as showing that, with the cynical manipulation of share options and refinancing, the companies' debts could disappear overnight.

They had effortlessly established the false passport offences, in which the only saving grace was that Stonehouse had uncharacteristically possessed the good sense to make his admissions and save the harrowing prospect of the widows of Mr Markham and Mr Mildoon having to attend to give evidence.

Finally, the Crown had now adduced the evidence relating to the insurance policies, amounting to £125,000.

On 28 May the focus of the case against Stonehouse shifted from chronicling his financial manipulation to the huge pressure that he had been put under in the months prior to his disappearance, with the prosecution claiming that it was the intensity of the financial burdens that he had ultimately tried to escape. While they chose to concentrate on that facet, it was far from the only aspect that had been gripping Stonehouse's mind in those months before he disappeared.

Stonehouse would have been acutely aware that Josef Frolík was due to publish his memoirs, which, written at the height of the Cold War, were eagerly anticipated. Tales of international espionage at home and abroad always held a grim fascination. His disappearance had prompted the resurrection of Czech spy allegations, a treacherous undercurrent against which Stonehouse had been swimming since 1969.

The jury heard that Stonehouse was being pressured to reduce the numerous overdrafts that he had generated as three bank managers gave evidence of debts exceeding £20,000 on each of the accounts held by them, equating to in excess of £400,000 today.

The first of these bank managers was Michael Fuller, manager of the Victoria Street branch of the Midland Bank, who stated that he had allowed Stonehouse to increase the overdraft facility for his company EPACS from £10,000 to £17,500, unaware that Stonehouse had opened another account at a neighbouring branch in the name of John Markham. He produced five cheques that had been signed by Stonehouse or Sheila Buckley, either for cash or payable to Stonehouse. By January 1975, the overdraft on his private account stood at £23,981 and Stonehouse's personal guarantee with EPACS stood at £17,500, a total personal liability exceeding £40,000. Unsurprisingly, the bank had run out of patience and had written to Stonehouse asking for the debt to be settled immediately.

Stonehouse tried to diminish yet more damning evidence. 'Did I ever deceive the bank about my personal bank accounts?'

'Well no, but that's because I hadn't asked Mr Stonehouse about any other accounts. By the time that the bank made its demand for payment in full we knew that Mr Stonehouse was in Australia.'

Next up was Barclays bank manager, Alan Mason, who said that Stonehouse had owed £22,000 in November 1974, rising to £28,000 with the addition of interest.

Through Mr Corkery's patient, persistent questioning, Mason confirmed that, throughout August and September 1974, he had become increasingly concerned that Stonehouse had exceeded his overdraft limit and had asked Stonehouse to cease drawing cheques on the account until the overdraft had been reduced below £20,000. He further advised Stonehouse that he would not allow the £20 per week standing order payable to Sheila Buckley to be honoured while the account remained as it was.

'Was this payment to Mrs Buckley as salary?' enquired Mr Corkery.

'M'lud,' Lord Wigoder clambered to his feet, 'it is admitted that the £20 was Mrs Buckley's weekly salary as Mr Stonehouse's secretary.'

Corkery moved on, detailing further concerns about Stonehouse cashing a £30 cheque.

'I had no idea that at this time Mr Stonehouse had opened an account and paid funds in the name of Markham,' Mason added.

Unusually, it was Lord Wigoder who spent the most time and effort in cross-examining Mason with the purpose of distancing Sheila from any suggestion that she was in some way complicit in the huge debts that Stonehouse had run up with Barclays.

'Mr Mason, did you not realise that Mrs Buckley was the parliamentary secretary to Mr Stonehouse?'

'No, I didn't,' replied the banker.

'It's the case that your subsequent knowledge of this fact was gained from what you had since read in the newspapers?'

'Yes, that is probably the case.'

'It is also the case from the bank records that Mrs Buckley has been receiving these payments since 1968?'

'Yes, that is possible.'

Slowly but surely the prosecution case was coming together, the increasing pressure during those suffocatingly warm summer days growing increasingly unbearable for Stonehouse and Sheila. It was only a matter of time before someone would snap.

3–4 June 1976

The Crown's case moved on to the further activities undertaken by Stonehouse under the name of Joseph Markham.

On 3 June, Arthur Jones, a representative from the London office of the Bank of New South Wales, was called to give evidence, relaying to the court an interview he had conducted with a gentleman by the name of Joseph Arthur Markham in 1974, though he was candid enough to admit that he would not be able to recognise Mr Markham and certainly could not identify Stonehouse as being that person.

However, Arthur Jones did at least recall the conversation between himself and Mr Markham, who had told him that he was considering emigrating to Australia and was approaching his bank as it was authorised to manage emigration finance. Mr Markham had explained it was his intention to emigrate in November 1974 and, giving his occupation as an export consultant, he produced the two pieces of headed notepaper and passport required to open a current account, into which he deposited £40.

Mr Jones had informed Mr Markham that a limit of £20,000 could be transferred from the UK to Australia by a single family. He described to the court how, by a series of transactions, Stonehouse had transferred £14,000 to the bank's Melbourne office.

The witness was shown an exchange-control form that had been exhibited by the Crown, which was completed by Mr Markham as part of the process of transferring funds and on which he had given an address at St George's Drive, London.

* * *

The following day, Margaret Reilly, the manager of the Astoria Hotel, Pimlico, was called by the prosecution, giving evidence that, between July and October 1974, a man whom she knew as Joseph Markham had booked single rooms once a week, purportedly when attending London on business.

'Do you see Mr Markham here today?'

Peering across the court, the witness's eyes settled on the smartly dressed figure in the dock. 'Yes, it's the gentleman sitting over there,' she said, pointing at Stonehouse.

She expanded on her account by telling the court that Mr Markham would telephone the hotel between visits to see whether any post had been delivered, explaining that the hotel received quite a lot of post addressed to him and that on one occasion he had come in a taxi to collect it.

She then remembered a telephone call she had received from Markham shortly after he stayed in the hotel on 16 October 1974 in which he informed her that he would not be returning as he was leaving for Australia.

Stonehouse then cross-examined Reilly. 'You agree that Mr Markham had made no attempt to hide and did not wear a disguise?'

'Yes,' was her response.

Further evidence of the movements of the mysterious Mr Markham was called, demonstrating the planned and systematic approach that had been adopted by Stonehouse, abetted by Sheila, the Crown asserting that this could not possibly be the chaotic work of someone who was having a breakdown.

Jane Grubb, a ticket clerk for Pan American Airways in London, reported a Mr Markham booking flights from London to Sydney via the United States, paid for using an American Express card and showing a passport as required. She went on to describe a conversation as to whether the ticket could be changed to include Miami instead of Houston as the stopover in the United States.

There followed Miss Mariella Zandstra, who held the position as secretary-receptionist at Highfield House Hotel in Fitzjohn's Street, Hampstead, who reported that, in October 1974, the hotel had been visited by Sheila Buckley. 'She came with a gentleman, whom I cannot now identify. I remember the gentleman said he wanted a room for his wife while he was away for a few months. I believe he said he was going abroad and would like his wife to stay there.'

She informed the court that Sheila Buckley's stay at the hotel lasted one day short of six weeks, during which time she had received external telephone calls, one being from Copenhagen. The call had been put through the hotel switchboard.

* * *

The prosecution had brought before the jury a powerful exposé: a sensational drama revealing evidence of Stonehouse's meticulous planning; his systematic emptying of the company bank accounts; financial mismanagement, including huge losses Stonehouse had incurred on the stock exchange resulting in further debt of upwards of £40,000; false identities; disposal of company assets; feathering his nest in Australia; and his damning disappearance had all now been presented in exquisite detail to the jury. The prosecution's show was nearly at an end. Finally, they turned to Stonehouse's conduct in Australia.

Detective Sergeant John Coffey of the Victoria State Police in Australia had made the long, arduous journey to give his evidence. The Crown had considered it worth the cost to taxpayers to deliver the spectacle of the events of the surveillance and arrest of Stonehouse.

44

TO THE CELLS

Another significant witness relied on by the prosecution was the *Daily Telegraph*'s South-east Asian correspondent, Ian Ward, who had 'befriended' Stonehouse after his discovery in Australia. Ward had covered a number of conflicts in the region, but the Australian, just like any other reporter, was always on the lookout for the next big scoop.

He recounted to the court the singularly bizarre episode – more in keeping with Stonehouse's defence that he had suffered a breakdown than the prosecution's narrative – when he had visited Stonehouse at his rented apartment in Melbourne just before Barbara was due to arrive. There he had found Stonehouse unpacking women's clothes from the trunk: 'At one stage he said they were Mrs Sheila Buckley's clothes. He took the black slip from the trunk, put it up in front of him, and started to dance round the room with it.'

Expanding on the strange scene, he pressed on. 'I suggested that it would be unwise to have Mrs Buckley's clothing in the apartment with his wife coming. I then arranged that I take the clothing to my mother's home. I stored it there until Mrs Buckley arrived.'

'Did it seem to you that Mr Stonehouse was emerging from a breakdown?' he was asked.

'That's not something I can really comment on as I don't have the medical experience. Mr Stonehouse told me that he was emerging from a breakdown and I do recall that he would have breakdowns from time to time.'

As with many previous witnesses, Ward's evidence was not completed that day, and he was instructed to return the following morning.

Day twenty-seven of the trial was to prove explosive.

Stonehouse, who required glasses to read, would scan a document with his spectacles on and, when he questioned the witness, he would remove them, using them as a prop to accentuate the point he was making.

He began to quiz Ward, quoting from newspaper reports that had been published in the *Telegraph* in the weeks after Stonehouse's discovery in Australia.

No more than ten minutes into his cross-examination, the judge, who had been growing increasingly restless, could no longer restrain his impatience. 'This is not the way to prove the contents of these reports, Mr Stonehouse.'

Stonehouse, ignoring the intervention, continued to question the witness. The judge interrupted again, his tone strained. 'One of the reasons why I have not clamped down on you doing this is because it takes longer to do so than to let you have your head. But if you think you are scoring over the court by this, I shall mark it in letters large to remind the jury at the end of the day of what I am saying now and what you are doing now. Don't forget that.'

'I won't forget,' Stonehouse responded. 'I have no wish to score over this court or anyone else. All I wish is the totality of the facts.'

The judge cut him short, raising his voice. 'The totality of the facts will come out by evidence which is admissible, and you must be well aware of what is and what is not admissible.'

'But my lord, I am anxious to examine this witness.'

'Do you wish everything to come out in every conceivable way, relevant or irrelevant?' the judge snapped back.

'I am concerned with relevancies . . .' Stonehouse was determined not to be cowed, but before he could continue the judge cut across him.

'You see, we may accede to your request and we will be here until Christmas.'

Stonehouse could contain himself no longer and a roar of pent-up frustration erupted from the dock. 'NO!' he bellowed. 'IT IS NOT MY WISH TO BE HERE UNTIL CHRISTMAS. I didn't request this witness to be brought here all the way from Singapore. It was the Crown's decision . . .'

'Take Mr Stonehouse down to the cells.'

The abrupt bluntness of the order caused everyone momentarily to freeze. Although the judge had previously threatened Stonehouse with this sanction, this was a new twist. The dock officers stepped forward, one placing a hand on Stonehouse's arm, and escorted him to the cells immediately beneath the court.

The judge turned to the jury, apologised, and asked them to retire. Having watched them silently file out of court, the judge announced that the case would be adjourned for a short while.

Stonehouse spent the next hour in a cell, a forlorn and isolated figure. He returned to the court chastened and calm, apologising to the judge with whom he spoke briefly before the jury returned and the trial continued.

Stonehouse resumed his cross-examination of Ward, in particular regarding what had now been referred to in the press as the 'Dance of the Black Slip'.

'The clothes belonged to my wife, Mrs Barbara Stonehouse, and it was said with jocularity. "Wouldn't it be fun if the press thought that these were Mrs Buckley's clothes?"'

'That is not my recollection,' Ward responded, guardedly.

Stonehouse pressed him. 'Wasn't the atmosphere between us at this time one of friendly badinage?'

'My impression was that we were having a serious conversation. I don't recall any remarks being jocular.'

'It is not possible that Mr Stonehouse was just joking about Mrs Buckley's clothes being there?'

'I don't think so. In fact, I'm definite about this because in the end the clothes were taken to my mother's home to avoid an embarrassing situation when Mrs Stonehouse arrived.'

Stonehouse had clearly considered that their relationship was more one of friendship than professional. 'Isn't it the case Mr Stonehouse regarded you as a friend, not as a journalist?' Stonehouse asked, straining to hide the frustration and anger in his voice.

'No, that wasn't the case. I am a journalist and I was there to put over Mr Stonehouse's side of the story.'

Infuriated by this response, Stonehouse demanded, 'So you had throughout this period one object, namely to get a scoop for your newspaper, whatever the cost in personal relationships?'

'I was doing a job,' Ward replied.

'The fact is that you were prepared to stoop to any trick in order to get an exclusive story of public interest?'

'I don't think I stooped at all,' the journalist responded.

Stonehouse persisted. 'You wheedled your way into Mr Stonehouse's confidence by saying you were not one of the pack in the newspaper world prepared to do anything to get a story?'

'I contacted Mr Stonehouse though his lawyer and then Mr Stonehouse suggested that we meet.' Ward shrugged as he answered.

Re-examining the journalist, Michael Corkery asked about the 'secret code' that Stonehouse and Sheila Buckley had developed to evade detection.

'Mr Stonehouse told me about the code which he used. It was used for telephone conversations and written correspondence.' Ward expanded: 'Mr Stonehouse had used the code when telephoning Mrs Buckley at her Cornwall hideout. He had urged her four or five times to come out to Australia, however she was hesitant to do so.'

The journalist divulged that Mrs Stonehouse had informed her husband she would not be prepared to live in Australia so long as Mrs Buckley was there. 'Mr Stonehouse then suggested that

Mrs Buckley went to New Zealand, thus allowing a "cooling off" period for all concerned.'

Changing tack, Corkery asked, 'In your various conversations with Mr Stonehouse, did he ever discuss his movements between his disappearance from Miami Beach on 20 November 1974 and his reappearance in Australia on Christmas Eve the same year?'

'Very little,' replied Ward. 'I frequently questioned him on this period, but his stock answer was "that material will be good for the book", and that was the end of the conversation.'

45

TAPES

10 June 1976

With Stonehouse's discovery in Australia and the revelations about his business affairs, the Department of Trade and Industry had undertaken its own investigations concentrating on London Capital Securities and related companies. Department inspector Michael Sherrard, QC, had flown to Australia to interview Stonehouse. The interview had been recorded and the prosecution now wished to play some extracts from the tape.

This was unusual at the time. When the police or other investigatory authority interviewed suspects, rather than recording them on audiotape, a transcript or account would be made in writing. The statement would be read back to the suspect and signed as being accurate.

Had Stonehouse been legally represented, it is quite possible that the admissibility of this evidence would have been challenged but, having chosen to dispense with his lawyers, a hugely damaging piece of evidence was to be admitted by the judge. He permitted the prosecution to cherry-pick the sections of the interview that they wished to play, which led inevitably to further conflict between judge and defendant.

The jury heard Stonehouse giving an account to the inspector about the financial transactions that his businesses had undertaken before he disappeared.

At the beginning of the recording, Stonehouse had made it very clear that he was bitterly resentful of the suggestions made in the press and elsewhere that sums of money were missing from EPACS. He complained caustically that he found it unacceptable that there had been leaks to the press about missing money.

'One of the reasons why I have been cooperating is because I want to deal with a particular matter . . . Any suggestion of criminal charges against me is so ludicrous, as against either Mr Stonehouse or Mr Markham. I completely and utterly refute it.'

The recording played on, Stonehouse's face growing dark with dismay.

'The suggestion people have implied, and it has appeared in the press, that I have taken money out illegally or have been involved in some sort of fraud is utterly wrong and it is something that is totally against my whole life . . . I want you to know that every single one of these transactions are legitimate. Although I was moving over to the Markham personality, as I have already told you, it was my intention to get the bank organised in a way that it would survive and prosper.

'Money that I took out and put into resources of a new personality as Mr J. A. Markham was money that I was fully entitled to from legal and moral points of view.'

Further on he commented, 'Whether as Mr Markham or Stonehouse, I had great respect for Mr Stonehouse. I loved him, I admired him and certainly would not want him to go down in death or disappearance with any cloud over him. Certainly, if you are asking me if I lost interest in Stonehouse behaving as a respectable human being I must say, "No." I wanted his actions to be perfectly proper.'

The prosecution also played an extract highlighting the financial irregularities, in particular the details regarding the proof that was available in the bank accounts to show legitimate expenditure. The DTI investigator asked, 'Would you be good enough to tell me this – in relation to each of the cheque items referred to, and that we discussed at length yesterday, are you telling us that there will be proper entries in the books or records of the company showing the purpose of the expenditure so that one can obtain a true and fair view of the state of the company's affairs in that connection or to explain that transaction?'

Stonehouse responded, 'What I am saying is that I kept a record, and it is either on the counterfoil of the cheque or in other documents in my desk or in the safe at 26 Dover Street. I am not saying that they were written into the books because the accountant, Mr Le Fort, left some weeks before and I am not sure that these accounts were written up in the way they normally would be.'

When challenged whether he could give the names of agents to whom money was paid and withdrawn from the company's loan account, he advised them that he could not remember, but such information could be found in the safe or in his desk.

With the salient sections of the interviews played and objectives achieved, Corkery asked for the tape to be stopped. Stonehouse immediately rose to his feet to express his indignation. 'My lord, it's vital that the jury should hear the whole of the recording.'

'Mr Stonehouse, can you specify why the jury should hear the whole tape?' The judge gritted his teeth in an effort to conceal his irritation.

'My lord, I don't see that I need to give a reason,' Stonehouse declared with scorn, flinging his glasses down on the table next to him. The assembly held their breath as they clattered against the tabletop, the judge staring at him in disbelief.

Unable to prevent his rising anger, he chastised Stonehouse. 'If you make defiant gestures in this court when I am seeking an answer before deciding whether evidence is admissible or not, if you throw down your spectacles, or whatever you have in your hand in a defiant gesture, I have the means to make you behave properly and will not hesitate to use them. Bear that in mind.'

Stonehouse, following his brief period in the cells, was under no illusions as to what the judge was prepared to do but he was finding it increasingly difficult to contain his frustration and stress. His carefully rehearsed act of calm confidence had slipped on a number of occasions and it was to do so again.

In an attempt to counter the damage, Stonehouse chose to refer to another tape of which a transcript had been made, though doing so came at a price. As he read the passages of the call he had made to Barbara on the Christmas Eve he had been arrested, the emotion was evident in his voice, each line seeming to choke him. He was only barely managing to hold himself together until the moment Barbara put their son Matthew on the phone to him. The memory felled him like a blow to the stomach and, unable to go on, the stricken figure collapsed on to his chair in the dock and wept.

The prosecution case was drawing to a close and what remained of June was spent tying up the 'loose ends' with evidence called in relation to the credit cards Stonehouse had obtained in his and the Markham name.

30 June 1976

It was late afternoon, the prosecution's last witness had been heard and the last statement read. Michael Corkery rose to his feet, declaring solemnly, 'My lord, that is the case for the Crown.' With that, he settled back on to the bench, his job, for the time being at least, done.

There was a pause as Mr Justice Eveleigh turned his attention to the figures seated in the dock. Stonehouse rose to his feet to be addressed by the judge.

'I think the point has been reached where you, as it were, have come to your turn to bat. For that reason, your bail must now cease.'

Stonehouse bit his lip, his shoulders slumped and his head bowed at having to face the prospect of prison with all the miseries of slopping out, terrible food, early morning calls for the prison van and the cramped, uncomfortable journey to and from court.

Even though it was standard practice for such a step to be taken at that time, it did appear a rather arbitrary and unfair step to take and one Stonehouse suspected the judge had taken some satisfaction in, especially as Sheila remained out on bail. The concept of an accused having an automatic right to bail was not yet enshrined in law. The Bail Act, the terms of which Stonehouse had been actively engaged with over the previous year in parliamentary debates, had not yet come into force. Stonehouse was led down to the cells and taken from there to Brixton prison.

Fortunately for Stonehouse, his solicitor Michael O'Dell was still assisting him. The lawyer immediately sent a telegram to the home secretary and the prison governor protesting Stonehouse's remand in custody. He then rushed to Brixton prison in order to hold a conference with his client. But perhaps unsurprisingly, O'Dell was denied access to his client, the prison stating that appointments needed to be booked and clearances obtained.

Some of the following day's court time was spent dealing with legal submissions; Stonehouse made an application for bail, but this was refused by the judge. The die was cast and Stonehouse would have to spend the remaining period of his trial in custody.

The proceedings had taken their toll. The tanned and relaxed figure that had appeared at the beginning of the trial was now pale and drawn, looking considerably older than his fifty years, a decline which would only be exacerbated by incarceration.

46

THE DEFENCE

1 July 1976

At that time, when conducting a defence the accused had three options. The first was to go into the witness box and give evidence under oath, where Stonehouse would be subjected to exacting cross-examination by Corkery. The second was not to give evidence at all and simply submit that the prosecution had not proved their case. This was not an option for Stonehouse given the strength of the evidence. The third option was to give a dock statement, unsworn and untested by cross-examination. This peculiarity was abolished in 1982 in a decision that was in no small part due to the Stonehouse case. One of the judges providing evidence to the Law Commission charged with looking at its abolition was none other than Mr Justice Eveleigh.

Stonehouse stood, soberly informing the court that he proposed to make a statement. The judge warned him that giving evidence on oath in the witness box would carry more weight, but Stonehouse was not to be dissuaded. The tiny table at his side was overflowing with papers, with some bundles now resting precariously on the ledge of the dock.

Studying the faces of the eleven members of the jury, Stonehouse's words rang out clearly across the hushed, expectant chamber. The journalists were primed, ready to take down every word.

'Ladies and gentlemen, I think I should say at the outset that I decided to represent myself because it was better for you not to be obscured by a baffle-board of legal gentlemen between you and me.' Keeping his tone measured, despite his depth of feeling, he elaborated. 'I wanted you to understand me as a human being and not merely be dealing with the dry dust of legal cases being argued according to the professional game between barristers.'

Using the prosecutor's jigsaw analogy, he continued, 'The case that has been presented by the Crown has been like a jigsaw puzzle. They have fitted a lot of the pieces together correctly, but they have got the essential theme of the jigsaw entirely wrong. By forcing bits of the story into the wrong places there is a misleading impression given of the jigsaw puzzle that they have put together. Of course the picture is grotesque, but they want it like that. I would ask, ladies and gentlemen, that you put that puzzle together correctly so that you can really see the depth of the picture and try and understand what lies behind it and not just use a superficial judgement, which the police appear to have done, who might want to win their medals.'

Thumping, with a theatrical flourish, one of the tightly bound bundles on to the small desk, its legs groaning under the weight of papers, he exclaimed, 'Most of these documents are irrelevant but still they are all produced.'

Much of his address focused on what he considered to be a press and political witch-hunt; it was he who was the victim of malicious media and government interference. Referring to the Commons select committee set up to investigate his conduct, whose determination was that there was no justification for his expulsion, he suggested that this was not the desired outcome of those in power, 'because I had become a political embarrassment to the Labour government and party.'

Elaborating further on what he considered to be the politicisation of his case, he explained how his status as an MP and privy councillor meant any decision to prosecute him had to be made by the attorney general, who was himself a political appointment. 'We do not know what other political influence may have been brought to bear, because these things are not advertised by the government, but what you have to bear in mind is what the government does, from time to time, in order to protect its position.'

This purgatory continued for six days. A seasoned orator, he made it a feature of this speech that he would finish each day on a cliffhanger. If the judge had thought that Stonehouse's incarceration would in some way foreshorten matters, he was to be sadly mistaken. Prison provided the politician plenty of time to ruminate on further issues with which to regale the jury. Even the judge did not escape the politician's ire. No doubt Stonehouse considered this payback time for the humiliation he had suffered throughout the proceedings.

Not even the distinguished surroundings could prevent the atmosphere from becoming oppressively wearisome. The heat and monotony had taken its toll on those in court. One newspaper article had turned its attention away from the speech to the audience, noting that one of the junior prosecuting counsel was seen to nod off, snapping to attention as he fought back against the fatigue. The judge, seeking to avoid succumbing to sleep, pulled at his earlobes and gazed down the sleeves of his robes. Occasionally, he yielded to moments of judicial impatience when he considered that Stonehouse had overstepped the mark in his statement.

Blinded by his sense of injustice and hurt, Stonehouse appeared oblivious to the effect his speech was having. He continued to lambast the press, police, prosecution and government. His wilting audience endured a detailed description of how his bank, the British Bangladesh Trust, had begun to fail, in no small part due to an article that had appeared in the *Sunday Times*, which had affected public confidence. In its subsequent guise as London Capital Securities, it continued to suffer as a result of interference by the president of Uganda, Idi Amin. Those who managed to resist drifting off heard him refer to being blackmailed into buying more shares by the solicitor director of Hanover Barclay, Mr Gorman. Stonehouse insisted that the threats had a profound and devastating impact on him, forcing him to undertake actions he would never previously have contemplated.

Endeavouring to explain why he had relieved his companies of tens of thousands of pounds in the weeks and months immediately before his disappearance, Stonehouse subjected the jury to the minutiae of his company loan account for the preceding four years. He tried to convince them that the fluctuations in the balance were in large part due to payments that had to be paid as 'sweeteners' to various agents to smooth the way for his export business. He continued, to anyone still caring to follow, to explain that this loan account had subsequently been used by the company accountants to post any transactions that did not have a natural home in any other accounts. It was, as he put it, 'a matter of accountancy convenience', nothing more. This peroration, exacerbated by the summer heat as London sweltered in Mediterranean temperatures, which the court's air-conditioning was quite powerless to cope with, lulled many to sleep.

Stonehouse had lost his audience but, as he was apt to do, he recaptured their attention when he focused on his disappearance, enthralling them and in particular the journalists who recommenced their notetaking. They recorded the 'bizarre, extraordinary and incredible' tale of how one of his fake identities had taken over from John Stonehouse, the MP, who described the anguish of the battle between his two personalities: Stonehouse versus Markham. This was the first time that they had heard an account of this from Stonehouse himself.

'It's hard even for me to explain what happened. In the months leading up to my disappearance in November 1974, John Stonehouse, ex-cabinet minister, privy councillor and chairman of companies, was composed of ninety-five per cent John Stonehouse and five per cent Markham. But then the proportion of Markham began to increase.'

A number of the journalists noted that Stonehouse almost choked at the recollection of this moment, whether it was genuine or part of the performance only he knew.

'By the middle of 1974, John Stonehouse had become an intolerable burden to me . . . he was the man who had all the pressures on him . . . the front man. Like so many people in public life he was putting on a facade, an image where the real person behind it is different. Mr John Stonehouse in 1974 was a humbug and a fraud, not in the sense that the prosecution have alleged, but in his political and business life.'

Stonehouse painted the picture that the creation of new identities and travelling to Australia was not planned, but a 'dream'. He described how, when booking airline tickets in the name of Markham, he had been filled with 'incredible joy and relief'.

Caught again by the emotion of the moment, his voice cracking, Stonehouse said, 'It was Markham, not Stonehouse, who sat in the breakfast room of the Astoria Hotel in London. It was this body, the body of Stonehouse, but it was really Markham, Joe Markham . . . it was Markham who sat in the queue at the passport office in London . . . Stonehouse does not like queueing,' he remarked wryly.

Stonehouse went on to describe how on his first business trip to the United States at the beginning of November 1974, Markham had taken control, boarding a flight from Miami to Houston and then Mexico, intending to go on to Australia, but missing the connecting plane and returning to San Francisco in order to take another flight to Australia. 'This parallel personality of Markham confronted Stonehouse in the toilet of a jet in the skies over the west coast of America . . . I was screaming, screaming, screaming . . . on that occasion Stonehouse won the argument but there were other times when he lost.'

Then he recounted how the Stonehouse personality had reasserted itself, returning to Miami and his life as an MP and businessman. However, he recalled, by mid-November 1974 matters finally came to a head. 'Although I kept the image of a successful, dynamic man the pressure was intolerable. I was drawn irresistibly into the personality of Joseph Markham. This was a psychological device for me to get relief. Markham was a way of helping John Stonehouse to survive.'

It was Markham, he claimed, who had entered the US and flew to Australia via Hawaii. The reporters noted the defendant gazing upwards to the ornate ceiling as if trying to recapture that moment when Stonehouse had allowed his alter ego to consume him entirely. 'Markham is in control, wonderful, Stonehouse has gone, wonderful, Markham loved Stonehouse, a man misunderstood, persecuted, but a good man.'

For a moment it was as if the entire assembly held its breath. Even the motes of dust seemed to pause in their dance, suspended in the shafts of sunlight that entered the court room. Mesmerised by the fantastic saga, many almost willed themselves to believe it.

But Stonehouse suddenly digressed into the tale of his relationship with Sheila, snapping them from their reverie. It was Sheila, he told the jury, whom he had phoned when he had disappeared. It was she whom he had made arrangements to meet in Copenhagen to talk things over. Most damningly, while the world believed he was dead, Sheila had known that he was very much alive. The conundrum was that the man making the telephone call to Sheila was Joseph Markham.

'It must have come as a big shock to her – being the great woman she was, she coped and did what she was asked . . . not to tell this terrible thing to anyone.'

Sheila showed no emotion, gazing fixedly into the courtroom, acknowledging nothing.

Stonehouse tried to sum up the nature of their relationship in as matter of fact a manner as possible. 'The situation between Mrs Buckley and myself is that we were very close in our political work for many years . . . she was doing an excellent job for me as a constituency secretary and, after her husband left her, an intimate relationship grew up between us.'

He returned to describing the inner conflict between the two egos battling for supremacy in his mind and how the friction affected him while in Melbourne. He claimed that this resulted in his unconscious assuming of the further personality of Clive Mildoon, to act as a foil to the contentious personalities, the three personalities coexisting uncomfortably until his arrest on Christmas Eve, 1974.

'It is now 100 per cent John Stonehouse who is stood in the dock of the Old Bailey pleading not guilty to twenty-one charges of forgery, theft, conspiracy and fraud. Joseph Markham began to disappear the day he was picked up by the Melbourne police on Christmas Eve, 1974. That has left John Stonehouse a better and stronger man.'

It was surely with some relief that Stonehouse abruptly ended his speech, informing the jury that he would be resigning from politics whatever the outcome of the trial.

47

THE THREE FACES

13 July 1976

Once the waffle and irrelevancies had been discounted, there appeared to be at least two facets to Stonehouse's defence. The first concerned his management of the companies, his argument appearing to be that the prosecution had overstated their case against him and that all his transactions and manoeuvres with the companies and their financial affairs were legitimate.

During his statement from the dock, Stonehouse had announced that he would be calling a number of witnesses, including another MP, declining to divulge who it would be, saying that he did not wish to draw unwelcome press attention to the individual concerned.

On the morning of 13 July, the first of Stonehouse's witnesses, Bruce Douglas-Mann, stepped into the box. The MP for Merton and Morden had been minister for housing in the 1974 Wilson government. He was a solicitor by profession.

The purpose of his evidence was partially to provide a character witness, but also to supply some background on factors that may have triggered Stonehouse's breakdowns.

He told the jury that he had known Stonehouse since 1947 and that they had got to know each other better when he had been elected to parliament in 1970, going on to describe how he and Stonehouse had been in Bangladesh in April 1971 to witness for themselves what was going on, both being particularly concerned about the Pakistani government crackdown.

'We were both emotionally shattered at seeing people dying and wounded, the disease and filth and intense poverty everywhere. People were telling us stories of the atrocities, and the concern which Mr Stonehouse then showed was completely genuine.'

He spoke of how Stonehouse had left a previously despondent and depressed Bangladeshi leadership filled with hope and optimism for self-government and that, on their return to London, they had described what they had found to various political colleagues and friends in order to seek help for the cause. They gained considerable cross-party support, which made their task to promote recognition for this fledgling state easier.

Douglas-Mann characterised his colleague approvingly. 'I have no doubt in that period his activities were directed to a very idealistic concern to ensure that the terrible things we had seen and heard about were put right and prevented from being continued.'

Michael Corkery rose slowly from his seat, rearranging his robes and wig and peering over the top of his spectacles as he regarded the witness. 'You would agree that Mr Stonehouse is a highly intelligent and resourceful man?'

'Yes, I would agree,' Douglas-Mann responded without hesitation.

'Would you agree that Mr Stonehouse is highly adaptive and quick to react to changing circumstances?'

'I'd say that he is very capable and very much aware of people's problems.'

'Would you say that he is a man who finds it difficult to accept criticism?' asked Corkery.

'Yes, he did find it difficult to take criticism,' Douglas-Mann admitted. 'He always had to be right, backing his own judgement rather than that of others.'

Stonehouse called his personal accountant, John Marks, to rebut the prosecution suggestion that, as part of his financial mismanagement and dishonesty, he had failed to pay his income tax on £10,000 in director's fees he had received from EPACS. Marks confirmed that the £10,000 had been included in the Stonehouse tax returns for the period 1972 to 1975, that he had paid all the tax he was required to pay after making allowances for a tax rebate he was due on a tax overpayment and therefore had no outstanding tax liability, as suggested by the Crown.

* * *

The second facet of Stonehouse's defence proposed that his disappearance had come about because he was mentally unwell and that any wrongdoing in respect of his business affairs had been conducted by his alter ego, Joe Markham.

The Crown had made a compelling assertion that the disappearance had been elaborately planned and executed in the months before, but Stonehouse was desperate to demonstrate that the responsibility lay entirely with his alter ego, Joseph Markham.

The problem was that this was not a recognised defence for the charges that Stonehouse faced as he wasn't arguing insanity, which had been a long-established defence, and the psychiatric evidence that he produced was not intended to propose such a suggestion. Over a period of a week, a number of psychiatrists and psychologists were called to support Stonehouse's contention that, while not certifiably insane, he had not been mentally fit.

The first witness he called was an Australian psychiatrist, Dr Gerard Gibney, who had examined Stonehouse when he was in Australia in the early part of 1975. He expressed that in his opinion Stonehouse had suffered a severe reactive depression, which had started in 1971, shortly after he had become involved with the plight of Bangladesh.

Dr Gibney further suggested that Stonehouse developing an alter ego, Joseph Markham, was a classic symptom of that type of depression which he considered akin to a type of suicide, an attempt to mentally escape the John Stonehouse personality and his associated troubles, complemented by paranoid ideations manifesting themselves in feelings of bitterness and resentment towards society, and in particular British institutions connected with business and parliament.

The next witness called was the East Kilbride MP, Dr Maurice Miller, who confirmed that he was experienced in understanding mental health problems from his involvement with air crews in the Second World War. In 1973 he had spent time with Stonehouse and recounted a conversation during which Stonehouse had described suffering with recurring nightmares. 'I had suspected for some time that it was not a physical condition but that there was mental strain, and I came to the conclusion that he was suffering from an anxiety state with an element of depression.'

Dr Miller expressed concerns that, after a sustained press campaign in 1975, with what he knew of Stonehouse's medical history, he was in danger of committing suicide.

Next, Stonehouse called consultant psychologist Lionel Haward, who, in evidence that took two days to complete, began by explaining to the jury the psychological tests undertaken on Stonehouse based on a popular book of the time *Three Faces of Eve*. As the title suggested, the tests aimed to identify the three faces of John Stonehouse: the first being his view of himself in 1974; the second as he saw himself in 1976; and finally, how he regarded himself in the personalities of Markham and Mildoon.

Assessments had been undertaken in August 1975 while he was in prison, at his home in October 1975 and finally that July 1976, while Stonehouse had returned to jail. Perhaps unsurprisingly, the outcome suggested he regarded Mildoon and Markham as ideal personalities while John Stonehouse reflected all that was negative. The results also showed that he had a very high IQ of 140 but that he was suffering from emotional disturbance, displaying indications of hysteria with symptoms of amnesia, and/or limb paralysis and even a change in identity.

The following day Mr Haward told the court how he had, over a twenty-year period, developed a specialism in studying the artwork of psychiatric patients, explaining that psychiatric patients were encouraged to use painting as a type of therapy. They would often start using bright colours as a way of trying to regain the relish in the world that they had known, this being overtaken by their depression seeping into their paintings, often manifesting itself in the use of dark colours, especially dark browns and blacks.

In Haward's opinion Stonehouse had a hysteroid personality, explaining that, 'A hysteroid chooses the most appropriate form of escape from his present circumstances when these become too much for him.'

A number of paintings were produced, temporarily lending the courtroom the appearance of the Tate art gallery, displaying artworks in the abstract style, painted by Stonehouse over a period of years.

Haward recounted the visit he had made to Stonehouse's home in October 1975 where he had observed several paintings on display of which Stonehouse confirmed that he was the artist, the artwork having been produced before November 1974.

The jury was shown five of the Stonehouse paintings as the psychologist provided them with a running commentary interpreting the use of colour and shapes in them. One of the canvasses was emerald green stained with a black blot at its centre and with a grey circle to one side, while another showed bright crimson with smears of black, leading Haward to voice his opinion that when Stonehouse had painted them he was suffering from acute anxiety generally only recognised in psychiatric patients.

In order to circumvent any suggestion that the condition that Stonehouse had been diagnosed with was feigned, he called an expert in the field of divided personalities, Dr Ronald D. Laing, who had spent twenty-five years developing ways of detecting whether a patient was in fact malingering. He described a practice among prisoners on remand awaiting trial where they would fabricate mental breakdowns or exaggerate and lie about past medical conditions so that they would seem to be mad in order to evade justice when the reality was that they were perfectly fine. 'In the case of Mr Stonehouse, his account was plausible,' was the doctor's opinion. 'It would seem to me that, over a period of time which is not easy to set, Mr Stonehouse's personality became very disturbed . . . He began to feel an increasing sense of unreality and futility and irrational emotions. He felt he was being persecuted.'

The next witness Stonehouse called was his daughter, Jane, whom he asked to give evidence about the changes she had witnessed in her father. She described the years her father served in the Wilson cabinet in the 1960s. 'He was a very busy man. I seemed to see him rarely, but when I did, he always had time for me.' She painted a glowing picture of a happy, functional familial relationship before portraying how things changed from about 1970 onwards. 'I noticed he was shutting himself off a great deal and becoming more difficult to communicate with and to relate to. He had always had time for me and my problems but, as time went on, he had less time.' She learned that he was suffering with stress brought about by his many business activities, in particular with the unfair article in the *Sunday Times* and the DTI investigation, and reflected sorrowfully how he would react with anger at the slightest of things, storming out of rooms and slamming doors, going on to report how, during their brief time in Australia, she had witnessed several emotional outbursts. She had found the shock at seeing her father completely out of control a terrifying experience.

Corkery rose to cross-examine Jane, choosing to concentrate on her involvement in the questionable business affairs of her father's bank and referring to a visit that she and her friend, Susan Hill, had made to the British Bangladesh Trust. Jane confirmed that the visit had taken place and that she and her friend had been invited to become nominee shareholders without liability. In pursuing this line of enquiry, there came a point where the judge felt that he needed to interject and warn Jane that she need not answer a question in case it should incriminate her. The point related to the form Miss Hill had completed for the purpose of becoming a shareholder. Mr Corkery suggested to her that it was Jane who had advised her friend to list her occupation on the form as a dress designer, when she knew that she was a shop manager. Jane looked a little nonplussed. 'I did not know there would be any case of that . . . I suggested a dress designer because she had designed dresses for me. It was as simple and as unimportant as that.'

With this evidence the Stonehouse defence was complete.

* * *

Sheila's defence followed. She also chose to give a speech from the dock, thus depriving the prosecution of the chance to cross-examine, though she made no attempt to emulate her co-defendant's six-day saga, managing to keep her address to a concise forty-five minutes. Reports suggested she took no more than 5,000 words, after three long, sweltering months, to attempt to persuade the jury of her innocence. Her speech was poignant and at times emotional, her voice was quiet, indeed so quiet that a number of the jury later complained that they could not hear and were subsequently provided with a transcript of the speech. Those who were able to hear could not help but be moved, and there is no doubt that it had a marked effect on the way the judge dealt with her later. She described how she had started to work for Stonehouse in 1968 at the age of twenty-two, saying that she had married in 1969, but that the marriage had faltered. In 1971, she sued for divorce on the grounds of her husband's adultery.

'Some time after I parted from my husband, my friendship with Mr Stonehouse grew . . . Eventually I developed a very personal and intimate relationship with him,' she admitted, her voice cracking.

She denied knowledge of Stonehouse's activities concerning EPACS, although she did accept that she had signed two cheques from the EPACS loan account that formed part of the funds fraudulently transferred to accounts held by Stonehouse, maintaining that she was not aware of their significance. 'I did, in fact, sign, which certainly does not surprise me because I signed many hundreds of cheques during my employment as part of my regular duties, in practically every case Mr Le Fort would ask me to sign. I knew of the existence of the loan account because Mr Le Fort told me. I became a director of EPACS and two of the other companies in 1970 at the request of Mr Stonehouse, but I was regarded as having no real say in the running of the companies. I occasionally signed letters as a director and secretary, but they were drafted by others. I had to rely on the professionals in the company for the accuracy of the documents.'

She mentioned that the flat that she occupied belonged to Stonehouse, explaining that she had been trying to save for her own property when, on discovering this, Stonehouse had sold a valuable stamp collection to help provide a deposit for her. With this capital at her disposal, she had given notice to her landlord in anticipation of moving into a new property and had viewed alternative accommodation, but nothing came of them.

'I had to leave on 30 October, so on 23 October I went to see a flat in Golders Green, but I was not successful. We saw the Highfield hotel and Mr Stonehouse went ahead of me into the hotel. I didn't hear him say that he was looking for temporary accommodation for his wife while he was abroad. Then I moved in on 27 October.'

Sheila moved on to Stonehouse's trip to Miami and how she understood that this was to meet potential investors in the bank. She recalled receiving a telephone call just after midnight on 21 November from Mr McGrath, who informed her of Stonehouse's disappearance. She described being 'stunned and shocked at the news . . . Fleetingly, suicide entered my head as a possibility, but the thought was too grotesque to think about and anyway, I felt his presence. I felt sure that I would know if he had been taken from me, if he were dead. I had no evidence or knowledge at that time to back that feeling. It was simple intuition.'

Pausing to blot the tears that had spilled over at the memory, she resolutely carried on. 'On, I think, Friday 22 November 1974, I was in my room when I was completely bowled over to receive a telephone call from Mr Stonehouse. I asked him where he was but he did not reply to this question. He was incoherent and I thought he sounded suicidal. He said things like, "Help me, Sheila."'

She described a second call she received on 4 December and how worried she was for his safety, and the difficulties she was facing in his absence. 'I believed at the time that I might be pregnant, wrongly as it turned out, and that Mr Stonehouse was the father.'

Sheila recounted their meeting in Copenhagen and spoke of how, on being informed that Stonehouse was in Australia, she was told that she should write to him in the name of Mildoon, divulging that the code she used was not prearranged, but had simply been devised to confuse a 'nosey post office clerk'.

Her address to the jury ended, Lord Wigoder announced that this concluded her case. No further evidence would be called.

* * *

The defence cases complete, the end was in sight, but not before what, for many, are the most notable set pieces of a criminal trial: the closing speeches. The last opportunity to be heard, they are often highly dramatic but predominantly present a vital opportunity for the advocates to find a hook on which to hang their argument, a soundbite that encapsulates the essence of the case.

Michael Corkery rose to his feet to address the courtroom one final time. His task was to try to help the jury make sense of the vast amount of evidence that they had heard in the previous almost sixty days. Over the course of three days, his closing remarks described Stonehouse as a 'man of political ambition' enjoying the high life, quoting Stonehouse's remarks to a detective that 'everybody in business and politics, if they are going to succeed, has got to take risks . . . They have to keep all the balls in the air and if somebody starts pushing him in the elbow and they begin to drop the balls, they have bloody well had it.'

Little did Corkery, or anyone else in that courtroom, know what other balls Stonehouse had desperately been striving to juggle, such as fraternisation with an Eastern Bloc country, a Cold War enemy, to help realise his political ambitions.

Corkery reminded the jury of the evidence that seemed to show the MP borrowing huge amounts of cash for himself and his companies, and how that money was being moved around, or as we know it today, 'laundered', the veteran prosecutor describing it as a 'money-go-round' and that Stonehouse's 'elbow was jogged'. A number of events that occurred, chief among them the economic downturn at the beginning of the 1970s, meant Stonehouse faced the prospect of economic ruin. Looming bankruptcy, with the resulting humiliation of expulsion from parliament, led to his frenzy to escape. Recruiting Sheila as his willing accomplice, he methodically set out to make a new life for himself, plundering his companies of money, setting up secret bank accounts, robbing dead men of their identities and ruthlessly faking his death in Miami. He asserted that Stonehouse's medical defence did not amount to insanity or diminished responsibility, and there was certainly no medical evidence to support that. What medical evidence had been presented attempted to suggest that he was suffering with a depressive illness that caused him to act recklessly.

With the prosecution speech complete, the focus turned to Stonehouse. Speculation buzzed about how he could deal with such damning evidence and what tack he would take. Determined not to disappoint, Stonehouse rose inimically to the occasion. Addressing the jury from the dock, with his years of training in the bear pit of parliamentary debate having honed his oratorical skills, his two-day speech was eloquent, passionate and emotional. He held forth surrounded by the mountains of counsel's notepads that had built up through what the judge would later refer to as his noting brief's 'industry'. The court was once again his stage.

Stonehouse began by reminding the jury that, some fifteen weeks before, they had been told by the prosecution that they must decide the case on the evidence. Prodding the tower of notepads with his forefinger, the MP remarked drily that herein lay the evidence. He recalled having been advised to have a lawyer speak for him, to abide by the rules of 'the game'. 'I don't want to participate in any game. What I wanted to do, for the sake of my own health, was to ensure that the whole of the story came out as fully as possible, warts and all. I certainly do not want an acquittal in this case based on some verbal game.'

He characterised the prosecution's presentation of the case against him as nothing but 'lying, deceit, cheating and trickery . . . The lying and cheating is as bad as anything I have seen in the House of Commons, but the humbug is even worse, because it is dressed in this decorum and in that way you are not supposed to notice it.'

He attacked the prosecution's suggestion that Sheila had been actively involved in the conspiracy, that Barbara had known he was still alive after his disappearance, or that his daughter, Jane, knew of his scheme. 'There was no pre-planning. All the evidence points to Mrs Buckley not knowing anything about Mr Markham and being totally confused after she got to know about him.'

The letters she wrote showed 'no pre-knowledge . . . just a great deal of confusion' and, while she had signed cheques, there were others, like his personal assistant Mr Bingham and his accountant Mr Le Fort, who had done the same, but who were not in the dock facing any charges. He contended that the reason for this was the intimate relationship that existed between himself and Sheila. It is worth noting that Ian Mayes, the DTI junior, considered that there would have been others in the dock if there had been more time to investigate.

On the second day, the speech became more impassioned. As Jane sobbed, he thumped the desk in the dock and exclaimed, 'Convict me of every damned charge. Send me to prison for the rest of my life. All I know is that I am innocent, and I know I had a breakdown because I really suffered it.'

He reiterated his assertion that his disappearance was not designed, pointing out that, had he planned it, he could have been far more successful. 'I could easily have defected and have had a life of ease in the Soviet Union, where there is no extradition treaty. I could have chosen a hideaway in the United States or in Brazil as a political defector . . . all this was possible, but it did not happen like that because it was not a "planned" disappearance.'

The journalists noted that in his passion Stonehouse used his fist to emphasise each phrase, striking the desk as he spoke and causing his listeners to jump. 'It is all very well for these well-ordered and mechanical people to dismiss it . . . it happened . . .' Bang! 'It happened.' Bang! 'It happened.' Bang! 'I know because I suffered it.'

This time, instead of the expected thump, he paused, relying on the effect of silence. 'Would it be likely that I would have rushed across America in that mad, insane way if I had not had a breakdown? Then it is dismissed by these people who have only one interest . . . to get a conviction. They just dismiss all this breakdown business as though it is some wonderful concoction. Is it possible, members of the jury, that this highly intelligent, 140 IQ MP would have invented this breakdown here at the Old Bailey as a marvellous excuse? All they can think about is that this man is a criminal, a criminal, a criminal,' once more punctuating his words by banging down his fist.

By the end of the speech he was physically spent, collapsing into his seat, head bowed. He had given the performance of his life.

The final address was given by Lord Wigoder. His aim, despite his speech lasting two days, was to keep his client's defence as simple as possible. Reminding the jury that they were not there to judge Sheila on her morals but to decide on the charges before them, he summed up the case against his client, deriding the notion of her being involved in some 'grand plot' to effect Stonehouse's disappearance and then flit off to Australia to live happily ever after.

'Even if the prosecution were right about that, it does not involve Mrs Buckley in being guilty of any of the charges she faces. There is no charge that she was a pretty girl who fell in love with a married man. That is not a crime.'

Her counsel took into account that some members of the jury may be scandalised by her conduct, particularly her behaviour after her divorce, with all the emotional upheaval that it would cause. 'You won't, I hope, blame her for that . . . it is something that can easily happen to many, many people,' he appealed.

His speech straddled a weekend, which is generally regarded as far from ideal. On Monday, he took the time to remind the jury of the salient parts of the case and to emphasise that, as the secretary, the cheques that Sheila had signed off had been prepared by the company accountant and were only a fraction of many of the hundreds of cheques she would have approved. While insisting that the fact that she had signed those cheques did not make her Stonehouse's accomplice, in accordance with his client's instructions, he was careful not to tread on Stonehouse's defence, restraining himself from going as far as to say that she had been duped by this man. Instead, he sympathised with Stonehouse's 'breakdown', referring to him as being a 'charming and pleasant man' and an 'impressive and powerful figure in the world of politics', cleverly inviting the jury to read between the lines of his speech with its inescapable implication.

The final act called for the judge to sum up the case, a legal device which involves directions on the law and a summary of the evidence called in respect of each of the prosecution and defence cases. Mr Justice Eveleigh brought to bear the full weight of his years as a veteran of the justice system in the three days he spent summarising the case.

Clearly the eloquence and passion of the Stonehouse closing speech had unsettled the judge, who was perhaps concerned that the jury would be taken in by it. He used the summing up to enhance the prosecution case and undermine the defence cases of both Stonehouse and Sheila, instructing the jury to 'keep their eye on the ball', suggesting that the defence put forward by Stonehouse was an attempt to divert their gaze on to irrelevant and extraneous matters. He went so far as to raise in his summing up aspects of the prosecution that even Mr Corkery had overlooked, in particular when referring to various items of correspondence as well as highlighting a couple of items missing from the exhibits that he felt should be brought to the jury's attention. His summing up of the defences was not helpful as he outlined their respective cases, dismissing the psychiatric aspect of Stonehouse's case out of hand and expressing incredulity at Sheila's explanation on certain aspects such as the telephone calls she received from Stonehouse in Hawaii shortly after his disappearance.

When the judge was satisfied that his job had been done, the jury ushers were sworn in and the eleven jurors retired to consider their verdicts at 10.55 a.m. on 5 August.

48

VERDICT AND AFTERMATH

5 August 1976

The jury were out for a full day, deliberating on each of the twenty-eight charges that the two defendants faced between them. Separately, the accused attempted to alleviate the excruciating tension, Stonehouse sitting and pacing in the court cell, lost in thought; Sheila confined to the precincts of the court, wandering the corridors of the Old Bailey seeking some respite in distraction as the hours ticked sluggishly by.

Dusk fell and still the jury were deliberating until, just after 8 p.m., the judge received a note informing him that verdicts had been reached in respect of counts three and four against Stonehouse. The court reconvened, the jurors filing silently into their places under the eyes of the packed, expectant court, which seemed to take a collective breath.

'Will the foreman of the jury please stand?' the court clerk asked.

One of the women jurors stood.

'Madam, will you please answer only yes or no. Have you reached a unanimous verdict on count three?'

The woman answered, 'Yes.'

'On count three, do you find John Thomson Stonehouse guilty or not guilty of uttering a forged document?'

'Guilty,' she replied.

'Have you reached a verdict of count four?'

'Yes,' came the response.

'On count four, do you find John Thomson Stonehouse guilty or not guilty of theft?'

'Guilty,' she responded.

Realising that the court clerk had omitted to ask the question, the judge inquired if they had reached a unanimous verdict, to which the woman answered, 'Yes.'

Stonehouse's shoulders slumped, but that was the only indication he allowed to reveal his disappointment. He kept his dignity and composure intact, his emotional turmoil in check.

The court clerk went through the remaining charges, to which the juror responded that they had not reached agreement. Realising that there was division within the jury, the judge decided to give them a majority verdict direction: provided ten of the eleven jurors agreed, the majority would prevail.

Hoping this would break the deadlock, the judge then asked the jury to retire again to continue their deliberations the next morning. As was the custom in those days, the jurors were not permitted to go home for fear of outside influence so instead they retired to a hotel under the supervision of the two jury ushers, leaving the two defendants to endure an agonisingly anxious night.

6 August 1976

The jurors returned for a 9.30 a.m. start, spending the rest of the day deliberating on the remaining twenty-six charges. While Stonehouse had been convicted on some of the charges, nothing had yet been determined regarding Sheila's fate and the most serious charges were still being debated. The pair clung to the prospect that there was still hope, Stonehouse optimistically taking the view that the time that it was taking boded better for him.

After over sixteen hours of deliberations, the jury reached agreement on the other charges and a message was conveyed to the judge, who asked for the parties to be recalled to court. The two defendants took their place in the dock to await their fate as Court 1 filled quickly to capacity. Stonehouse's daughter, Jane, sitting impassively at the back of the court, had cut a haunting figure at every session since giving evidence. The creak of ancient wood reverberated through the room as she and all present rose in unison when the sharp rap on the door announced the judge's entry.

Anxiety was etched into the faces of each of the defendants as the jurors shuffled into place and time seemed to slow. The forewoman stood, the weight of expectation manifesting itself in her formal demeanour as the clerk of the court asked if they had come to verdicts in which they were agreed. They had, was the response. Each charge was read and, to all but one of the charges, a single word resounded: 'Guilty'.

Having determined each of these judgments by a majority of ten to one, it was a pyrrhic victory to hear that one of the conspiracy-to-steal charges returned a unanimous not guilty verdict.

The journalists noted that Stonehouse looked crestfallen, and Sheila, deathly pale, crumpled into the arms of a prison officer, who, having seen her knees buckling, had rushed forward to catch her as she fell.

A hubbub immediately erupted in court as the assembly took in the full impact of the verdicts. As the murmuring died down, Jane, hunched in her seat, her shoulders shaking, could be heard quietly sobbing. Heartbroken, she could contain her frayed emotions no more.

There remained some outstanding issues regarding the money that was held in Swiss bank accounts and DCS Etheridge was called back to give evidence on this particular aspect to advise as to what steps now needed to be taken to secure that money on behalf of the Crown.

The MP gave a final statement in mitigation to the judge, the epitome of dignified eloquence, though it failed to impress Mr Justice Eveleigh. In turn Lord Wigoder spoke on his client's behalf, giving a cryptic address, being conscious that Sheila did not wish anything he said to exacerbate the predicament that her lover was in, though his guarded language did little to conceal where he considered the blame lay.

In sentencing Stonehouse, the judge made a number of comments condemning the politician. 'You were not an unlucky businessman escaping from undeserved financial problems. That all arose from your own initial devious behaviour, whatever the object might be.' In case he had not made his distaste clear enough he added, 'You are not an ill-fated idealist. You committed fraud when you intended to provide for your future comfort.'

Satisfied that he had expressed his views on the matter, the judge imposed a total of seven years' imprisonment and a criminal bankruptcy order.

Turning to Sheila, he began sternly, 'I have no doubt that you were fully aware of what was going on.' Modifying his tone a little, he made it quite clear as to where he attributed the blame for her situation. 'You are a person of good character up to now and I have no reason at all to believe that, if you had not met Mr Stonehouse, you would not have committed any kind of criminal offence. I have no reason to believe that deviousness is in your nature. I think you were extremely unfortunate to meet this persuasive, deceitful and ambitious man.'

In sentencing her to two years' imprisonment, suspended for two years, he added, 'I do recognise that John Stonehouse's influence must have been tremendous. One had only to see the manner in which he sought to mesmerise the jury in this court to know that he could have told you anything, and while it is clear, as I say, that you knew the situation, I have no doubt he persuaded you your duty was to go along with him, and while you regretted having to do it, you did it.'

Jane's distress had intensified with the sentence that was passed and, as Stonehouse turned to be led away, he glimpsed her tearstained face at the back of court. The journalists noted that he smiled weakly and put his hand up to wave, drumming his fingers on the glass panel that surrounded the back of the dock in an effort to reassure her that he was all right before disappearing into the bowels of the court.

* * *

For days following the verdict, the newspapers continued to emblazon their front pages with stories of the 'Casanova' MP, the wronged wife, the fraudulent businesses. Stonehouse formally resigned from the House of Commons and bankruptcy proceedings were finalised. The criminal courts ordered the seizure of large sums of money held in Swiss bank accounts and he was declared bankrupt later that year.

Having had a taste of the proceedings first hand, it had not been difficult for Michael to anticipate the outcome and feel the urge to protect his two eldest children from the salacious headlines he had no doubt would infest the newspapers, whatever the verdict. To that end, he had arranged to travel with my sister and me to stay with friends in France as a respite from the madness, of which we remained innocently ignorant.

In the court cells, Stonehouse had requested a meeting with Geoffrey Robertson, informing him that he wanted to appeal. His counsel thought he may have some grounds and an appeal was swiftly lodged that would set precedents that still stand as law today. However, despite the best endeavours of his QC, Louis Blom-Cooper, the appeal was insufficient to overturn the conviction.

Among a number of legal principles established by the case, the first related to the Stonehouse defence, in which he had professed that it was his alter ego, Joe Markham, who had committed the offences, not John Stonehouse. It is suggested that the reason Stonehouse and his advocates parted company was because he was insistent on presenting this defence. His advocates may well have taken the view that he was attempting to build his house on sand as, with no psychiatric evidence to suggest that he was insane or suffering diminished responsibility, the closest condition one could say his syndrome related to was automatism, implying that, while his body may have committed the offences, his mind was not responsible because he was not 'conscious' of doing so. But Stonehouse's condition did not amount to automatism either. In his summing up, Mr Justice Eveleigh had withdrawn this from the jury, stating that it did not amount to a defence and directing them to discount it. In return, the Court of Appeal announced that it had been improper for the judge to have made such a statement and that, whether it legally amounted to a defence or not, it was still a matter for the jury to decide and not for the judge to withdraw it, reiterating the right of pre-eminence of the jury as the arbiters of facts and not the judge. A second principle was to establish that it was perfectly feasible to stand trial for offences that were planned and/or executed outside of the jurisdiction of the courts of England and Wales.

Further insight into Stonehouse's personality was reported to the Court of Appeal by Francis Etang, the chief medical officer at HMP Blundeston in Suffolk. After Stonehouse had informed the doctor of his breakdowns and diagnosis of psychiatric suicide, Etang noted, 'I find him alert and well orientated. He has normal memory and does not show any signs of a psychotic illness. He has "doubtful" insight into his condition and I think he has a tendency to exaggerate the normal stresses and strains of life and to wishfully think that he had a nervous breakdown which gave rise to his irresponsible conduct, and as such, wants to be pitied. He has an attention-seeking personality.'

The DTI investigation continued long after the trial. Ian Mayes, the fresh-faced barrister instructed to assist the inspectors led by Michael Sherrard, QC, had attended every day of that long, hot, stifling trial to note its drama and twists. He recalls the eight days that the inspectors spent interviewing Stonehouse at Wormwood Scrubs in the autumn of 1976. There was some sympathy for this once-proud man who had been so reduced to the day-to-day humiliations of prison life, prison food and slopping out. Indeed, during the course of the interviews, Stonehouse had asked that his interrogators delay to the afternoon, as his weekly shower was due the next morning and, if he missed it, he would have to endure another week without one.

The pervasive view on the cause of Stonehouse's downfall was that his ego was to blame. Having invested so much of his time, effort and reputation into the British Bangladesh Trust, he refused to let it fail, with the consequence that, rather than admit defeat and allow the venture to be closed in an orderly fashion, he stumbled from one crisis to another, fighting fire after fire.

As Mayes said, had the DTI inspectors been allowed the time, it is almost certain that others would have been in the dock with Stonehouse, but they had not been afforded that luxury, the complex political ramifications requiring an expedited police investigation. So it was only the captain who went down with his ship, condemned to drown in the waters of his pride, weighed down by the millstone of the British Bangladesh Trust, his personal mission that he refused to relinquish even as it dragged him to the depths. When the *Sunday Times* report inflicted such devastating damage, intensified by the downturn in the world economy, wreaking havoc with the secondary-bank industry, Stonehouse should have cut his losses, but hubris was his downfall.

A year later, there followed a DTI report on the management of Stonehouse's businesses, which was damning of many of those who had featured in his trial, in particular his accountants, but his nephew, Michael, came in for no criticism or sanction as he, like a number of others, was perceived as a victim of Stonehouse's fraudulent plans, the unscrupulous MP employing his position and charms to manipulate various youngsters do his bidding.

As for the impact on Michael personally, it is of little surprise that the whole chaotic episode affected him profoundly. Having been very close to his uncle, he felt the betrayal was unforgivable, especially as it had exposed him to the full media glare even before it reached the confines of Court 1 of the Old Bailey. Michael became a more morose and distant figure to his family, occasionally finding solace in alcohol, and his mental absence from us all, particularly his wife Patti, upset her considerably. By nature a happy and positive woman, the strain took its toll.

Barbara divorced Stonehouse as the family struggled to adapt to their new, diminished circumstances, and Michael was charged with the task of helping her clear up the detritus of what had been their family life. Not only was Michael instructed to act as Barbara's solicitor in her divorce, there were practical aspects that needed to be resolved. I recall spending a day with him at the farmhouse in Andover, sorting through the contents of the home that had seen so many happy family memories, now a melancholy monument to those carefree days. Michael brought much of Stonehouse's record collection home and I still have half a dozen or so albums, a mixture of modern jazz, classical and film music.

Stonehouse's mother, Rosina, never quite recovered from the shock. The stigma of his disgrace enveloped her like a cloud for the rest of her life. With the enforced absence of her son, my mother, Patti, took it upon herself to regularly visit her at her ground-floor flat in Shirley, also to invite her to join us for Christmas and other family occasions. As the eldest, I would be asked to tag along. Rosina had developed a very hard, cold exterior and for those who didn't know her she might be described as 'difficult' and 'obtuse', but such a carapace is often a shield against the vicissitudes of life, hiding a kind and generous spirit. Having been a former mayor of Southampton, she would still be invited to various civic functions and so it was that, shortly after her son's conviction, Rosina was at a reception for the Southampton 1976 FA Cup-winning side at the Guildhall, Southampton. With her son's enforced absence I was asked to chaperone her to the event, her first public appearance after the scandal of the trial. As she took my arm as we entered the event, I observed the surprised and uncomfortable glances from the other guests. Not to be deterred, she tightened her grip and we glided through with a steely grace, stopping occasionally for her to exchange pleasantries with an old associate. Later, I observed her from the balcony of the hall, lost in thought, alone in the crowd.

As for the others involved in that momentous trial, Mr Justice Eveleigh continued a distinguished career on the bench and may be considered to have been instrumental in having the right to make a dock statement removed from criminal trial procedures. Six long days listening to Stonehouse may well have caused Eveleigh to reflect, and the right was abolished in the early 1980s. Michael Corkery and Lord Wigoder continued with lengthy and notable careers, while Ian Mayes has always maintained that the Stonehouse case was the making of him, going on to enjoy a long and successful time at the bar, as has Geoffrey Robertson. Michael Grieve achieved silk and now sits as a Crown Court judge. He reflects that the insight he obtained into Stonehouse's character in those three long months has been of immense value, leaving him under no illusion that, while Stonehouse was always deferential to him, he perceived that the politician had a very clear agenda, displaying traits of narcissism and self-absorption, characteristics we perhaps recognise in many of our current politicians.

Detective Chief Superintendent Etheridge could never quite throw off the whiff of scandal that hit the Metropolitan Police in the early 1970s and, having been passed over for promotion despite numerous commendations, he left the police in 1977 to take up a position with Tiny Rowland and his Lonrho empire, causing – perhaps not unintentionally – some consternation in police circles that the gamekeeper had now become poacher.

With his appeal unsuccessful, Stonehouse settled down to serve the rest of his sentence. Sheila remained steadfastly loyal, pledging herself to him. No doubt the immense strain had left its mark on the man, as evidenced by the fact that while in prison he suffered a number of heart attacks and ultimately had to receive heart bypass surgery. Patti Hayes took Rosina to see him at Wormwood Scrubs shortly after the operation.

Tragically, his elder brother George, suffering with a similar condition, endured the same operation, almost to the day, but did not survive. Poignantly, George had tried to help his brother and on Stonehouse's prison file there is a letter asking the authorities to consider his brother's early release for health reasons and suggesting that he had suffered enough.

Stonehouse was eventually transferred to an open prison and, for health reasons, was released early, though he could never quite shake off the press, who continued to display a morbid fascination with his story and its aftermath, even filming and reporting on his release from prison on 14 August 1979.

49

FINAL FROLÍK

6 October 1980

Josef Frolík had been watching events unfold in London from his new home in the United States with a furious sense of betrayal. He had read the statement made by Harold Wilson to parliament on 17 December 1974, which effectively labelled him a liar. In May 1975, a meeting took place between the Czech and a senior MI5 officer, along with his CIA handler in Washington, during which he was questioned further, later claiming that the MI5 officer had been given authority by Wilson to convey an apology for the statement he had made to parliament.

In the aftermath of Stonehouse's conviction, the Czech spy allegation was reviewed, with questions continuing to be raised in parliament about the affair, particularly revolving around the statement made by Wilson in December 1974 exonerating Stonehouse. Meanwhile, Frolík was still infuriated by the British government's failure to acknowledge their error and in exasperation he wrote to the prominent Czech activist and journalist Josef Josten, detailing his concerns and relaying details of the meeting with the MI5 officer. In December 1977, the MP Stephen Hastings raised the issue during a parliamentary debate, which was swiftly followed with letters to the prime minister, Jim Callaghan (who had taken over from Wilson in 1976), as the controversy simmered on, with members of the opposition parties insinuating that Wilson had lied to parliament.

Frolík agreed to meet with another MP, Patrick Mayhew, who conducted two days of interviews with the defector in a hotel room in Miami, recording six hours of tapes, which still exist but remain subject to the Official Secrets Act. Yet, when Callaghan called a cabinet meeting to address the matter, the ministers failed to resolve the debate.

The Labour government had, since their election in February 1974 and re-election in October of that year, limped from being a minority government to one with a tiny majority of just three, a situation that deteriorated further with Stonehouse's conviction and the death of a sitting MP, which whittled that slim majority to almost nothing. The 'winter of discontent' with binmen, firefighters and grave diggers simultaneously striking finished off the Labour government and at the general election in May 1979 Margaret Thatcher swept into Downing Street on a mission to clear up what she regarded as the mess left by the previous administration.

Conscious of the controversy that the Anthony Blunt and Cambridge spy affair had caused a year earlier, the Thatcher government now faced an additional politically sensitive issue with the emergence of another Czech intelligence service defector. In 1980, Karel Pravec, codename Pelnár, defected to the United States, revealing himself to be the operative who had ambushed Stonehouse in his room at the Hotel Kosodrevina, later pursuing him across the continent to the Labour Party conferences in the late 1960s.

Pravec provided information that he had been Stonehouse's handler in 1968 and 1969, prior to which the MP had been handled by Robert Husak, the agent with whom Frolík had conducted personal dealings while stationed in London. Pravec also claimed to have seen Stonehouse's file and had suggested the MP had been on their 'books' from the mid-1950s, confirming that Stonehouse was a paid informer from about 1962, providing information on technological innovations and aviation. The dilemma now was whether the government would take steps to remove this thorn in their side, or cover it up with a sticking plaster and hope it went away.

On 6 October 1980 a meeting was convened by the prime minister with her home secretary, Willie Whitelaw, Attorney General Michael Havers, and cabinet secretary Sir Robert Armstrong, to discuss a minute that had been prepared by Sir Robert regarding the Stonehouse affair.

It had been a niggling issue that the prime minister had thought had died a death with Stonehouse's imprisonment. However, the latest revelations on his alleged activities required handling robustly but with sensitivity, the potential implications for her government and the security services being considerable. There had been great consternation when she had revealed the Blunt affair to the House of Commons in November 1979, and Thatcher was determined to avoid a repetition of the suggestions made in the press of a government cover-up and protection of the political elite, especially as Blunt had been given immunity from prosecution in return for a confession and information.

Gathered around the table in the cabinet room, the prime minister listened intently as her advisors updated her, weighing up the legal and political consequences of any action they should take. It was the consensus that the information Pravec had provided irrefutably proved that Stonehouse was a spy. Pravec, who was safely ensconced in his new life in the US, did not wish to come to the UK to give evidence. Perhaps not surprising, given the fate of poor Georgi Markov, a Bulgarian dissident writer who had claimed political asylum in London only to be poisoned by a pellet laced with ricin administered through the tip of an umbrella as he waited on a tube station platform some eighteen months earlier.

They could not offer immunity to prosecution in return for an admission as they had done with Blunt. However, they saw little point in confronting Stonehouse, taking the view that he had served his time, was in poor health and, if they were to prosecute, given his conduct before his trial, he would only use the media to claim another government witch-hunt, heaping yet more embarrassment upon them. They chose to let sleeping dogs lie.

A final minute of the meeting was prepared, confirming what had been agreed, stamped 'secret', filed and then sent for archiving.

So ended any government interest in prosecuting John Stonehouse for treason. With hindsight, it was a politically astute decision, not only for the reasons given in the meeting, but also in the wider context, considering the embarrassment that would be caused to the government with revelations of treason, corruption and subterfuge at the highest level. These were flames that would undoubtedly be fanned by a belligerent ex-minister with the capacity to betray further secrets in the course of the trial in pursuing the claim that it was a conspiracy against him. It is clear that the Labour Party was riddled with informants and agents such as Lee, Knight and Skot, to name but a few. These were people who had access to the very highest level of political influence and information, so this is more shocking now than the Cambridge spy ring.

It is a fact that John Thomson Stonehouse was recorded in the StB files as an agent with the codename of Kolon and later Twister but, though it was alleged that Stonehouse was in their pay and that he had passed to the Czechs information to which he had been privy as a minister, he consistently denied any involvement. There does not appear to be any evidence of a honey trap; if there had been, it is certain that the StB would have relied upon it to 'compromise' their man when he wasn't cooperative. They didn't, strongly suggesting they never had it in the first place.

Stonehouse was not a spy or agent in the terms that we understand them in the novels of John le Carré and Ian Fleming. He hadn't provided the Czechs with anything significant and the disappointment in their filed reports is palpable. The Czechs invested considerable time and money nurturing their 'agent', supplying him with 'cash for questions' to assist the Czech cause as well as funds for political insights and information, and in return Stonehouse provided them with technical information (some documents are indisputably in his handwriting, as confirmed by a handwriting expert). That information, however, could easily have been obtained through other means. Stonehouse had been blinded by ambition and had used the Czechs to pursue his aims in a Faustian pact that came back to haunt him in the late 1960s and no doubt contributed to his political decline and ultimate downfall. His exclusion from the shadow cabinet and the Labour cabinet of the 1970s inspired him to pursue the business interests that resulted in his ruin after he allowed himself to be compromised from the moment he accepted the first payment in the back of his chauffeur-driven Daimler in early 1960. He did 'work' for the Czechs, but on his terms and, once he had achieved cabinet status, he led them a merry dance, playing up to his codename Twister, though by then the damage had been done and his integrity was lost. If Owen's case was anything to go by, then it is highly unlikely, even today, that there would be a successful prosecution, given that, even though it was proven that Owen had received money from the Czechs, the jury was not satisfied that he had in fact obtained and passed any secrets to them. In Stonehouse's case, without the principle witnesses, the Czech counter-intelligence officers, the prosecution would not even be able to establish that payments were ever received by Stonehouse.

Frolík settled in the warm climes of Florida, remaining there until his death in 1989, although an inevitable conspiracy theory arose that he is still alive, living anonymously. Pravec also settled in the US, having adopted a new identity. In 2019, an old man was tracked down by journalists to his New Jersey home. He was confronted with information from an StB file for agent Pelnár. Denying that he was one and the same person, he brought a wry smile to his interrogator when exclaiming, 'a good spy would never answer your stupid questions'.

Arguably, the StB had been one of the most effective Eastern Bloc counter-espionage organisations of the 1950s and 1960s, but when Soviet paranoia caused them to mishandle the Prague Spring, its brutal suppression led to purges within the Czechoslovak security services. This led to highly skilled and dedicated operatives such as Frolík, Pravec and Husak speaking out against the new regime, inevitably leading to their dismissal. Men and women who had remained loyal chose to take that most drastic of steps: betrayal of their homeland.

50

THE FUNERAL

February 1981

Patti Hayes was hurtling down the road at breakneck speed, the frost-rimed trees a blur as she raced to reach the church on time.

It was a big day for the family. Rosina Stonehouse had passed away and, having been a mayor of Southampton, she was afforded the honour of a civic funeral, which not only meant that the cost was met by the local authority, but also included police escorts and road closures. All of this was eclipsed by the fact that her son, John Stonehouse, would be present, for which spectacle the press were excitedly preparing. There had been a reconciliation, of sorts, between Patti and Stonehouse at the hospital in Rosina's final days.

As she sped towards the Chilworth roundabout she felt the car shudder and, recognising the thumpity-thump-thump of a flat tyre, her heart sank. Inspecting the damage, she wondered what to do. Thankfully, Michael had already dropped their sons at St Boniface's church on Shirley High Street, where they were engaged as altar servers at the requiem mass. As she sat by the roadside contemplating her bad luck, a police car pulled up and an officer approached and asked what the problem was. Within ten minutes, the spare wheel was on and she had the benefit of a police escort for the final four miles to the church.

As anticipated, the media were out in force to record the first public appearance of Stonehouse since his release from prison in August 1979, perhaps hoping to witness any altercation or reconciliation between the disgraced politician and his estranged nephew Michael.

Under the gaze of the world's press, the mass and graveside service passed without incident. Patti informed the gathered mourners that the wake was to be held at our family home and extended the family's invitation to all present, an invitation which Stonehouse accepted.

Michael did not join the wake. After a brief discussion he agreed with Patti that it was the right thing to have Stonehouse back to their home but it was just too much for him to face. He asked that everyone be informed that he had some urgent business to attend to at his newly opened practice and slipped away before his uncle's attendance.

When Stonehouse arrived it was almost as if he was on one of his ministerial visits. He hadn't lost the gravitas, the aura, although it was observed by another of his nephews that he was wearing odd shoes, one brown and one black. Patti played the kind and dutiful hostess and was heartened to see Stonehouse's son Matthew engaging with me in the kitchen, exchanging guitar chords on an old acoustic I had been given the Christmas before, lending some normality to the whole event, unaware that it was to be the last that we ever saw of Stonehouse.

Stonehouse married Sheila, they had a son and life settled into a 'normal' family routine. Stonehouse focused on writing novels, three of which were published. It has been suggested that his novel *Ralph* revealed the fabled 'honey trap'. However, perhaps most telling was his book, *The Baring Fault*, where the story's central character, Charles Baring, had become prime minister, whilst all the while spying for the KGB. Was Stonehouse tipping a nod to the StB plans all those years earlier? To the extended family he seemed much more relaxed, no longer troubled by the vicissitudes of political and business life, finding a quiet contentment in the simpler things in his life.

My parents maintained contact with Barbara and every Christmas we would visit, looking forward to seeing her as she showered us with the quiet, loving attention that is integral to her character.

EPILOGUE

In addition to embarking on a career as a novelist, Stonehouse's notoriety attracted innumerable invitations to appear on various television chat shows, discussing the events of his disappearance. While attending one of those shows in April 1988, he collapsed with what was diagnosed as another heart attack. He was discharged from hospital but, within days, suffered a further massive cardiac arrest. On 14 April, I had arrived home from work and, cup of tea in hand, turned on the BBC six o'clock news to be confronted with the leading report: 'John Stonehouse dead'. Heart attack. His story retold.

His death was perhaps timely, as the following year the old communist regimes of the Warsaw Pact collapsed in a domino effect following Gorbachev's *perestroika* and the thaw in relations between East and West. Czechoslovakia was freed from its shackles and, unlike the Balkan states, where civil war prevailed for years, the Czechs and Slovaks agreed that the two nations should be re-established, and separated amicably. Another aspect of the process of reconciliation with the past was the opening up of the StB archives in Prague, which, since being made accessible to the public in the early 1990s, have been a source of fascination, regularly plundered by the world's press. There isn't a year that seems to go by without further discoveries. Research of the archives for this book divulged revelations about Harold Wilson's

Labour government of the 1960s and 1970s, for instance those concerning Ted Short, later to become Lord Glenamara, who had escaped any allegations of spying during his lifetime. In 1975 he had been instrumental in the attempts to have Stonehouse removed as an MP, knowing of the spy allegations against Stonehouse, yet all the time he hid his alter ego as agent Skot with the StB, leading to the question as to whether he was really acting in the interests of the Labour government in 1975 or was motivated by other incentives.

The opening of the archives revealed the full extent of Stonehouse's involvement though, even today, some members of his family refuse to accept that he had been engaged in such work, suggesting that the story has either been concocted by the Czechs or that it reveals nothing other than his attempts to pursue his ambitions to twin his constituency with Kladno and to promote trade between Britain and Czechoslovakia. The evidence reveals otherwise, exposing a man whose ambition for political and financial gain was to be his downfall, a man who had shown so much promise ultimately undone by his ego. Kugler perceived this flaw in those pivotal months in 1959 when he recruited Kolon.

As someone once said of him, Stonehouse had created ripples in time, ripples that don't appear to be about to dissipate soon. There is not a year that goes by when his case is not referred to, when there are no revelations about disappearances or Cold War spy allegations. He was a complex man who did some good, not only in his constituency work but by doing much to promote the newly independent African countries, formerly British colonies, as well as contributing considerably to the recognition of Bangladesh as an independent state. That was the public face; in private he was a man devoted to his family and children, generous and kind, and we cherish fond memories of family visits and parties while remaining mindful that those have to be tempered with the love affairs and his subsequent betrayal of Barbara, Michael and other members of the family.

Stonehouse left his mark on all those who touched him; he was a man who 'launched a thousand headlines'. Many of those who were closest to him have remained silent to this day, some choosing to protect their cherished memories, others maintaining a dignified silence as his life and times still hold a grim fascination. Over the years, I have spoken to many people who had been involved. Sheila, understandably, declined to discuss matters, but our brief email correspondence left a very telling impression, particularly in her recollection of receiving a visit from an old childhood friend of her husband shortly after his death: 'He just wanted to say that he thought I should look after myself and the best way of doing that was to stop fighting for John, now he had died. Although I didn't really know the man, I decided that he was right and that, if I wasn't careful, I could spend a lot of the rest of my life continuing to defend John. It was such a hard thing for me to do.'

It seems that history is littered with such characters, polarising opinion, invoking absolute loyalty and devotion in those closest to them and contempt from those whom they cross. Where did Stonehouse's drive and ambition come from? Was it innate or had it been instilled in him? Despite all the deeply personal, embarrassing and disastrous revelations of 1974 and 1975, it is his mother, Rosina, whom he wished to avoid disappointing the most, as expressed in a simple personal inscription in one of his books, which perhaps says it all:

To
My Mother on her birthday
With many happy returns
From her son who has been re-born
Love from John
6 November 1975 London

ACKNOWLEDGEMENTS

Writing *Stonehouse* has been a long, fascinating, cathartic and at times frustrating process. It has been an odyssey that commenced in December 1969 when I first recall ever meeting John and Barbara as a child and has gathered apace in particular over the last five years with the development, research and writing of this book.

I endeavoured to approach the project much like I would do any of my cases, with objectivity, forensic analysis and sensitivity. In that process I have considered thousands of pages of source documents, speaking with some of those who witnessed the events, as well as using my own legal knowledge and experience. In that process I spoke with some of the finest legal minds, in the form of Ian Mayes, QC, HHJ Michael Grieve, QC, and Geoffrey Robertson, QC, all of whom represented a number of the protagonists in the criminal trial and DTI investigation. Their knowledge and recollection of the case after so many years was astounding and their insights and anecdotes fascinating. Geoffrey Robertson's two books, *The Justice Game* and *Rather His Own Man*, also provided some helpful information detailing his perspective on the case.

I would like to thank my mother, Patti Hayes, who has been an invaluable source of many stories and facts pertaining to this saga; my uncle, Philip Hayes, whose knowledge of the Hayes/Stonehouse family tree is second to none and my uncle, David Hayes, for his memories.

The journey has also allowed me to understand what my parents had gone through and, in particular, my father, Michael Hayes, with whom I have had a difficult relationship. It has given me a fresh perspective and appreciation of the man that he is. Over the years he would occasionally speak of those events and gave some interesting insights and perspectives. My career in law was initiated with his support and whilst there are some regrets, I have been blessed with pursuing a vocation that I enjoy and for that I thank him.

I must also recognise the help that my aunt, Raili Taylor, and, posthumously, my uncle David Taylor, provided me with: some invaluable source documents and invaluable tips on the fine art of writing when I first embarked on the process. Sarah Williams, my original introduction to the world of publishing, must also be mentioned and thanked for her kind and gentle encouragement and guidance. I would also like to thank Katherine May for the editing of the first draft of the book. Thank you, Justin Penrose for your kind advice and for also putting me in touch with my literary agent Robert Smith who has been hugely influential in finally allowing the book to see the light of day.

The love and support of my children, Christian, Patrick and Rachel, has sustained me through the more difficult times over the years. Their inquisitiveness and desire to learn more about their family history has inspired me to pursue the project to its end.

I also acknowledge and appreciate the infinite patience of my business partner, Seema Dosaj, Lesley Hayes, and all those involved with my firm, Berris Law.

I have been privileged to have had help, support and encouragement throughout this expedition. In particular, Sabina, who provided so much laughter and light in dark times. I have cherished the time you have given me. Thank you.

I acknowledge the kind assistance provided by the staff at both the StB archives in Prague and the National Archives for their patience as well as the translation and handwriting experts who were very helpful and prompt with the work they undertook on my behalf.

Finally, I must thank all those at Little, Brown for their professionalism and guidance – in particular, Duncan Proudfoot, Howard Watson and Amanda Keats.

Without you all this would not have been achieved. Thank you.

INDEX

Admiralty 72
Aeromaritime Ltd 100–1
Africa 9, 10, 13, 54, 59, 76, 196, 248
African National Congress (ANC) 9, 13, 28
Ahmed, Mr 95
Airbus 37, 44
Allies 21
Ambulant Finance 95
American embassy, London 35
Amin, Idi 321
ANC *see* African National Congress
Andover, Hampshire 77, 89, 96, 107, 242, 285, 347
Anglo-American relations 47, 51
Anglo-German relations 51
Ankara 47
Archer, Jeffrey 95
arms trade 85
Armstrong, Sir Robert 352
Arthur Anderson 206, 207
Astoria Hotel, Pimlico 99, 306–7, 323
Atlanta 109
August (agent) 138
Australia 101–2, 109, 127–32, 136, 140, 142–8, 149–56, 157–8, 160–2, 168–70, 171–6, 177–88, 191, 202–3, 204–6, 208–9, 210–13, 215–22, 224, 232, 233, 234–5, 241–2, 247–8, 257, 265, 273–4, 282, 298, 304, 306–8, 309–10, 312–13, 314, 323–5, 328, 331, 334, 338
Australian Department of Immigration 177
Australian House of Representatives 208
Australian Migration Act 161, 173, 175
Australian (newspaper) 186
Austria 67, 68
Awami League 83–4
Awdry, Mr 251

Bacon, Francis 262
Bail Act 1976 239, 318
Baird, John 17
Balkan states 359

see also specific states
Ballard, John 168, 172, 173, 175, 218
Bangkok 130
Bangladesh 83–7, 93, 122, 179–80, 231, 249–50, 290, 295–6, 326–7, 360
Bangladesh Relief Fund 133
Bangladesh 'Shrangri-La Project' 281
Bangladeshi High Commission 180
Bank of England 280
Bank of New South Wales 100, 101–2, 131–2, 143, 306
Bank of New Zealand 131–2, 143, 173, 174, 192
Barclays bank 304–5
Bartholomew, Allen A. 2, 220
Bayswater 34
BBC *see* British Broadcasting Corporation
Beale's restaurant 28
Beaverbrook, Lord 169, 174
Bedford, Edward 281
Beirut 54
Belfast 79
Belgravia 44
Bengal 83–4, 249
Benn, Tony 37
Bentley's Oyster Bar and Grill, London 14, 16–17
Berlin Blockade 10
Berlin Wall 10, 31
Berman, Alfred 262
Biggs, Charmian 148
Biggs, Ronnie 148, 172
Bingham, Philip 294–5, 296–7, 336
Black Horse Inn 28
Black Sea 64
Blair cabinet 232
Blom-Cooper, Louis 344
Blunt, Anthony 351–2
BOAC *see* British Overseas Airways Corporation
Boeing 39
Bow Street Magistrates' Court 224, 227, 228, 229–33, 236, 243
Bow Street police station 229